SOCIAL EXCLUSION IN EUROPE

PZ .

900425093 2

Social Exclusion in Europe

Problems and paradigms

Edited by
PAUL LITTLEWOOD
Department of Sociology, University of Glasgow, UK

with

IGNACE GLORIEUX
Vakgroep Sociologie, Vrije Universiteit Brussel, Belgium

SEBASTIAN HERKOMMER
Institut für Soziologie, Freie Universität Berlin, Germany

INGRID JÖNSSON
Sociologiska Institutionen, Lunds Universitet, Sweden

Ashgate

Aldershot • Brookfield USA • Singapore • Sydney

Published by
Ashgate Publishing Ltd
Gower House
Croft Road
Aldershot
Hants GU11 3HR
England

Ashgate Publishing Company
Old Post Road
Brookfield
Vermont 05036
USA

Ashgate website: http://www.ashgate.com

British Library Cataloguing in Publication Data
Social exclusion in Europe: problems and paradigms
   1. Marginality, Social - Europe 2. Socially handicapped -
   Europe
   I. Littlewood, Paul II. Glorieux, Ignace III. Herkommer,
   Sebastian IV. Jönsson, Ingrid
   305'.094

Library of Congress Catalog Card Number: 99-73316

ISBN 1 84014 717 2 ✓

Printed in Great Britain by
Antony Rowe Ltd, Chippenham, Wiltshire

Contents

Preface

THE EDITORS

This book is the outcome of the sustained collaboration of a group of colleagues working in areas of sociology, social policy and politics at a number of European universities. It originated in the establishment of an ERASMUS funded programme at the end of the 1980s, designed to facilitate staff and student exchange between a dozen institutions. This also involved running annual intensive courses, at which various combinations of colleagues would lecture and conduct seminars. The collaboration this involved was the stimulus to the preparation of a volume of papers on a variety of aspects of identity, conflict and social justice in Europe (Erskine *et al*, 1996)*, drawn from the themes of the courses we held in the early 1990s. But in 1996 we decided to develop a new, more focused theme for the courses, this time based on the increasingly topical issue of social exclusion, and with the explicit intention of producing a second volume.

We come from a wide variety of different academic traditions, which is no doubt reflected in this book. It is clear that the contributors to this volume do not pretend to share identical sociological perspectives or concerns, except in their common interest in the notion of social exclusion. We also have very different research interests, and a number of the chapters report the findings of various projects conducted in the recent past, while other chapters are more concerned with the development of competing theories seeking to explain the phenomenon of exclusion. Each chapter is designed to stand by itself, but what binds the volume together is the way in which a whole series of issues and themes are inter-linked. The end of full employment and the prevalence of high levels of unemployment, the ubiquity of new, less secure forms of paid employment, and the polarization of wealth between the rich and the not-so rich on the one hand, and the impoverished on the other, have had profound effects throughout Europe. The late twentieth-century trend in the reduction of welfare benefits is another crucial cause of these effects, which the authors proceed to analyse in various ways in each of the chapters. Another of the effects is arguably the emergence of new social tensions and conflicts, although the authors of this volume are generally in agreement that these cannot be separated from those traditional divisions which still give European social structures their basic character - class, gender and ethnicity.

The book begins with a review of some of the literature on social exclusion by Littlewood and Herkommer, in which they explore the origins and the multiplicity of meanings and uses of the term, some of the perspectives and paradigms which inform them, and what the dominant uses seem to have in common. The chapters which follow explore in more depth many of the principal features of social exclusion described in the opening chapter. They have been ordered in such a way as to give the volume an explicit trajectory. First there are four chapters which focus on social exclusion in the context of *economic* change, given the fundamental role of economic restructuring in the genesis and maintenance of social exclusion. Then the direction of the volume swings more to issues relating to *social policy* and *state welfare*. In the last three chapters the direction changes again, focusing on issues concerning *cultural* and *political identity*.

Vobruba sets the scene for what follows by examining the rise of unemployment. He argues that we are living through a period of epoch-making social change, now that our society is no longer founded on full employment, but faces a two-fold crisis of paid work: - the *lack* of it, in both quantitative and qualitative terms. He proceeds to analyse the consequences of this in relation to income mixes and claims for a basic income. Next van Kooten gives an account of one of the enormous changes in the nature of work - flexibilization - and its ramifications for emerging patterns in the division of labour. He considers these in relation to various classificatory schema combining income, relations to the labour market and duration of unemployment. Although his arguments focus on the Netherlands, the global nature of the trends he analyses give his model a much more general applicability. The following chapter by Glorieux describes some detailed findings of a survey conducted in Flanders about the meanings which different categories of people - men and women, paid and unpaid workers, give to their activities, stressing the gendered nature of work. Adopting a perspective derived from the sociology of Durkheim, he demonstrates that work is a key means to social integration and that long-term economic exclusion is likely to have serious socially disruptive effects. Finally in this first group of chapters, Herkommer and Koch, working from a very different perspective, drawing on the work of Marx and contemporary Marxists, consider the nature of the widespread poverty in contemporary society. They survey a mass of research on the so-called 'underclass' and explore its relevance in the context of theories of social class and structural change.

The chapter by Jönsson provides a bridge between the economic and social policy themes mentioned above, by exploring the crucial role of gender in the context of paid and unpaid work, and rights to welfare. The chapter discusses the meaning of citizenship and draws on data from the whole of Europe concerning changes in patterns of work and welfare provision. It also provides the basis for an interesting comparison with Glorieux's study of perceptions of work, given the salience in each of the role of unpaid domestic labour.

Next, Pioch reports on the findings of some qualitative research she recently conducted into comparative perceptions of welfare in relation to social justice in Germany and the Netherlands. Blomberg and Petersson use the notion of stigma to analyse the effects of and responses to various forms of state welfare policy. They develop Goffman's original concept to explore its impact in terms of both the right to welfare benefits and the phenomenon of non-take up.

If state education is treated as a product of social policy as well as a means of cultural transmission, the chapter by Littlewood provides the link between the themes of social policy/welfare on the one hand, and cultural and political identity on the other. He draws on Parkin's and Bourdieu's paradigms of social exclusion to consider certain aspects of formal education in England, suggesting that over time schools have moved from exclusionary to self-exclusionary practices.

The last pair of chapters focus much more directly on the political and cultural facets of social exclusion. McGuinness locates his analysis of citizenship and exclusion in the context of debates about 'European citizenship' and the role of national identities as they affect various categories of resident in Europe. He looks at the ramifications of the growth of the intra-European co-operation for those with the status of 'third country nationals'. Finally, and very much on the same theme, M'hammed Sabour reports on his research into the attitudes and perceptions of a sample of refugees seeking to settle in a Finnish city in the 1990s. Drawing on the work of Bourdieu, he provides a graphic description of the racist exclusionary practices and the responses of the refugees, including, importantly, self-exclusion.

In this volume we have tried to address a readership of policy makers and commentators as well as academics and students. We have identified major trends characterizing the end of the twentieth century; we have sought to provide the basis for a deeper and more self-critical understanding of the origins of contemporary discourses on social exclusion; we have located them in their broader socio-economic, political and cultural contexts; and we have reported the findings of a diversity of original research activities. We hope the outcome is as useful and challenging to the reader as its preparation was to the team which produced it.

*   Erskine, A., M. Elchardus, S. Herkommer and J. Ryan, (1996), (eds), *Changing Europe: Some Aspects of Identity, Conflict and Social Justice*, Avebury, Aldershot.

Acknowledgements

The contributors are indebted to two colleagues in the School of Social Sciences at the Erasmus University of Rotterdam. The first is Mart-Jan de Jong, without whose initiative and drive the network would never have come into being, let alone thrived for the whole decade. The second is Marianne Otte, whose superb administrative skills have ensured the smooth running of to date seven intensive courses and a similar number of planning meetings, in a variety of locations scattered throughout Europe.

We are also grateful to all the other colleagues who have taught on the intensive courses and who, while not having contributed directly to this book, have nevertheless given us the benefit of their constructive criticisms in its production. Similarly we would like to acknowledge the contribution of all the students who have attended the courses, providing a remarkably high level of critical inquiry and commentary.

Finally we wish to thank two colleagues for their help in preparing the manuscript: Barbara Littlewood of the Sociology Department at the University of Glasgow, who showed unstinting good humour and patience in proof reading drafts at varying stages; and Lesley McMillan for her magical skills at solving seemingly intractable computing and word-processing problems, while quelling the panic in those around her.

Contributors

Staffan Blomberg is Assistant Professor of Social Policy and Economics at the School of Social Work, Lund University, Sweden. His research focuses on changing user patterns of older service recipients in the context of changes in the delivery of public social services at the local level.

Ignace Glorieux is Professor of Sociology at the Free University of Brussels, Belgium. His main research interests are the temporal dimension of social life and the analysis of culture, especially with regard to the meaning of work.

Sebastian Herkommer was until his retirement in 1998 Professor of Sociology at the Free University of Berlin, Germany. His main research interests are social theory, class and stratification theory, and political and industrial sociology.

Ingrid Jönsson is Associate Professor of Sociology at Lund University, Sweden. Her main research interests are class and gender segregation in the Swedish school system and the relationship of work and family life for women in different welfare systems.

Max Koch works in the Department of Sociology of the Free University of Berlin, Germany. His main research interests include the Chilean social structure, and social exclusion and marginalization in comparative perspective.

Gerrit van Kooten is Associate Professor of Labour and Organization in the Department of Sociology, Erasmus University in Rotterdam, the Netherlands. His main fields of interest are labour market policy, quality of work, industrial relations, collective bargaining and industrial conflict.

Paul Littlewood is a lecturer in the Sociology Department and a member of the Youth, Education and Employment Research Unit at the University of Glasgow, Scotland (UK). His main research interests include schooling in Britain, comparative education and processes of educational selection.

Mike McGuinness is Senior Lecturer in Politics at the University of Teesside, Middlesbrough, UK. His main research interests are the impact of European integration and nationalism with particular reference to racism, and sport, nationalism and identity.

Jan Petersson is Associate Professor of Social Policy and Economics at Lund University, Sweden. He is currently engaged in research on priorities in social policy, particularly the social services, in an increasingly decentralized and shrinking welfare state.

Roswitha Pioch has recently left the University of Leipzig to become a lecturer at the Institute of Social Policy and the Centre of European and Northamerican Studies at the University of Göttingen, Germany. Her main research areas are social policy and social theory, welfare states from an international and comparative perspective, and qualitative methods.

M'hammed Sabour is Professor of Sociology at the University of Joensuu, Finland. His main research interests are the sociology of Pierre Bourdieu, and migration, ethnicity, racism and marginalization.

Georg Vobruba is Professor of Sociology and Social Policy at the University of Leipzig, Germany. His main research interests include social theory and social policy, the impact of unemployment on welfare, and transnational processes within society.

1 Identifying Social Exclusion
Some problems of meaning

PAUL LITTLEWOOD and SEBASTIAN HERKOMMER

The term 'social exclusion' has come to be very widely used by politicians, policy makers, practitioners and academics in the course of the 1990s. Although various conceptions of social exclusion were being developed as far back as the 1960s and 1970s, the very end of the millennium has witnessed an upsurge in the publication of a wide range of books and articles on the theme. Most have concentrated on various aspects of economic exclusion, or more precisely, the exclusionary effects of economic restructuring - see, for example, Brown and Crompton, 1994; Paugam, 1996a; Lawless, Martin and Hardy, 1997. Others have restricted their use of exclusion to analyses of poverty (see Rodgers, Gore and Figueiredo, 1995; Room, 1995; Walker and Walker, 1997). Yet others have explored social exclusion along other dimensions such as the political (Roche and van Berkel, 1997), while others - most famously perhaps, Jordan (1996), although his central focus is also poverty - have sought to develop holistic theoretical approaches based on the concept. There is also a growing body of literature on the overlapping theme of the 'underclass' (MacDonald, 1997). This list is very far from exhaustive, as we demonstrate in the following review of the relevant literature.

Closely associated with the explosion in the use of the term by academics, 'exclusion' has come to hold a prominent place in the political discourse of all governments in the European Union and in the European Commission itself (Levitas, 1996). It figures importantly in various research agencies' funding priorities, attracting researchers to develop and conduct major programmes. As such, 'exclusion' is proving to be much more than just the flavour of the month, but promises to provide a central organising framework for social research well into the next millennium. We need to ask, however, three fundamental questions. Why should the term have acquired such salience in recent years? What do those who use the term understand by it? And what are its origins? In what follows, we seek to answer these questions before attempting to provide an outline of what social exclusion has come to mean in general terms, according to most research in the area.

The emergence of the exclusion discourse

Arguably the growth in popularity of the term marks attempts to understand and interpret new patterns of social cleavage emerging during the last third of the twentieth century, particularly in relation to changing patterns in employment and unemployment, modifications to welfare-state provision, changing patterns in demographic mobility, both nationally and internationally, and changing definitions of eligibility for a variety of civil rights and duties. The contributors to this volume of writings seek to explore the nature of these changes, how they have occurred, and what implications they have for those who are most at risk of being excluded from employment, state benefits and other civil rights. The focus is largely on Europe, both generally and specifically, although many of the trends we seek to describe and explain can be found in societies throughout the world. But first we need to explore the implications of the changes listed immediately above, before investigating what exactly is meant by the expression 'social exclusion' and the different uses to which the term has been put.

The latter half of the twentieth century has been marked principally by a series of inextricably intertwined trends:

- changing patterns in the nature of work, both paid and unpaid;
- concomitant changes in the demand for and supply of different forms of labour;
- developments in and modifications to the provision of welfare support, particularly for those in low paid work or without paid work;
- changing patterns in interpersonal relations in the home, at work and in the locality;
- new patterns in inter-relations between ethnically, nationally and culturally diverse groups;
- changes to the definitions of the juridical rights and duties of those living within both national and supra-national boundaries.

Turning our focus towards the forces of social exclusion, from among all these changes we would draw particular attention to the following emergent trends:

- the presence of high rates of endemic unemployment and underemployment, particularly among the young, and the growth of insecure or precarious employment;
- the relative and absolute diminution in the availability of manual work and the corresponding growth in the availability of white-collar work;
- the increasing participation of women in paid work;
- the introduction of ever more sophisticated technological innovations both within and outside the workplace;
- a growth in the demand for and supply of an ever greater number and diversity of educational and vocational qualifications;
- growth in the flow of population movement across national boundaries, and indications of a rise in resistance to such movement among sections of indigenous populations.

These massive changes to the world we live in have led to major changes in the explanatory models developed by social commentators. Many have argued for some time that traditional forms of explanation, particularly those giving central place to social class, are no longer adequate, as is evident in feminist and post-modernist critiques. Thus some approaches are predicated on the axiom that as society has become more classless, the major social divide is one which demarcates the poor, the dispossessed, the marginalized, the excluded. (This is not to say that these approaches are identical; as Room (1995) among others has pointed out, there is a marked difference between Anglo-Saxon and continental, predominantly French, treatments of poverty and exclusion respectively.) The application, particularly among scholars in North America and continental Europe, of perspectives informed by Durkheimian and Parsonsian models of social integration to the treatment of exclusion, are also clearly prevalent. So too are approaches which draw on libertarian precepts of the centrality of the choice-making individual, with their development of the notion of 'underclass'. The focus on either or both social integration and individualism lends itself readily to a conception of society made up of the included and the excluded. As we shall see, however, those for whom social class as an organising concept retains its validity have also incorporated exclusion into their analyses. In sum, then, exclusion has become a very popular term.

The meanings of social exclusion

But what exactly does it mean? To anyone reading the literature on social exclusion, it soon becomes apparent that different authors mean very different things when they use the term - hence our inclusion of 'paradigms' in the title of this book. In a recently published volume, Roche distinguishes between broad and narrow definitions. The former refers to the ways in which particular sections within society at large can be deemed to be more or less excluded from a variety of economic, social, political and cultural resources and activities; and the latter depends more specifically on economically rooted inequalities in the sphere of work and income (Roche, 1997, p. 4). But behind this difference in the application of the term lie much more profound contrasts in the ways 'social exclusion' has been and is conceived. Hence, too, the inclusion of 'problems' in our title, because these different ways in turn determine how the 'problem' of social exclusion has been defined, and the various solutions to the 'problem' which have been proposed.

Perhaps the clearest account of the conceptual confusion surrounding the term is that by Silver, who writes, 'By all accounts, defining exclusion is not an easy task' (Silver, 1994/5, p. 535). She goes on to say that 'exclusion appears to be a very vague term..., loaded with numerous economic, social, political and cultural connotations and dimensions' and that 'the expression is so evocative, ambiguous, multidimensional and elastic that it can be defined in many different ways' (*ibid.*, p. 536).

She proceeds to identify three dominant paradigms, reflecting different theoretical perspectives, political ideologies and national discourses. She labels them the *solidarity, specialization* and *monopoly* paradigms, each attributing exclusion to a different cause and being grounded in a different political philosophy: in turn, Republicanism, Liberalism and Social Democracy. To make these distinctions clearer to a more general audience, however, it might be easier to link them to major schools of sociological thought: respectively, Durkheimian functionalism, pluralism and the conflict theories of Marx and Weber (we discuss these paradigms at some length here because of the help they can give in identifying the similarities and contrasts between the diverse approaches in the following chapters. See in particular the chapters by Glorieux, Herkommer and Koch.).

Silver identifies a number of key differences between the paradigms. At a very general level there are contrasting *conceptions* of integration - in a sense the other side of the coin from social exclusion. For the solidarity paradigm this means an emphasis on social cohesion through group solidarity and cultural boundaries, whereas that of specialization centres on the interdependence of separate, specialized spheres, and that of monopoly relies on a conception of social closure. Next, Silver distinguishes the paradigms in terms of the *sources* of integration they identify: moral integration, exchange and citizenship rights respectively. She also distinguishes between the *discourses* through which the paradigms are predominantly expressed. The term exclusion itself is basic to the solidarity discourse, whereas for specialization, terms such as discrimination and underclass figure widely. Underclass has also permeated the discourse of the monopoly paradigm, along with an emphasis on 'new poverty' and inequality more generally.

Following Silver, within the solidarity paradigm 'the "social" order is conceived as external, moral, and normative, rather than grounded in individual, group, or class interests. A national consensus, collective conscience, or general will ties the individual to the larger society through vertically interrelated mediating institutions' (p. 541). Integration is attained by assimilation into the dominant culture or in more contemporary contexts, the mutual adaptation of dominant and minority cultures to each other. Exclusion on the other hand is 'inherent in the solidarity of nation, race, ethnicity, locality, and other cultural or primordial ties that delimit boundaries between groups. Yet applications... include discussion of cultures of poverty and long-term unemployment and of trends toward "flexible specialization" in political economy' (p. 542).

The key defining characteristics of the specialization paradigm is a social order made up of 'networks of voluntary exchanges between competing individuals with their own interests and motivations' (p. 542) and the consequent separation of social spheres. 'Specialized social structures are comprised of separate, competing, but not necessarily unequal spheres, which leads to exchange and interdependence between them. Social groups are voluntarily constituted by their members, and shifting alliances between them reflect their various interests and wishes' (p. 542). Exclusion as a consequence 'results from an inadequate separation of social spheres, from the application of rules inappropriate to a given sphere, or from barriers to free movement and exchange between spheres' (pp. 542-3). Because of the separation of social spheres, there is a multiplicity of causes and forms of social exclusion, related fundamentally to individual choice and initiative, or the lack of them. In terms of economic strategy, emphasis is placed on the acquisition of skills, and on work incentives and disincentives.

The monopoly paradigm rests on a very different set of axioms, with the social order being essentially coercive and imposed downwards through a set of hierarchical power relations. According to this paradigm, 'exclusion arises from the interplay of class, status, and political power and serves the interests of the included' (p. 543). Social entities delimited by class, status and political power enjoy a monopoly of scarce resources which gives them a shared interest and which they seek to preserve through processes of social closure, whereby others are kept out against their will. In turn, the excluded seek to gain access through claims of citizenship and equal rights. While traditionally this paradigm has given primacy to social class, some proponents have incorporated the notion of underclass into their analyses.

Silver goes on to indicate the cultural embeddedness of the concept of exclusion, noting the different concerns expressed in debates at different times and in different countries. This not only leads to problems in cross-national comparison, but also points to the need to unpack the meaning of the term in all instances of its use. Her subsequent account also makes clear that the three sociological paradigms she identifies are a] ideal types - which by implication means that students of exclusion may well merge tenets from two or even three of them; and b] not exhaustive of all uses of the term - demonstrated by her account of a number of *organic*, non-sociological models of integration and exclusion. She also indicates that applications of exclusion differ in terms of whether it is treated as an identity or condition, a dynamic process or an institutionalized outcome. They also differ in terms of the dimensions they explore, whether they are economic, social political or cultural. In fact the rest of her article is a rich and illuminating illustration of the applications of the three paradigms to the economic dimension of exclusion, but because of this specificity it need not concern us here.

More recently, it has been suggested that we need to recognize another, fourth paradigm, evident in the work of such authors as Bauman, Beck, Giddens, Touraine, Lash, Wacquant and others, and conceptualizing the key means to integration as that of reflexivity (Virtanen, 1996, p. 150). We shall not explore this 'fourth paradigm' in any more depth here, since it has little relevance for the other chapters in this volume and serves only to muddy the waters further. Indeed, given the plethora of meanings and applications of the term 'social exclusion' already in circulation, one might be tempted to suggest that it would be better to rid ourselves of the term and start again; but this would be to ignore its extraordinary salience in current discourse and its importance in framing our understanding of a vast array of social issues, and in proposing various solutions. In addition, by exploring the genesis of its rise to such salience, we can identify more easily a number of social trends underlying its explosive growth; and we can better reveal the various assumptions being made, often only implicitly, behind it.

The dominant paradigm?

It would appear that the current prevalence of exclusion discourse originated in France at the end of the 1980s or at least the early 1990s. Room writes of the degree of discomfort French researchers for the European Commission felt with the British model of poverty lines, based on issues of distribution, preferring to develop an exclusion model centred on relational issues of inadequate social participation, lack of social integration and lack of power (Room, 1994, p 5). Yépez del Castillo goes on to cite Gaudier's survey of current uses: 'social exclusion is considered by many of the authors consulted to be a typical mechanism of poverty in the industrialized countries, especially in the case of the increased numbers of the new poor. The many varieties of exclusion, the fears of social explosions to which it gives rise, the dangers of social disruption; the complexity of the mechanisms that cause it, the extreme difficulty of finding solutions, have made it "the major social issue of our time"' (Yépez del Castillo, 1994, p. 614).

It appears to be this conception which predominates in European studies of social exclusion. In the 1995 document *Thematic Priorities*, circulated by the Economic and Social Research Council - the principal state-funding agency for social science research in Britain - one of the nine themes identified is 'Social Integration and Exclusion'. In the 'Rationale' it says,

> The need to understand the major societal processes whereby *individuals* are either *integrated* into, or excluded from, society and the ways in which these processes are changing presents social science with an important and urgent research agenda. The problem of how to create *social order* and positive

social change which will *benefit society* is a traditional focus of social science research. However, the need to identify the factors which underpin stable societies is assuming a new and profound urgency. Rapid social change, the disruption of traditional political, cultural and societal allegiances, and changing forms of governance and political participation, is a source of great concern. Indeed, the scope for greater marginalization in society may be increasing. Technology, suggests the findings of the Technology Foresight Panel, may further divide society through the creation of an *underclass* of people with neither access to nor understanding of new technologies. The prospect of such widening gaps within society suggests an urgent need for a greater sense of responsibility and *cohesion within communities* (ESRC 1995, our italics).

The document then goes on to list a series of 'Research Issues', one of which is called 'Social exclusion':

The factors which underpin social exclusion and an *individual's* response to that exclusion are key research topics. Also, the extent to which increasing crime and violence can be viewed as an indicator of *failing social and political cohesion*; and the effectiveness or otherwise of political representation, pressure groups and economic safety valves such as the 'black' and 'grey' economies in diffusing (*sic*) the effects of exclusion. Are social and welfare policies doing more harm than good in *integrating individuals within society*? (*ibid.*, our italics).

It can be argued that the way in which these research priorities are expressed indicates a distinct set of social research paradigms predicated on a particular view of the world which is fundamentally at variance with the view underlying other paradigms used in the analysis of social exclusion. The italicized terms above highlight the way in which research analysis is to be tied to the place of individuals in society at large, with particular stress on social cohesion and integration. Society is viewed as ideally a cohesive, integrated whole - essentially a functionalist framework, in which the key concern is a perceived *dys*function: the apparent exclusion of certain categories of individuals and the possibility of social disorder emanating from their exclusion, and the key aim of research is morally prescriptive - to promote greater degrees of integration and social order. This framework is closely tied to the first of Silver's paradigms discussed above (as well as to the perspective adopted by Glorieux in this volume).

The ESRC is not alone in championing this particular sense of social exclusion. Levitas (1996) arrives at a similar interpretation of its use in, among other documents, two of the European Commission's White Papers (1994a and 1994b). She suggests that social exclusion is here conceived as in opposition to social integration and cohesion, and is used to refer predominantly to the unemployed - thereby ignoring issues about the nature of unpaid and low paid work, of poverty and material inequalities. Thus the excluded as a category is more or less identical to the unemployed, whose integration would be achieved through paid employment (Levitas 1996, p. 13).

Yet if this view does predominate in social exclusion research, it is not the only one available to sociologists. What is intriguing in Yépez del Castillo's coverage is that, despite claiming 'to place the French concept of social exclusion within its context' (p. 613), she does not cite the work of Bourdieu. Yet arguably it is through the influence of earlier work by Bourdieu and others that much current exclusion discourse originated, even although their senses of the term might differ markedly from that of other French researchers. (Certainly, Bourdieu's conception of exclusion has profoundly influenced two of the chapters in this volume, Chapter 9 by Littlewood and Chapter 11 by Sabour, although in somewhat different ways.)

Earlier uses of social exclusion

In the 1960s, fairly early in the development of his massive holistic theory of domination, Bourdieu and his collaborator Passeron developed their Foundations of a Theory of Symbolic Violence, which crucially involve the notion of exclusion - in this case of the pupil by the teacher for failing to be inculcated into acceptance of dominant cultural forms as presented through formal education (Bourdieu and Passeron, 1997). Exclusion and the associated concept of self-exclusion have come to occupy a central position in the whole of Bourdieu's work - see in particular his writing on student culture (1968), cultural capital (1977), taste (1984), French universities (1988), cultural production (1993a), school certification (1993b), academic discourse (1994), the *grandes écoles* (1996a), its graduates and more generally the 'state nobility' (1998), and the genesis and structure of what is deemed to be great literature (1996b). Bourdieu's treatment of exclusion clearly falls within the monopoly paradigm, as elaborated by Silver (1994/5).

Another sociologist who was writing of exclusion before the term came into widespread usage in the 1990s is Parkin - again, clearly located within the monopoly paradigm, and another influence on Littlewood's approach in Chapter 9 of this volume. Parkin's thesis on exclusion draws its inspiration from Weber's conception of social closure - a process or strategy whereby members of more or less any social collectivity try to restrict access to resources and opportunities of the collectivity, by reference to a group attribute - ethnic identity, language, social origin, religion and so on. The denial of access to outsiders contributes to the nature of the distributive system, including the distribution of power. Parkin goes on to develop this thesis by identifying and analysing 'the two main generic types of social closure, the latter always being a consequence of, and collective response to, the former' (Parkin 1979, p. 45): *exclusion* and *usurpation*. Exclusion is the strategy adopted by the excluders and usurpation that adopted by the excluded, in an attempt perhaps to be included: 'Modes of closure can be thought of as different means of mobilizing power for the purpose of engaging in distributive struggle' (*ibid.*, pp. 45-6). Parkin goes on to claim that 'exclusion is the predominant mode of closure in all stratified societies' (*ibid.*, p. 47) - in striking contrast to the treatments of social closure examined above, with their reticence to acknowledge the existence of social stratification, at least in the form of social class. In capitalist society, however,

> the process of class formation and social reproduction of the bourgeoisie is significantly different from that of preceding classes in that the conditions for membership are, in principle at least, attainable by all. Exclusionary rules and institutions must always be justified by universal criteria that are indifferent to the pretensions and stigmata of birth. There is thus a permanent tension within this class resulting from the need to legitimate itself by preserving openness of access, and the desire to reproduce itself socially by resort to closure on the basis of descent (*ibid.*, p. 47).

Quite clearly Parkin's conception of exclusion, in terms of strategies of social closure, is radically different from that currently employed by such institutions as the European Commission and various economic and social research agencies. This is principally because, first, his conception presupposes a fundamental role for social class. This is not to say that closure strategies are not used by groups and categories other than classes - indeed, Parkin goes on to consider intra-class exclusionary activities, particularly within the working class, based on ethnic, gender and religious identities. Second, Parkin gives an identity to those excluded, whether they be a class or a class fraction or a status group; they are not treated as an amorphous mass of discrete individuals with no common identity of their own.

Common themes in exclusion discourse

So far in this introductory chapter we have sought to establish the rise in the use of the term 'social exclusion', the socio-economic, political and other changes which have lead to this rise, and the array of meanings which have been accorded to it. One might well be tempted to jettison such a confusing term in the interests of clarity, but that would be like shutting one's eyes in the futile hope that what can't be seen isn't there. The term is now firmly embedded in official discourse for the foreseeable future. An alternative approach is to stop seeking the 'right' or the 'best' meaning, and heed the warning of Serge Paugam, the French author of *L'Exclusion* (1996a), who elsewhere has written,

> On questions as socially and politically sensitive as poverty and exclusion, sociologists must first of all recognise the impossibility of finding exhaustive definitions. These concepts are relative, and vary according to time and circumstance. It is unreasonable to expect to find a fair and objective definition, which is distinct from social debate, without falling into the trap of putting unclearly defined populations into clumsily defined categories (Paugam, 1996b, p. 4).

(A more extended treatment of Paugam's work is given in the chapter by Herkommer and Koch). This is an important point to bear in mind when reading studies about exclusion, poverty and the underclass. In what follows, we wish to follow Paugam's advice and instead try to identify *what most uses of exclusion and related terms actually have in common* - that is, to focus on *consensus* in the various analyses rather than on *differences*. We have identified several interconnected and overlapping features about which most analyses would seem generally to agree.

The 'newness' of social exclusion

First, what most uses of 'social exclusion' have in common is a sense that it refers to *new phenomena*. Social research reports are predominantly concerned with *new* poverty, *new* cleavages, *new* dimensions of social inequality; and *new* phenomena need new terms. One reviewer of reports from the European Union writes, 'All the reports emphasise the newness of the term "social exclusion"' (Chamberlayne, 1996, p. 1). Against the background of a long period of economic prosperity, the poverty, mass unemployment and widening gaps within today's society (i.e., polarization between the rich and poor) *seem* to be 'new' in that they were more or less unimaginable in the affluent or welfare society. While old aspects of earlier capitalist society are now re-emerging, other divisions have been observed to be new in the sense that they cannot be explained by class theory and traditional theories of social stratification.

> The end of the class struggle paradigm and the retreat of Marxist categories that provided both an analysis of social conflict and a vision of a social order without classes, leaves us without the theoretical means to analyse the phenomena that survived the death of the paradigm (Procacci, 1996, p. 10).

Poverty and exclusion from work are such survivals, she goes on, but these forms of exclusion

> do not represent so much an aggregation or a class, but rather the result of a social decomposition, the indicator of a low degree of integration and the rupture of social ties. 'Exclusion' reflects a holistic conception of society, in which social cohesion is undermined by the polarisation of inequalities (*ibid.*, p. 11).

Those cleavages which are not primarily explained by class structure are characterized by ascriptive features such as gender, race and ethnicity, which are used to discriminate against competing social groups and categories, immigrants and other minorities. As Parkin makes clear in his notion of closure, the strategies of both exclusion and usurpation involve intra-class activities, particularly within the working class, based on ethnic, gender and religious identities.

But are these cleavages consequent on exclusion really so new? It is not so long ago that women were not allowed to vote or participate in public life; and in many ways that discrimination continues in the present. And the fate of newcomers to the United States, getting the worst jobs and the meanest housing as described by Park and the Chicago School back in the 1920s - is it so fundamentally different today? However we answer these questions, it is clear that there is novelty in some of the *theories*, for example on 'gender and class', 'ethclass' and 'ethnic stratification'

(Körber, 1998). These at any rate reflect some of the cross-cutting and overlapping elements in the class structure, and of intra-class exclusion.

These forms of competition and exclusionary activity between social groups, and hence the debates about integration and marginalization, are therefore perhaps *new* only in the sense that they are re-emerging after a long period of prosperity and welfare.

Another aspect of current society which might be termed 'new' relates to the increased possibility of *déclassement*, of downward social mobility for those placed in once secure middle-class occupations such as highly qualified engineers, who now find themselves unemployed with little prospect of finding another position. Sociologists conceive of this phenomenon as a 'transversal category' (Newman, 1988; Bude, 1998; Sennett, 1998). So now there are losers on all levels, sharing the fate of those unskilled, superfluous workers, excluded even from exploitation. Again, however, there is nothing utterly new about downward social mobility for members of the petty bourgeoisie; perhaps what makes it seem new is the fact of its occurrence after an extended period of full employment.

Social exclusion as the effect of economic and social restructuring

There seems to be broad agreement about the underlying causes of social exclusion - the massive economic changes, particularly over the two or three decades, at international, national and regional levels, the concomitant intensification of competitive conditions and the consequent restructuring of social and political institutions. As Weber recognized, when and where such intensification occurs,

> Usually one group of competitors takes some externally identifiable characteristic of another group of (actual or potential) competitors - race, language, religion, local or social origin, descent, resident, etc. - as a pretext for attempting their exclusion. It does not matter which characteristic is chosen in the individual case: whatever suggests itself most easily is seized upon. Such group action may provoke a corresponding reaction on the part of those against whom it is directed (Weber, 1968, cited in Brown and Crompton, 1994, p.5).

For Mollenkopf and Castells, Marcuse, Davis and others, it is the economic changes in capitalist society which are fundamentally responsible for the recent trends in polarization and pluralization, and the consequence of exclusion. In an urban context according to Marcuse, 'The post-Fordist city results from four inter-linked processes: technological change, internationalization, concentration of ownership and centralization of control' (Marcuse, 1996, p. 176). The post-industrial city 'has been transformed from a relatively well-off, white and blue-collar city into a more economically divided, multi-racial, white collar city' (Mollenkopf and Castells, 1992, p. 8).

Social exclusion as a process

Social exclusion, however, has not merely been treated as a result or a consequence of other societal changes. Importantly it has also been widely treated as a process. *Déclassement* provides an excellent example of the treatment of social exclusion as a temporal process, in the sense of the *making of superfluousness*. Seen from the point of view of the individual, this involves first, the experience of losing one's job and not finding another one; second, the absence of subsidizing, supportive institutions such as the family and neighbourhood; third, the humiliation of the control procedures related to public welfare; fourth, possible physical reactions in terms of apathy, alcoholism, drug dependency and so on (Bude, 1998, p. 378), Sennett, 1998, p. 202). Here too we can see the process of *self-exclusion*, in the sense of despair, a feeling of being of no use to anybody.

One of the advantages of treating exclusion as a process is that it allows us to avoid strict 'either/or' definitions. Some schools of sociology adhere to system logic which necessitates the treatment of people as being either members or non-members - leading to the ultimately absurd argument that all individuals in a multifunctional society are included in the legal, economic, etc. subsystems, even the poor and those resorting to criminality (see the critical discussion of the all-inclusion theses of Luhmann and Nassehi by Kronauer, 1997). For others, however, the temporal aspect of exclusion allows them to take into account the experience of changing situations, of precarious conditions, of being periodically excluded and included, leading to a conception of indefinite boundaries separating the included from the excluded. In Germany, both the 'dynamic' school of poverty studies (Leibfried *et al.*, 1995) and the 'life course' studies of Kohli (1999) explored the finding that many more people have experienced poverty than are presently poor. From this, Kronauer draws a distinction between the notions of social exclusion and underclass: exclusion is a process, whereas underclass is a more or less stable situation which results from the exclusionary process. And Marcuse too gives a processual, dynamic connotation to exclusion in his account of the effects of globalization, the concentration of private economic power, the retreat of state power and the reduction in welfare programmes, which may all combine to lead to latent and manifest victimization. In the end of this process there is the concentration and isolation of the excluded in the urban ghetto (Marcuse, 1996). We shall return to this theme shortly.

Social exclusion as multi-dimensional

Another very common aspect of the treatment of exclusion is its *plurality*. Kronauer gives an almost exhaustive list of the most important dimensions. First and most commonly, there is *exclusion from the labour market* - long-term unemployment with no prospect of new work. Second, there is *economic exclusion* in a more general sense of poverty, conceived of in relation to social and cultural values about standards of living. Third, there is *cultural exclusion*, in which the nature of dominant patterns of values and behaviour has an exclusionary effect on those who adhere to and express different patterns. Fourth, there is *exclusion by isolation*, manifested by the restriction and circumscription of social contact, social relationships and group identity exclusively to the marginalized and stigmatized. This dimension is also close to the fifth, *spatial exclusion*, such as the confinement of the excluded within distinct neighbourhoods or zones of a city or region. And Kronauer's sixth dimension is *institutional exclusion*, manifest in and consequent on the retreat of private and public institutions from welfare programmes, the inclusionary conditions of access to welfare institutions and the direct exclusion from access to such public services as schooling (Kronauer, 1997).

But this list is not exhaustive, as other proposals for classifying the dimensions of exclusion reveal. The most general is that which identifies the *economic*, the *social*, the *cultural* and the *political* (including restrictions on citizenship rights). Of the political, Roche writes that '"Social citizenship" refers to those rights and duties of citizenship concerned with the welfare of people as citizens, taking "welfare" in a broad sense to include such things as work, education, health and quality of life' (Roche, 1992, p. 3). He goes on to relate this to social exclusion:

> Poverty is antithetical to full citizenship... Poverty represents a strategically important limit for the concept of social citizenship. Beyond this limit in some respects people are not full and participating members of society, and also

they are not full citizens. Beyond this limit people are politically and civically as well as socially 'excluded', they are 'second-class citizens' or less (p. 55).

Social exclusion as cumulative

The multiplicity of dimensions of exclusion is closely related to its cumulative nature. 'Exclusion is a multi-dimensional, cumulative and sequentially combined process of exclusion from a plurality of functional systems' (Stichweh, 1997, p. 123). Paugam too talks about an 'accumulation of handicaps' (Paugam, 1996b), and Scherr gives a simple example of a person with no income not being able to consume in a culturally acceptable way, to guide their child through schooling or to find a lawyer to defend their rights, and so on (Scherr, 1998). What is particularly important here is the way in which a multiplicity of deprivations combine to reinforce the state of social exclusion. Room writes that 'Deprivation is caused not only by lack of personal resources but also by insufficient or unsatisfactory community facilities, such as dilapidated schools, remotely sited shops, poor public transport networks and so on; indeed such an environment tends to reinforce and perpetuate household poverty' (1995, p. 238). And children subjected to this multi-dimensional and cumulative set of forces are unlikely to be able to escape, given the spatial segregation they experience. This dimension occupies such an important place in the literature on social exclusion that it deserves separate attention.

The spatial dimension of social exclusion

Accumulation of exclusionary effects is most obvious and in fact most visible in the case of its spatial concentration. But paradoxically exclusion is at the same time made *invisible* for the majority of people. This is because of the underclass being hidden behind the walls of the modern ghettos, no-go areas, from the hyper ghettos in the USA and the Latin American favellas to the less dramatic housing schemes in some European countries. Research into segregation within modern cities has been undertaken by a variety of urban sociologists and human geographers, such as Wilson, Wacquant, Sassen, Harvey, Soja, (Mike) Davis, Marcuse and many others.

> On both sides of the Atlantic, the theme of dualization, or polarization, of the city has taken center stage in the most advanced sectors of urban theory and

research, as the extremes high society and dark ghetto, luxurious wealth and utter destitution, cosmopolitan bourgeoisie and urban outcasts, flourished and decayed side by side (Wacquant, 1996, p. 122).

Marcuse combines the concepts of segmentation and segregation with economic functions and housing areas in such a way that he can identify five types within the post-Fordist metropolis: *luxury housing spots* - not really part of the city but enclaves of isolated buildings, occupied by those at the top of the economic, social and political hierarchy; *the gentrified city* - the city of those who are making it, occupied by professional, managerial and technical categories, whether yuppie or muppie without children; *the suburban city* - sometimes single-family housing in the outer city, at other times apartments near the centre, occupied by skilled workers, middle-range professionals and civil servants; *the tenement city* - sometimes cheaper single-family areas, most often rented, occupied by lower paid workers, both blue and white collar, and generally including a substantial proportion of social housing - although less so in the USA; and finally *the abandoned city* - the city of the victims, the end result of trickle-down, left for the poor, the unemployed, the excluded, where particularly in the USA, housing for the homeless is most frequently located (Marcuse, 1996, p. 196). Marcuse's chief interest here is the spatial segregation 'between what used to be called the "working class" and those poorer than they, largely excluded at least from the formal economy, more and more often impoverished and even homeless'. Significantly, he desists from using the term 'underclass' preferring to talk of the excluded:

> the victims of economic change, the very poor, squeezed more and more out of the mainstream of economic activity, presumptively no longer needed even as a "reserve army of the unemployed", with no perceptible long-term prospects of improvement through normal economic channels (*ibid.*, pp. 205-7).

The spatial dimension is also central to the conceptualization of New York as a 'dual city' in the work of Mollenkopf and Castells (1992). 'The "two cities" of New York are not separate and distinct' (p. 11), given the cross-cutting and fragmentary complexity of the divisions between the rich and poor, blacks and whites, men and women, and the variety of ethnic and cultural identities. Nevertheless, there is a fundamental duality. The city is divided into two antagonistic forces: at the centre, the overwhelmingly white, male elite of top managers and professionals at the centre of power, well organized in a global network of economic decision-making; and on the periphery, fragmented segments and groups without common interests and values, and lacking shared instruments of organization and influence. The authors conclude, 'This differential capacity for social organization is expressed and reinforced in the cultural, spatial and political structure of New York' (p. 403).

Other approaches also give primacy to the spatial dimension, such as Fassin's use of three pairs of *oppositions spatiales* in analysing new forms of poverty: inside/outside, high/low and centre/periphery (Fassin, 1996). There is also Offe's spatial model involving the differentiation of three 'topographic metaphors' of base (or bottom), outside and inside. Thus we can visualise a *vertical* dimension with the excluded at the bottom of the social structure, marginalized and superfluous; a *horizontal* dimension, with the ethnonationalist exclusion of immigrants from certain rights; and a dimension of *internal* exclusion involving the lack of universally shared norms and values. Offe proceeds to construct diverse cases of more or less severe consequences, dependent on the precise constellation of these three dimensions.

Consideration of the spatial dimension in the analysis of social exclusion leads one almost inevitably to studies seeking to classify and categorize those concentrated in usually urban based conditions of extreme poverty where long-term unemployment and dependence on welfare are endemic. We are referring to another, closely related notion that, like social exclusion, has become widely used in social research literature: the 'underclass'.

The 'underclass' as an effect of exclusionary processes

While some researchers into social exclusion, such as Marcuse, prefer not to use the term 'underclass', others, given the striking concentration of intense poverty in urban locations, have adopted the term while trying to free it from the moralistic and negative baggage which all too frequently accompanies it. Since the 'underclass' is the subject of a later chapter in this volume, we shall only deal with it summarily here. Suffice it to say that some of the most thorough research on the 'underclass' has been conducted by Wilson, who concentrated on the specifically American phenomenon of urban, inner city class formation of the poorest members of the African-American and Latino minorities (Wilson, 1987, 1993). The author argues that, in opposition to such New Right rational-choice analysts as Charles Murray, the 'culture of poverty' should be seen as a *response* to restricted opportunities facing the poor, a *consequence* of the crisis rather than its *cause*. Social isolation has to be seen as the result of two processes mutually reinforcing each other: race segregation and class division.

Others like Wilson also try to formulate a comprehensive conception of the 'underclass', including importantly Devine and Wright (1993) and Schmitter-Heisler (1991). Finally Roche extends his analysis of citizenship and the lack of it to incorporate the underclass:

> This relatively small but socially isolated, alienated and anomic category has come to be referred to as the 'underclass'. Members of the underclass are effectively not so much 'second-class' citizens as 'non-citizens' ... excluded from citizenship... The underclass, even more so than poverty in general, is thus a theoretically strategic 'limit case' for social citizenship (Roche, 1992, p. 57).

The various features we have been describing above can be seen to be both common to much of the literature on social exclusion and also closely intertwined. Thus the fundamental role assigned to socio-economic restructuring in the formation of social exclusion can be seen to be processual, cumulative, and multi-dimensional (including here crucially the spatial dimension). It is when all these features are seen in combination that the phenomenon of social exclusion assumes the particular salience that it has at the end and start of the millennium.

References

Bourdieu, P. (1977), *Outline of a Theory of Practice*, Cambridge UP, Cambridge.
Bourdieu, P. (1984), *Distinction*, Routledge and Kegan Paul, London.
Bourdieu, P. (1988), *Homo Academicus*, Polity, Cambridge.
Bourdieu, P. (1993a), *The Field of Cultural Reproduction*, Polity, Cambridge.
Bourdieu, P. (1993b), *La Misère du Monde*, Seuil, Paris.
Bourdieu, P. (1994), *Academic Discourse*, Polity, Cambridge.
Bourdieu, P. (1996a), *The State Nobility*, Polity, Cambridge.
Bourdieu, P. (1996b), *The Rules of Art*, Polity, Cambridge.
Bourdieu, P. (1998), *The State Nobility*, Polity, Cambridge.
Bourdieu, P and J-C. Passeron (1968), *Les Heritiers*, Editions de Minuit, Paris.
Brown, P. and R. Crompton (1994), (eds), *Economic Restructuring and Social Exclusion*, UCL Press, London.

Bude, H. (1998) 'Die Überflüssigen als transversale Kategorie', in P. Berger and M. Vester, (eds), *Alte Ungleichheiten - Neue Spaltungen*, Leske und Budrich, Opladen.

Chamberlayne, P. (1996): 'Social exclusion: sociological traditions and national contexts', Sostris Working Paper 1.

Devine, J. and J. Wright (1993), *The Greatest of Evils. Urban Poverty and the American Underclass*, New York.

Economic and Social Research Council (1995), *Thematic Priorities*, Swindon.

European Commission (1994a), *Growth, Competitiveness, Employment: the Challenge and Ways Forward into the 21st Century*, European Commission, Luxembourg.

European Commission (1994b), *European Social Policy: A Way Forward for the Union*, European Commission, Luxembourg.

Fassin, D. (1996), 'Exclusion, underclass, marginalidad', in *Revue francaise de sociologie*, XXXVII-1.

Jordan, B. (1996), *A Theory of Poverty and Social Exclusion*, Polity, Cambridge.

Kohli, M. (1999), 'Ausgrenzung im Lebenslauf', in S. Herkommer, (ed.), *Soziale Ausgrenzungen*, VSA, Hamburg.

Körber, K. (1998), 'Ethnizität und Wohlfahrtsstaat' in Berger and Vester, *op cit.*

Kronauer, M. (1997),'Soziale Ausgrenzung' und 'Underclass'.Über neue Formen der gesellschaftlichen Spaltung, in *Leviathan* 1.

Kronauer, M. (1998), 'Armut, Ausgrenzung, Unterklasse', in H. Häußermann, (ed.), *Großstadt. Soziologische Stichworte*, Leske und Budrich, Opladen.

Lawless, P., R. Martin and S. Hardy (1997), (eds), *Unemployment and Social Exclusion*, Jessica Kingsley: London.

Leibfried, S. *et al.* (1995) *Zeit der Armut. Lebensläufe im Sozialstaat*, Suhrkamp, Frankfurt/Main.

Levitas, R. (1996), 'The concept of social exclusion and the new Durkheimian hegemony', *Critical Social Policy* 46, Vol. 16, pp. 5-20.

MacDonald, R. (1997), (ed.), *Youth, the 'Underclass' and Social Exclusion*, Routledge: London.

Marcuse, P. (1996), 'Space and Race in the Post-Fordist City', in E. Mingione, (ed.), *Urban Poverty and the Underclass*, Blackwell, Oxford.

Mollenkopf, J. and M. Castells (1992), (eds), *Dual City: Restructuring New York*, New York.

Newman, K. (1988), *Falling from Grace. The Experience of Downward Mobility in the American Middle Class*, New York .

Offe, C. (1996), 'Moderne "Barbarei" Der Naturzustand im Kleinformat?', in M. Miller and H.G. Soeffner, (eds), *Modernität und Barbarei*, Suhrkamp Frankfurt/Main.

Parkin, F. (1974), 'Strategies of Social Closure in Class Formation', in F. Parkin, (ed.), *The Social Analysis of Class Structure*, Tavistock, London, pp. 1-18.

Parkin, F. (1979), *Marxism and Class Theory: A Bourgeois Critique*, London, Tavistock.

Paugam, S. (1996a), *L'Exclusion, l'état des savoirs*, Paris.

Paugam, S. (1996b), 'A New Social Contract? Poverty and Social Exclusion: A Sociological View', EUI Working Papers RSC No. 96/37, Badia Fiesolana.

Procacci, G. (1996), 'A New Social Contract? Against Exclusion? The Poor and the Social Sciences', *European University Working Papers*, RSC No. 96/41, Badia Fiesolana, San Domenico (FI).

Roche, M. (1992), *Rethinking Citizenship: Welfare, Ideology and Change in Modern Society*, Polity Press, Cambridge.

Roche, M. and R. Van Berkel (1997), (eds), *European Citizenship and Social Exclusion*, Ashgate, Aldershot.

Rodgers, G., C. Gore and J. Figueiredo (1995), (eds), *Social Exclusion: Rhetoric, Reality, Responses*, International Institute for Labour Studies, Geneva.

Room, G. (1995), (ed.), *Beyond the Threshold: The Measurement and Analysis of Social Exclusion*, The Policy Press, Bristol.

Scherr, A. (1998), 'Randgruppen und Minderheiten' in B. Schäfers and W. Zapf, (eds), *Wörterbuch zur Gesellschaft Deutschlands*, Leske und Budrich, Opladen.

Sennett, R. (1998), *The Corrosion of Character*, Norton, New York.

Silver, H. (1994), 'Social exclusion and social solidarity: three paradigms', *International Labour Review*, Vol. 133, No. 5-6: pp. 531-578.

Schmitter-Heisler, B. (1991), 'A Comparative Perspective on the Underclass. Questions of Urban Poverty, Race and Citizenship', in *Theory and Society*, 20, no. 4.

Stichweh, R. (1997), 'Inklusion/Exklusion, funktionale Differenzierung und Theorie der Weltgesellschaft', in *Soziale Systeme*, Vol. 3.

Virtanen, P. (1996), 'The making of a new underclass among the unemployed youth', *Labour Policy Studies*, Ministry of Labour, 150/1996, Finland.

Wacquant, L. (1996), 'The Rise of Advanced Marginality', in *Acta Sociologica*, Vol. 39.

Wacquant, L. (1996), 'Red Belt, Black Belt: Racial Division, Class Inequality and the State in the French Urban Periphery and the American Ghetto', in: E. Mingione, (ed.), *Urban Poverty and the Underclass*, Blackwell, Oxford.

Walker, A. and C. Walker. (1997), *Britain Divided: The Growth of Social Exclusion in the 1980s and 1990s*, Child Poverty Action Group, London.

Weber, M. (1968), *Economy and Society* (G. Roth and C. Wittich, eds), Bedminster Press, New York.

Wilson, W. J. (1987), *The Truly Disadvantaged. The Inner City, the Underclass and Public Policy*, Chicago.

Wilson, W. J. (1993), *The Ghetto Underclass*, Social Science Perspectives, Newbury Park.

Yépez del Costello, I. (1994), 'A comparative approach to social exclusion: Lessons from France and Belgium', *International Labour Review*, Vol. 133, No. 5-6: 613-633.

2 The End of the Full Employment Society
Changing the basis of inclusion and exclusion

GEORG VOBRUBA

Introduction

One should be cautious when social scientists speak about epoch-making social change, because they tend to overstate it. One reason for this might be that fundamental change is a better subject for social research than stable situations. Maybe it is just that normal times are simply boring compared to those of rapid change. But having issued this warning, I shall argue in this chapter that - with certain reservations - within established capitalist societies, epoch-making social change is indeed currently taking place.

During the last quarter of a century the epoch of full employment has come to an end. We are now living in the middle of a transition towards societies *after* full employment. This change affects the core mechanisms of social inclusion in modern capitalist societies, the labour market and the welfare state, since these mechanisms are based on full employment. Thus, with certain reservations, it is quite appropriate to speak about an epoch-making social change.

For some time the changes that have occurred over the last decades have been named 'the end of the work society'. The term 'work society' was coined in order to describe a basic feature of modern capitalist as well as socialist societies: that work is a central to these societies, providing their social integration (Arendt, 1981). Work structures individual life courses and the crucial institutions. Consequently the term 'end of work society' was aimed at a fundamental social change. The basic assumption was that in the long run, labour-saving technological progress will drastically reduce work in the work society. Work as a necessity but also as a souce of meaning and social integration, disappears - 'what could be worse?' (Arendt, 1981, p. 12).

The objection that soon followed pointed to an error of categorization: speaking about an 'end of the work society' is an exaggeration, because the expression 'work society' has acquired too broad a connotation. Currently societies are not running out of work, but of *paid work*. Equating paid work with work was - rightly - seen as discriminating against other kinds of work - primarily housework, but also other forms, such as DIY (Do-It-Yourself), etc. Thus public and scientific attention has been directed towards these kinds of work, resulting in the belief that there is 'little work, but a lot to do' (Dierkes and Strümpel, 1985).

At this point a more fundamental objection can be made: There is no empirical evidence for the prospective end of paid work. Neither work nor paid work will disappear. This is what the development of paid workers in almost all western industrial societies shows (see Figure 2.1).

In the long run unemployment in all industrial societies has increased. But employment has by no means decreased correspondingly. Indeed, the employment rates hide a growing variety of modes of paid work - first and foremost, a growing rate of part-time work. But this hardly indicates a long-term trend towards an end of paid work. I shall show at the end of this chapter that this fact forces us to find a new basis for discussions about prospects after full employment.

Societies do not face the end of work nor of paid work, even although the period of full employment is over. Nevertheless, far-reaching processes of social change and adaptation are on the way. In order to encapsulate this change in a short formula I shall speak about 'the end of the full employment society'. 'Full employment society' means that important institutions that are crucial for the inclusion or exclusion of people, such as the system of social security and the tax system, are based on full employment and regular work. It means also that normal life courses are centred on paid work. The full employment society is structured by full employment, but this does not mean that full employment necessarily exists. On the contrary: the basic features of the full employment society become visible only when full employment is over; only when full employment is nothing more than a target. Presently the full employment society is centred on a fiction - but one with real consequences.

First I shall discuss the improbability of a return to full employment. Basically it is caused by certain peculiarities of the supply side of the labour market, as distinct from other markets. One of these peculiarities is the reason why unemployment and employment can rise simultaneously. The improbability of full employment results from such peculiarities, as well as from the disappearence of the conditions for successful macroeconomic regulation and from the constellation of interests of the actors involved in empoyment policy.

Figure 2.1   Employment and Unemployment in Europe and the US 1966-96

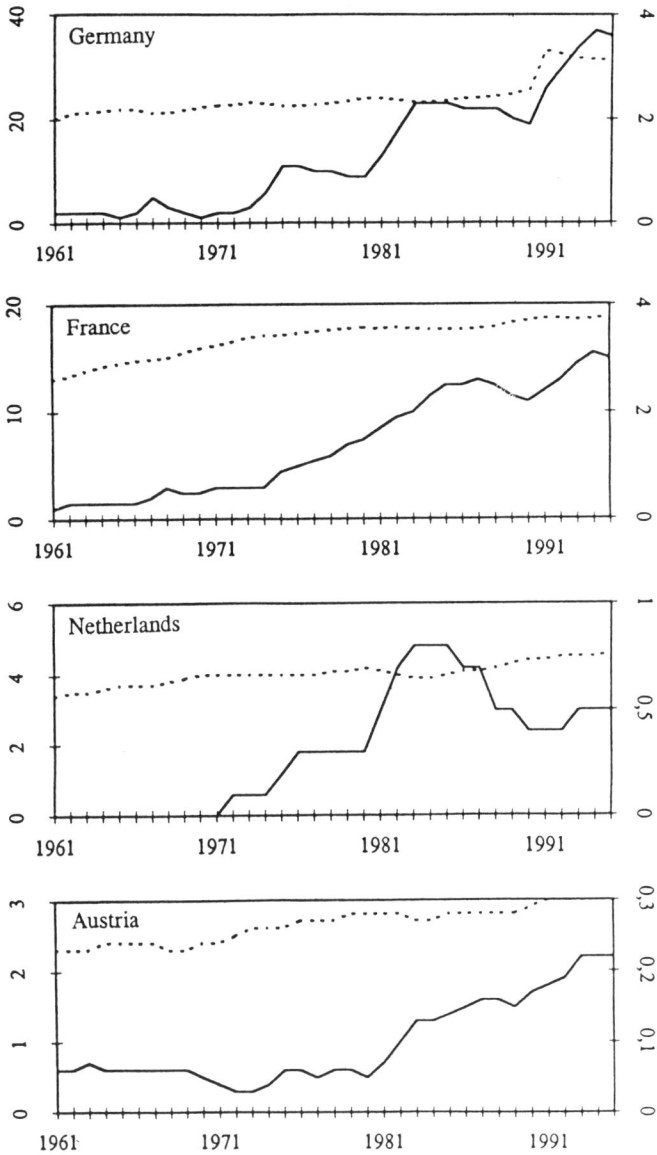

Figure 2.1 (continued)

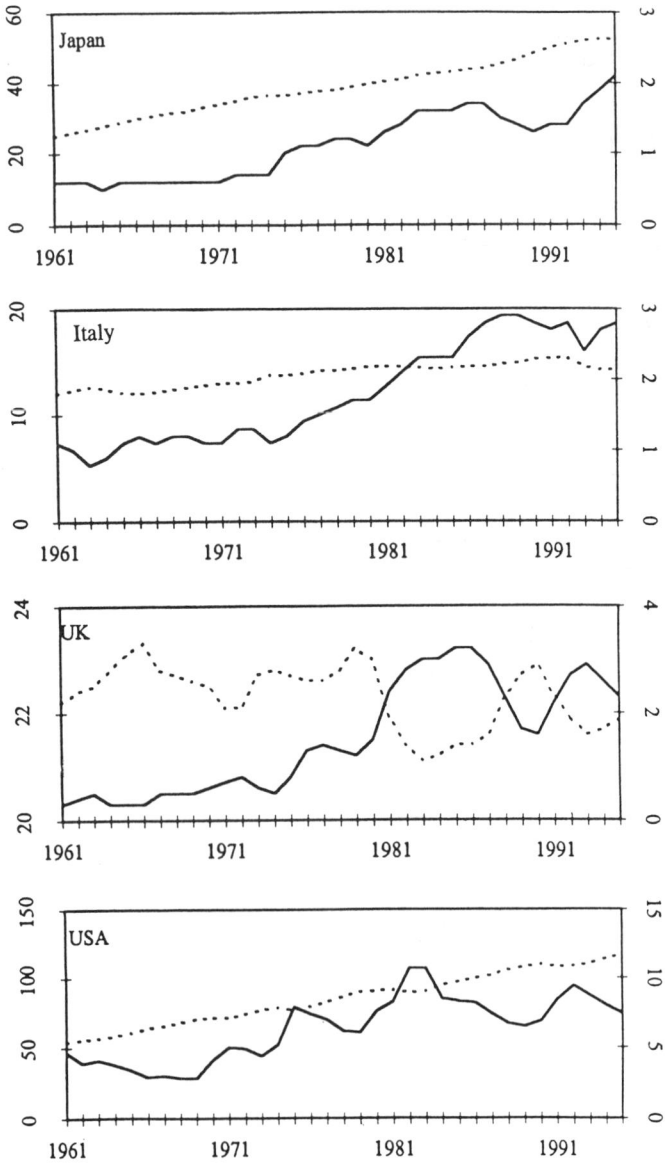

Source: Jahresgutachten 1997/8 des Sachverständigenrates zur Begutachtung der gesamtwirtschaftlichen Entwicklung

Then I shall offer a model of the phases of the long-term development of work and income, which exceeds the period of full employment in the past and in the future. Such a model does not prove anything, but taking such a long time period into account makes the historical location of full employment possible. This does not necessarily mean that full employment is definitely over. Rather, the result is that full employment can be seen as a phase in the long-term development of the relationship between paid work and income (Vobruba, 1998). This leads to a change of perspective: Full employment is no longer the standard constellation, which makes other phases appear as deviations (Burdillat and Outin, 1995). From the long-term perspective, full employment can be seen as a peculiar phase among others characterized by the lack of 'work for all'. This perspective triggers new questions concerning not just the possibility of regaining full employment but also other possibilities for the generation of work and income.

Finally I shall introduce a new element into the current debate on work and income, which until now has been limited to arguments about the gains and losses resulting from the end of full employment, and in particular, the condemnation of its exclusionary effects. That is, I shall adopt a much more optimistic and constructive approach, and argue that full employment is not the only basis for social inclusion; now that this basis has been rendered obsolete, we must seek other means to achieve social inclusion. The central concept in my argument is the 'two-fold crisis of paid work'. I shall use this term in order to link two influential theses. The first is that there are too few jobs in relation to the number of people who rely directly on paid work. And the second is that there are many workplaces which do not meet qualitative criteria relating to working conditions, especially ecological or peace requirements. All in all, paid work is lacking, in terms of both quantity and quality. I shall refer to this argument because it derives from a perspective which transcends full employment. If the analysis of the improbability of full employment is accurate, then one should expect a degree of realism in this discussion. In contrast, however, the countless proposals to regain traditional full employment that accompany the rise of unemployment are fascinating empirical phenomena themselves: What propels a discussion which holds up full employment counterfactually for more than a quarter of a century? This is not my subject here. But at least a few suggestions relating to it might be found in the analysis of the interests that lie behind full employment.

And what about the 'certain reservations' mentioned above? When I am talking about an epoch-making change from full employment societies to societies after full employment, this does not necessarily imply a dramatic and surprising process. Neither is it a process which society has not yet recognized. On the contrary, there are at least some indications that for a long time now, the public as well as the politicians have taken note of this change and have become resigned to it. I shall return to this point. Nor is it the end of a particularly long period. On the contrary, the end of full employment is the end of an exceptional period, notwithstanding its having been a period crucial to the formation of contemporary societies.

The improbability of full employment

Is the time of full employment in regular work over? I will deal with this question by considering three points: first some peculiarities of the supply side of the labour market, then the feasibility and necessity of full employment, and finally the interests relating to full employment. The outcome of this discussion will be evidence of the improbability of full employment within capitalism. (A strict proof of the impossibility of full employment is impossible, at least because there was once a time when full employment existed.)

Peculiarities of the supply side of the labour market

Labour supply is determined by various, not just economic, factors. The first important factor for the size of the labour supply is the birth rate. Cultural and institutional factors also play an important role: for instance, the development of labour-oriented attitudes of groups such as women who did not previously participate in the labour market, and the institutional developments that encourage or hinder diverse groups in offering their labour power, such as immigrants and guest workers. All such factors together make it impossible for the labour-supply to constitute itself according to purely market-stategic criteria, that is, according to anticipated relations of scarcity in the labour market. Forecasts of future labour market chances do not determine procreation and birth (Vobruba, 1989), thus quantitative adaptations on the supply side of the labour market are hardly possible. In addition, at present the mass migration of superfluous labour into world regions able to absorb them is no longer possible. Finally, there is only a limited number of possibilities to live outside the labour market. Thus a problem of existence emerges. In contrast to the superfluous supply of goods, there are no economic mechanisms in the labour market to make superfluous labour supply disappear. It remains a social problem within society: people without income. Until the middle of the twentieth century agriculture had the function of absorbing the unemployed who appeared from time to time in the course of the economic cycle, providing them with jobs and food - and sending them back into the industrial sector after each crisis (Lutz, 1984). But since within the Western industrial societies there is only a small industralized remainder of the agricultural sector left, this absorbing function can now only be fulfilled by systems of social security. These systems contribute - in some countries more and in some less - in a crucial way to the solution of an individual and a collective problem which faces all capitalist societies. The individual problem is the dynamic of impoverishment, and the collective problem is the emergence of deflationary processes.

The dynamic of impoverishment At least in the lower realm of incomes the labour supply tends to react inversely to the lowering of incomes. This means that reductions in the price of labour do not result in reductions in the labour supply, but in additional supply. Why? The closer the family's income approaches subsistence level, as 100% of the income has to be spent on consumption goods, so the more likely it will be for the family to try to compensate for losses of income by additional labour supply. Clearly this strategy guides the suppliers of labour into a prisoner's dilemma. The individual's rational strategy to offer more labour leads to collective self-damage. The widening of the collective labour supply causes a further weakening of the supply side - hence, further wage cuts. Without mechanisms limiting this downward competition, this peculiarity of the labour market implies the danger of a dynamic of impoverishment both within and outside the labour market.

Deflationary processes One major difference between labour and all other cost-factors in the enterprise lies in the fact that labour's price, the wage, is also an important part of the demand for goods (Vobruba, 1983, p 134). First, all enterprises face labour costs. And second, labour costs turn - in some cases to a quota of nearly 100% - into demand for goods. These facts have two consequences. First, if wages appear as costs in all enterprises, cuts of nominal wages might lead to a lower price level, hence higher real wage costs. Thus workers' 'wages presents' will not reach their addressees, the enterprises (Spahn, 1996, p. 143ff.). In other words, there is always the danger that a restrictive incomes policy leads to deflationary processes that thwart its redistributional aims. Second, wage cuts might unburden each individual enterprise as *producer* in the short run; but collectively, all enterprises, as *providers of goods*, will lose purchasing power. The two qualities of the wage, cost factor and part of the demand for goods, are mirrored in the two roles of the enterprise as producer (demand side of the labour market) and as seller (supply side of markets for goods). Thus successful cuts in real wages lead the enterprises into a prisoner's dilemma as well. On the one hand it is rational for each individual enterprise as producer to lower wages. But on the other, it is collectively self-damaging since, as suppliers of goods, all enterprises depend on purchasing power. The trade unions' wage policy, insisting on fixed minimum wages and a system of social security defining a reserve wage, preserve the enterprises (concerned in short-term unburdening from costs), from collective self-damage. From this persepective, Herny Ford II's famous phrase becomes less astonishing: 'If trade unions did not exist, they would have to be invented'.

We conclude that, due to the peculiarities on the supply side of the labour market, there are mechanisms that hinder balances between demand and supply in the labour market, by adaptation either of quantities or of prices. This is an important provisional finding, since the overwhelming majority of proposals aimed at regaining full employment are based on the assumption that mechanisms of economic equalization in the labour market exist. The proof of the exceptional characteristics of the labour market (Spahn and Vobruba, 1989) invalidates all proposals that basically consist in nothing but freeing market forces.

Necessity and feasibility

Usually such diagnoses result in arguments in favour of the necessity of state intervention for higher levels of employment. But arguing thus, most scholars barely see the systematic difference between the necessity and the feasibility of employment policy. On the contrary, this difference becomes simply bridged by recommendations aimed at the political systems, hence treating it as a 'black box'. In other words, in the context of such recommendations, considerations about possibilities and limits of state intervention play no role. This kind of interventionistic naivety is a common feature of almost all varieties of economic theory.

Introducing the distinction between the necessity and feasibility of employment policy enables us to formulate the two crucial questions: how has the feasibility and how has the necessity of employment policy developed?

The first question amounts to an examination of the preconditions of the success of Keynesian interventionism. These preconditions have dramatically deteriorated; for reasons that result from the shape of the economy, and for reasons that lie in the logic of Keynesian interventionism itself.

Keynesian interventionism has lost its preconditions of success with the end of fixed exchange rates, with the proceeding transnationalization of trade and financial markets (Scharpf 1987, p. 301ff.). In 1981 the Mitterrand government for instance discovered that under the condition of a fully internationalized monetary system, a national policy of low interest rates aimed at triggering higher employment leads to outflows of capital. In addition, high volumes of external trade lead to the danger that the disadvantages of deficit spending remain at home, while its advantages - the increased demand for goods - partly go abroad.

Practical experiences of Keynesian interventionism led to two kinds of entrepreneurial learning processes which turned out to be disastrous for the further efficacy of Keynesian interventionism. On the one hand, there was the experience that - in contrast to the Keynesian programmatic - there are no reductions in public deficits during periods of prosperity, mirroring the expansion of public deficits during periods of crisis. This led to the expectation for higher taxes in order to finance the public deficit as the price for Keynesian demand management. Additionally the asymmetry between expansion and reduction of public deficits caused a growing demand for capital, thus leading to higher interests and to an expansion of financial investments without any employment, at the expense of material investments that cause employment. On the other hand, Keynesian interventionism was wrecked on its own programmatic, of triggering long-term prosperity by short-term intervention. Entrepreneurs have learned to anticipate these interventions as short-term measures - and hence react accordingly by producing at the limits of their capacities instead of expanding investments, and by preferring overtime work to additional employment. These anticipations might be realistic or not - in any case, they led Keynesian interventionism into the trap of a self-fulfilling prophecy: they had solely short-term effects because everyone expected them to work that way (Vobruba, 1983, p 142). Unlike Scharpf (1987, p. 42) who states that the main reason for the failure of Keynesianism lay in 'the distinctive problems in popularizing Keynesian interpretations of the situation', I am stressing the point that just the awareness of the Keynesian functional relation undermined it.

I now turn to the question of the necessity of developing employment policy. But what does 'necessity' mean? One possibility is to start the argument by presupposing an 'objective' necessity of intervention. In this case, it is easy to answer the question as to how the necessity of employment policy develops: its necessity grows with the number of unemployed (Sheak, 1995). This is the usual approach. But such a term as 'objective necessity', imposed from the perspective of an external observer, is treacherous. It must remain unclear to the external observer, whether or not the relevant actors within the field of observation share his notion of necessity. A gap between the internal actors' and the external observer's notions of necessity is precarious for the latter. Either he does not recognize it or he cannot bridge the gap except by moral rhetoric. The following statement in favor of a reduction in work time is a telling example of the evident loss of realism among social scientists who base their political recommendations on 'objective necessities' instead of analysing how relevant actors perceive them. 'There is an incomprehensible (*sic*!) - not to say irresponsible - resistance from politicians, employers, trade unionists, but also academics, against the mathematical evidence of the need for a reduction of labour time' (Pacolet, 1997, p. 273). As a matter of fact, the abundance of different recommendations for a solution to the employment problem seems to be a hindrance to its success.

Treating the analysis of relevant actors as a part of the employment problem enables us to ask what different actors perceive as costs and benefits of different kinds of employment policy. Defining certain effects of employment policies as costs or benefits differs according to different actors' perspectives. Different actors will assess costs and benefits differently.

Interests in full employment

To cut a long story short: within the last twenty years, there has been a steady approximation of the notion of the *necessity* to that of the *feasibility* of employment policy. I shall cite three indicators to demonstrate this.

First one can observe that the political rhetoric has been gradually adapted to the existing situation of the labour market (Bleses and Rose, 1998, pp. 220ff.). The term 'full employment' has been replaced by 'more employment' and then by 'unemployment as our biggest concern'. Second, the level of unemployment that is regarded by politicians and economists as consistent with full employment has steadily increased, as has the NAIRU, the estimated level of unemployment necessary to forestall accelerating inflation. Considering increases in labour market flexibility in almost all industrial societies, the steadily increasing estimations of the NAIRU in the most important industrial societies are hardly plausible in economic terms, but rather look like legitimating the unavoidable (International Labour Office, 1996, p. 51ff.). And third, the main subjects of political and scientific publications that accompany developments in the labour market with commentaries, recommendations and laments have changed their character.

In the initial phase of unemployment after the first oil price shock, there were discussions about the desirability and feasibility of a 'right to work' in the sense of a legal claim. In the next phase, full employment was still highlightened as an aim and an obligation of the state. Then 'full employment' was dropped and replaced by 'more employment'. Meanwhile the production of texts on 'full employment' has virtually ceased. If used at all, 'full employment' now has a new sense, containing a large variety of deregulated forms of work beyond standard work. 'Full employment ... does not mean that everyone is in fact employed in a regular full-time job' (International Labour Office, 1996, p. 41). I shall return to this point in the next section on 'income mixes'.

It is worth noting that the political elite as well as the public (albeit reluctantly) have lost their ambitions regarding full employment. The old and almost forgotten forecast that mass unemployment will cause 'system-destroying' effects was wrong. High rates of unemployment had no political consequences; even that political early warning system, changes in the parliamentary majorities, did not result. Mass unemployment is not an obstacle to winning elections. This fact inevitably influenced the elite's perceptions of the importance of unemployment and employment policy.

All in all, learning processes to the disadvantage of the unemployed took place on all levels.

In order to analyse the interests of different groups with respect to full employment, one has to take into account the fact that different groups perceive different effects of employment policy as costly. Costs in this sense might be: empowerment of the supply side of the labour market, rising prices or interest rates, or income losses.

The interest of the owners of capital is clearly oriented against full employment. Full employment strengthens the bargaining position of the supply side of the labour market, hence increasing costs. A result of this interest is the connection between sinking unemployment rates and sinking stock prices.

The interests of entrepreneurs are ambivalent. On the one hand they must fear rising wage costs as a consequence of full employment, as well as rising interest rates as a consequence of inflation. On the other hand, the entrepreneurs' interests are more closely related to local conditions than are those of the capitalists. Thus entrepreneurs must be interested in maintaining social order at their places of production. They fear at least a dimension of unemployment that affects the social order.

Business associations as political actors are interested in full employment remaining as a recognized political aim. It is precisely the difference between the postulate of full employment and full employment itself which helps business organizations carry through their members' interests in different fields of conflict, like environment, technology, traffic or energy. It is easier to overcome environmental resistance against various investments by highlighting the expected gains in employment (Nissen, 1993) than by arguing about the desirability of the planned output.

The trade unions have the clearest interest in full employment. But this interest is not as clear-cut as one might assume at first glance. From the perspective of trade unions all those measurements are unproblematic which result in a widening of the volume of employment and/or in a redistribution of employment without a redistribution of incomes. At the same time, they must try to avoid all variants of employment policy that force their core membership to give up part of their work and income, or even just their income. There is little willingness to do so, because in reality the often discussed exchange of 'income for jobs' is a highly asymmetric arrangement - an immediate, definite renunciation by one group in exchange for future, uncertain gains of jobs for another group. Additionally, trade unions see the interests of their core membership affected by deregulation and a downward movement of wages. Generally, the interest of trade unions in measures favouring full employment has its limits, as soon as its members have to bear the costs of these measures. As these selective interests do not fit in with the claim of trade unions to represent the interests of all employed and unemployed workers, they are forced to insist on the postulate of full employment, at least programmatically. Thus, unwillingly, the trade unions are in accordance with the business associations' interest in maintaining a gap between the postulate of full employment and the actual labour market situation (Vobruba, 1997, p. 57ff.). Thus the trade unions contribute to a constellation in which they can be easily disciplined.

Income mixes

Full employment consisting of regular work is from a historical perspective not the rule but the exception. In order to demonstrate this I shall reiterate my distinction (Vobruba, 1998) of three stages in the long-term development of work and income within capitalism. First, in a long phase, the labour market as a distributional mechanism for work and income developed beside a traditional non-monetary sector, which subsidized it. Income mixes composed of incomes in cash, earned in the labour market, and incomes in kind, were dominant in this first phase. The family's earnings consisted in various proportions of men's unstable and often insufficient wages, of women's earnings in kind and, if necessary, of additional earnings of their children and the old. Roughly since the beginning of the 20th century, but differing from country to country, welfare payments came to assume a certain importance as additional income. But in the world economic crisis after 1929, possibilities to retreat into the primary agricultural sector were still of crucial importance (Lutz, 1984).

The next, relatively short phase started with the end of the Second World War. Rapid processes of urbanization led to the dissolution of primary economies, which had subsidized wage labour for a long time. Now almost everyone depends on incomes in cash. The related problem, that for the overwhelming majority this dependency required access to the labour market, did not become pressing because the fully monetarized society appeared as a full employment society based on regular work (Mückenberger, 1985). This means that all depended on wages in order to secure their material existence, and simultaneously the labour market offered regular work for all those who required it. In addition, the systems of social security expanded towards the provision of sufficient incomes. Nonetheless there was (and is) no free choice between the labour market and the system of social security, but a clear priority of the labour market, which is secured by administrative rules of access to welfare payments. Although the rigidity of these rules of access varies from country to country, they are always based on willingness to work, prior participation in paid work and level of income (Vobruba, 1990).

As a result, within the existing welfare states there are only few possibilities of combining wages and social security payments legally. This fact does not cause problems as long as there are enough opportunities to work and as long as the wages are at least above the level of subsistence. But it is exactly these preconditions that fade away with the end of full employment, with the increase in the prevalence of discontinuous work (Mutz et al., 1995) and with the expansion of non-standard work (Kalleberg et al., 1997).

One might describe the third phase that now appears in outline as follows: almost everyone still depends on an income in cash, but there is no longer enough regular work to provide everyone who needs it with a stable and sufficient income. Thus new income mixes, fully based on money, develop: in particular, mixes of wages and social security payments, and mixes of wages and capital earnings.

Wages and social security payments

In all capitalist societies which include a welfare state, income mixes of wages and social security payments expand. Until now the expansion of these income mixes predominantly have taken place in the realm of illegality. Illegal income mixes derive from different forms of illegal earnings beside social security payments (Jordan, 1992). Legal income mixes are possible if earnings are insufficient to lead to a total withdrawal of the social security payments. Within the systems of social security in most western industrial societies there is a slow trend in this direction. Relatively advanced examples are the Credit Income Tax in the US and some elements of a negative income tax in Austria.

Wages and capital earnings

An empirical indicator of the expansion of combinations of wages and capital earnings is the growing incongruence between the income distribution and factors of production. This incongruence indicates that a growing number of people receive wages and earnings from capital simultaneously. Programmatically the idea of a 'shareholder socialism' (Meade, 1986; Roemer, 1994) is a case in point. In principle the idea behind this is as follows. In capitalist societies the interests of capitalists have such a structural advantage that any political fight against them appears hopeless. This is the lesson from the history of social democracy. Simultaneously, the efficacy of capitalism in providing material well-being must be acknowledged. This is the lesson from the defeat of socialism within the competition of systems. The problem is that, without socio-political regulation, this advantage of capitalism only favours a minority of the population. If there is no possibility of realising the majority's interests against those of the owners of capital, and if a satisfactory redistribution by social policy is no longer possible, then this majority must become owners of capital itself. All these approaches result in dissolving the hitherto existing relation between social groups, income sources and interests. All in all, if capitalism has won, then everyone must become capitalist, at least in part, in order to have a share in the fruits of its victory. If there is not enough income from paid work, then it must be supplemented by income from capital. From this point of view the full employment society must change into a shareholder society.

Whether capitalism can endure such an enlargement of its social basis is an old question. The fear is that if people have enough income from capital they will refuse to work. But future developments might diminish this fear. In this respect at least the following aspects are important. There is no scarcity of workers, and the kinds of workers who are of central importance for future economic success are not only motivated by incomes.

Demonstrating the improbability of full employment and historicizing the phase of full employment together lead me to the question of what developments might be possible after full employment. There is only a little literature dealing with this subject. The only discussion that has treated this problem constructively has long since vanished.

The twofold crisis of paid work

At present there has been little consideration of whether the end of full employment might be seen as an advantage as well as a loss. Typically, most investigations focus exclusively on its being a loss, and concentrate on the living conditions of the losers, concluding with a condemnation of their exclusion. Conversely we know very little about people who have accommodated themselves successfully to the new conditions.

In a certain sense the discussion ten or fifteen years ago was already more advanced. At the beginning of the end of the full employment society, in the late 1970s and 1980s, there was a broad-ranging debate on alternatives to the industrial-capitalist mode of production and work, and - at that time implicitly - on alternative modes of inclusion and exclusion within society, in which the loss of jobs was treated not only as an evil but also as an opportunity. This discussion of alternative economics is relevant, because until today it has remained the only constructive response to the end of full employment. First I shall briefly summarize the discussion. Then I will explain why it was, just 'in a certain sense', more advanced. This will provide us with an answer as to why this discussion has broken down and suggest a way to restart it, with a greater chance of making it durable and effective.

Between the last years of full employment and the first oil price crisis the labour market situation changed rapidly. The end of full employment came to be recognized by a political and social scientific audience characterized by two convictions. On the one hand there was a permanent intensive critique of the industrial-capitalist mode of production. The main objections were targeted at the quality of work, the quality of products (the armament industry), external effects (ecology) and the industral-capitalist model of well-being in general (Schumacher, 1977; Biswanger, Geissberger and Ginsburg, 1979; Cooley, 1980). On the other hand it was taken for granted that the increasing number of unemployed is caused by a shrinking number of jobs. Unemployment was seen as caused by a decrease of labour force demand. As the years went by and unemployment continued to rise, this came to be perceived as an enduring phenomenon. The steady rise in unemployment became interpreted as the sign of the 'end of work' (Dahrendorf, 1980; Guggenberger, 1988). These two convictions led to the following interpretation of unemployment: industrial-capitalist work lacks quality and quantity. This is the constellation of the debate I am compressing in the term 'twofold crisis of paid work' (Vobruba, 1989, p. 23).

In this constellation all participants have faced certain problems in taking their stand in the discussion (Evers and Opielka, 1985). Opting unconditionally for a solution to the quantitative problem (i.e., employment policy) conflicted with the qualitative critique, involving consideration of the criteria of ecology, peace and health. Insisting on such criteria generated opposition in terms of the deprivation of the unemployed. This constellation, deriving from the 'twofold crisis of paid work', is the reason for the weakening of the informative impact of the political left-right-distinction, a strategic problem unresolved so far.

'Useful unemployment'

Facing growing unemployment, the first idea developed was to short-circuit quantitative failure and qualitative critique. To put it simply: if the quality of jobs is unacceptable then it is good if there are no more such jobs (Illich, 1978; Bahro, 1985). This interpretation might be seen as a simple combination of some ideas of Marx and Arendt. Marx's critique of alienation became ecologically widened and tied together with Arendt's idea of the transition from the work society to the *Tätigkeitsgesellschaft*, or 'active society'. The idea of changing the quality of industrial production and work came to be superseded by the image of an exit from the industrial society plus an entry into totally different ways of working and living. The empirical evidence fitting in with this image was found in the simultaneity of unemployment and changes of values (Inglehart, 1977; Vonderach, 1980; von Klipstein and Strümpel, 1984). This simultaneity fed the conviction that the economic and the cultural changes will reciprocally make each other unproblematic: the retreat from paid work leads to losses of income - but these losses become alleviated by the change of values. The change of values triggers desires for more self-determination - the retreat of the work society offers more room for manoeuvre. The debates were centred around questions like: what are the benefits of paid work for the workers? What kinds of activities can replace these benefits? In most cases those debates started by distinguishing between material and non-material benefits.

Most scholars did not expect that alternative forms of work could replace the losses of material benefits caused by unemployment. But they expected a compensation of losses of material benefits by increased leisure time - hence increasing non-material benefits. Thus less wealth was seen as being replaced by more well-being. This point of view was based on a critique of 'manipulated' needs, a critique of the 'monetarization' of all needs and on the saturation of demand. As a consequence one expected that losses of income and gains in leisure time would free authentic needs that are no longer distorted by capitalist society. These authentic needs are oriented towards fewer material goods - this was the assumption that led to the short-circuiting of the qualitative and the quantitative aspects of the twofold crisis of paid work.

Pragmatic dual economy

A more pragmatic reaction to the twofold crisis of paid work consisted of several proposals for a dual economy. These proposals start with the assumption that, while it is impossible to abolish industrial, alienated work, one can at least limit it (Adler-Karlsson, 1979; Gorz, 1982). The emancipation of paid work was abandoned, but in terms of its narrow limits this will do no harm.

For the development of the concept of a dual economy (Huber, 1984) the historical reconstruction of the tradition of cooperatives was viewed as being of crucial importance (Novy, 1978; Novy and Prinz, 1985). Also important was the literature which stressed the point that within capitalist-industrial societies a significant proportion of economic activity, especially housework, takes place outside the formal economy (Ostner, 1978; Cass, 1981). Much consideration was given to the question of how much the loss of welfare in the formal sector might be compensated for by work in the informal sector. Again, these considerations were linked with the thesis that the simultaneity of unemployment and a change of values alleviates the shift from the formal to the informal sector (Berger, 1982; Huber, 1979).

All in all, there was the conviction that informal work, while it cannot replace formal work, can, together with collective self-help, provide an important supplement (Gershuny and Pahl, 1980; Heinze and Olk, 1982; Grottian and Kück, 1983). These ideas focused less on a direct link between unemployment and the autonomous sector, but more on a redistribution of time for paid work and for informal work. This led to claims for a working time policy that would provide room for work outside the labour market (Vonderach, 1982; Gorz, 1983; Hegner, 1983).

By considering life beyond the labour market and beyond alienated paid work as an opportunity, the critique of industrial work ironically converged with neoclassical dogma. Neoclassical economic theory as everybody knows treats unemployment as a manifestation of preferences for an alternative use of time. The hopes of some alternative economists were - quite similarly - oriented towards informal work as a better alternative to the labour market.

The basic income debate

But the interpretation of unemployment as liberation did not lead to much in practice. The underlying assumption of unproblematic possibilities for inclusion outside the labour market in particular and into society in general appeared dubious. '*Autonomie oder Getto*' (Kraushaar, 1978), as rival characteristics of the autonomous sector, reflected such doubt. Thus the awareness oriented itself towards the actually self-evident fact that real possibilities outside the labour market depend on material conditions. After rather troublesome discussions it turned out that households do not really have at their disposal those options outside the labour market which neoclassical theory imputes to them. And what is more, it became clear that it is impossible to create the preconditions for such options individually or within small groups, as assumed by the theorists of an alternative economy. Thus some scholars concluded that these preconditions must be provided and secured by the state. This was the point of departure for the basic income debate (Schmid, 1984; Büchele and Wohlgenannt, 1985; Opielka and Vobruba, 1986).

All arguments for a basic income must offer answers to three questions. First, who is entitled to the basic income? Obviously this question has been seen as difficult and glossed over with the vague formula, 'for all'. More attention was devoted to the other two questions: what is the appropriate level for the basic income?, and what percentage of earnings should be deducted from the basic income? The debate first focused on the level of the basic income and later on the rules of deduction.

In its 'emphatic phase' the basic income debate was linked with the discussion on the alternative economy. The leading idea was to control the unavoidable 'decoupling of work and income' in such a way that it could provide preconditions for activities outside the labour market, by at least partially replacing wages. These proposals were based on diagnoses and motives that resemble the dual economy discussion. At the centre of these diagnoses were remarkable increases in labour productivity. Unemployment was seen as a consequence of the labour-saving technological progress. This assumption not only provided an explanation for unemployment but also offered a solution: increases in productivity lead to increasing wealth. Hence solving the social problem of unemployment is a matter of redistribution - through a basic income.

Later, however, the hope that technological progress would help to solve the problems of redistribution related to a basic income was dropped. But in the subsequent more pragmatic discussion the idea was maintained that a basic income makes it possible to resist protecting any given job, thus securing the state's political room of manoeuvre for modernization - economic, ecological etc. (Nissen, 1994). Whilst these considerations crucially depend on the guaranteed income, the more recent discussion refocused its interest on the combination of wages and parts of a basic income, thus on the technique of the negative income tax. Several proposals to introduce a negative income tax, or at least something like it, were put forward in order to develop a low-wage sector for the integration of low-productive workers into work without creating a working poor (Scharpf, 1995). In terms of the system introduced above, this is a proposal in favour of regulated income mixes.

For years the debates on how to handle unemployment were dominated by the misleading assumption that growing unemployment necessarily means falling employment. In other words one assumed there to be a zero-sum relation between employment and unemployment. This assumption was seriously damaging for the alternative-economy debate as well as the basic income discussion, because it led to misleading assessments of the usable room for redistribution. Why?

The interpretation of unemployment as being caused by decreasing employment and the average positive growth of the GDP inevitably implies that the reason for unemployment is a decline in the labour demand caused by high rates of productivity. Gorz (1983, p. 53) is a case in point: 'The microelectronic revolution launches the end of work'. This interpretation ignores the non-economic determinants of labour supply I mentioned above. It neglects the fact that within the last 25 years in almost all Western industrial societies, both unemployment and employment have increased. At best, only a small proportion of unemployment might be explained by a steady decrease in the demand for labour. One can speak of a lack of labour demand solely in this sense - that it does not absorb an increase in the labour supply.

The basic problem facing people who enter the labour market as an additional labour supply lies in the fact that they have to work *first*, in order *then* to get an income, hence increasing the demand for consumer goods and thus stimulating investment. The responsiveness of the economic system to the unemployed willing to work would be possible only if it could anticipate their additional demand for goods. But as long as those seeking additional employment have nothing to offer but their ability to work, they cannot attract attention in an economic sense.

The shift from the demand side to the supply side of the explanation for unemployment must cause disillusionment about the amount of room for redistribution. The hopeful assumption that the appropriate use of space for distribution is provided by technological progress is untenable, because it is simply a matter that more people need money within the given space for distribution.

The discussion of the twofold crisis of paid work suffered from two deficits. First, it imputed an unrealistic amount of space for redistribution, and it overestimated incomes from outside the labour market. Generally speaking, it underestimated the material aspects of the twofold crisis of paid work. Secondly, the discussion was more normative than analytical. This is especially true for the basic income discussion. For a long time, analyses of motives of relevant actors and of constellations of actors that could have been used strategically have been neglected (although for an exception, see Pioch, 1996). Instead, more or less elaborate attempts at normative argument were made (van Parijs, 1992) - not a good sign for the political relevance of a discussion (Vobruba, 1997, p. 113). The discussion about the alternative economy focused more clearly - but not clearly enough - on empirical evidence. This discussion could cite practical illustrations, but these were of relatively small groups. Recognition of the character of the real existing alternative economy as a 'model' had often been emphasised, but nevertheless, far-reaching hopes were still linked to it concerning solutions to unemployment. Thus a small group's way of life became implicitly treated as a model for everyone. But it turned out not to be open to generalization.

To sum up: the remarkable peculiarity of the discussion of the twofold crisis of paid work is that it treated the end of full employment constructively, instead of just complaining about it. But the discussion was wrecked on its two weaknesses: illusions about the possibilities of redistribution on the one hand, and illusions about possibilities of realising an alternative way of life more generally on the other.

Thus analyses of the development of societies after full employment must centre on distributional problems and on people's own perceptions of problems and opportunities after full employment. We still have little knowledge about people's income strategies and well-being after full employment. We still have little knowledge about how people cope with the present shifts in the conditions of exclusion and inclusion. Perhaps many of them have already made arrangements to deal with the new situation.

References

Adler-Karlsson, G. (1979), 'Gedanken zur Vollbeschäftigung', in *MittAB* 4.

Arendt, H. (1981), *Vita activa oder vom tätigen Leben*, Piper, München.

Aronowitz, S. and W. DiFazio (1994), *The Jobless Future*, University of Minnesota Press, Minneapolis.

Bahro, R. (1985), 'Kommune wagen!' in M. Opielka., (ed.), *Die ökosoziale Frage*, Fischer, Frankfurt.

Berger, J. (unter Mitarbeit von Lore Voigt) (1982), 'Zur Zukunft der Dualwirtschaft', in Benseler, F., R. Heinze and A. Klönne, (eds), *Zukunft der Arbeit*, VSA, Hamburg.

Biswanger, H., W. Geissberger and T. Ginsburg (1979), (eds) *Wege aus der Wohlstandsfalle. Der NAWU-Report: Strategien gegen Arbeitslosigkeit und Umweltkrise*, Fischer, Frankfurt.

Bleses, P. and E. Rose (1998), *Deutungswandel der Sozialpolitik*, Campus, Frankfurt.

Büchele, H. and L. Wohlgenannt (1985), *Grundeinkommen ohne Arbeit*, Europaverlag, Wien.

Cass, B. (1981), 'The Social Impact: Changes in Paid and Unpaid Work', in J. Wilkes, (ed.), *The Future of Work*, George Allen & Unwin, London, Boston, Sydney.

Cooley, M. (1980), 'Produktion für gesellschaftliche Bedürfnisse', in *Technologie und Politik. Das Magazin zur Wachstumskrise*, Band 15, Rowohlt, Reinbek bei Hamburg.

Dahrendorf, R. (1980), 'Im Entschwinden der Arbeitsgesellschaft', in *Merkur*, 34.

De Grip, A., J. Hoevenberg and E. Willems (1997). 'Atypical Employment in the European Union', in *International Labour Review*, Vol. 136, No. 1.

Dierkes, M. and B. Strümpel (1985), (eds), *Wenig Arbeit aber viel zu tun*, Westdeutscher Verlag, Opladen.

Evers, A. and M. Opielka (1985), 'Was heißt hier eigentlich sozial? Kleiner Leitfaden zur Orientierung in einer verwirrenden Auseinandersetzung', in M. Opielka, (ed.), *Die ökosoziale Frage*, Fischer, Frankfurt.

Gershuny, J. and R. Pahl (1980) 'Britain in the decade of the three economies', in *New Society*, January.

Gorz, A. (1980), *Farewell to the Working Class. An Essay on Post-Industrial Socialism*, Pluto Press, London.

Gorz, A. (1983) *Wege ins Paradies*, Rotbuch Verlag, Berlin.

Grottian, P. and M. Kück (1983), 'Modell Berlin: 10 000 neue Arbeitsplätze im Selbsthilfe- und Alternativbereich', in M. Bolle and P. Grottian, (eds), *Arbeit schaffen - jetzt!*, Rowohlt, Reinbek bei Hamburg.

Guggenberger, B. (1988), *Wenn uns die Arbeit ausgeht*, Hanser, München.

Hegner, F. (1983), 'Strukturen und Verhaltensorientierungen privater Haushalte als Rahmenbedingungen der Arbeitszeitpolitik', in F. Scharpf and M. Brockmann, (eds), *Institutionelle Bedingungen der Arbeitsmarkt- und Beschäftigungspolitik*, Campus, Frankfurt.

Heinze, R. and T. Olk (1982), 'Arbeitsgesellschaft in der Krise - Chance für den informellen Sektor?', in *Österreichische Zeitschrift für Soziologie*, Nr.3-4.

Huber, J. (1979), 'Anders arbeiten - anders wirtschaften', in J. Huber, (ed.), *Anders arbeiten - anders wirtschaften*, Fischer, Frankfurt.

Huber, J. (1984), *Die zwei Gesichter der Arbeit*, Fischer, Frankfurt.

Illich, I. (1978), 'Nützliche Arbeitslosigkeit - eine gesellschaftliche Alternative', in *Technologie und Politik. Das Magazin zur Wachstumskrise*, Band 10, Rowohlt, Reinbek bei Hamburg.

Inglehart, R. (1977), *The Silent Revolution*, Princeton University Press, Princeton.

International Labour Office (1996), *World Employment 1996/97. National Policies in a Global Context*, International Labour Office, Geneva.

Jordan, B. *et al.* (1992), *Trapped in Poverty? Labour-Market Decisions in Low-Income Households*, Routledge, London, New York.

Kalleberg, A. *et al.* (1997), *Nonstandard Work, Substandard Jobs. Flexible Work Arrangements in the U.S.*, Economic Policy Institute, Washington.

von Klipstein, M. and B. Strümpel (1984), *Der Überdruß am Überfluß*, Olzog, München.

Kraushaar, W. (1978), (ed.), *Autonomie oder Getto?*, Verlag Neue Kritik.

Lutz, B. (1984), *Der kurze Traum immerwährender Prosperität*, Campus, Frankfurt.

Meade, J. (1986), *Different Forms of Share Economy*, Public Policy Centre, London.

Mückenberger, U. (1985), 'Die Krise des Normalarbeitsverhältnisses - Hat das Arbeitsrecht noch Zukunft?', in *Zeitschrift für Sozialreform*, 31. Jg. Nr. 7 und 8.

Mutz, G. *et al.* (1995), *Diskontinuierliche Erwerbsverläufe*, Leske und Budrich, Opladen.

Nissen, S. (1993), *Umweltpolitik in der Beschäftigungsfalle*, Metropolis, Marburg.

Nissen, S. (1994), 'Arbeitsplatzangst und politischer Immobilismus', in *Zeitschrift für Sozialreform*, 40. Jg., Nr. 12.

Novy, K. (1978), *Strategien der Sozialisierung*, Campus, Frankfurt.

Novy, K. and M. Prinz (1985), *Illustrierte Geschichte der Gemeinwirtschaft*, Dietz Nachf, Berlin, Bonn.

Offe, C. (1984), *'Arbeitsgesellschaft': Strukturprobleme und Zukunftsperspektiven*, Campus, Frankfurt.

Offe, C. and K. Hinrichs (1984), 'Sozialökonomie des Arbeitsmarktes: primäres und sekudäres Machtgefälle', in C. Offe, op cit.

Opielka, M. and G. Vobruba (1986), (eds), *Das garantierte Grundeinkommen*,

Fischer, Frankfurt.

Ostner, I. (1978), *Beruf und Hausarbeit*, Campus, Frankfurt.

Pacolet, J. (1997), 'Beyond the Veil of Macro-Economic, Social and Political Integration: Care for the Dependent', in W. Beck, *et al.*, (eds), *The Social Quality of Europe*, Kluwer Law International, The Hague, London, Boston.

Van Parijs, P. (1992), (ed.), *Arguing for Basic Income. Ethical Foundations for a Radical Reform*, Verso, London, New York.

Pioch, R (1996), 'Basic Income: Social Policy After Full Employment', in A. Erskine, (ed.), *Changing Europe*, Avebury, Aldershot.

Roemer, J. (1994), *A Future for Socialism*, Verso, London.

Scharpf, F. (1987), *Sozialdemokratische Krisenpolitik in Europa*, Campus, Frankfurt.

Scharpf, F. (1995), 'Subventionierte Niedriglohn-Beschäftigung statt bezahlter Arbeitslosigkeit', in *Zeitschrift für Sozialreform*, 41. Jg., Nr. 2.

Schmid, T. (1984), (ed.), *Befreiung von falscher Arbeit*, Wagenbach, Berlin.

Schumacher, F. (1977), *Die Rückkehr zum menschlichen Maß*, Rowohlt, Reinbek bei Hamburg.

Sheak, R. (1995), 'U.S. Capitalism, 1972-1992: The Jobs Problem', *Critical Sociology*, Vol. 21, No. 1, pp. 33-57.

Spahn, H-P. (1996), *Makroökonomie*, Springer, Berlin.

Spahn, H-P. and G. Vobruba (1989), 'Das Beschäftigungsproblem. Die ökonomische Sonderstellung des Arbeitsmarkts und die Grenzen der Wirtschaftspolitik', in G. Vobruba, *Arbeiten und Essen*, Passagen, Wien.

Vobruba, G. (1983), *Politik mit dem Wohlfahrtsstaat*, Suhrkamp, Frankfurt.

Vobruba, G. (1989), *Arbeiten und Essen*, Passagen, Wien.

Vobruba, G. (1990), 'Lohnarbeitszentrierte Sozialpolitik in der Krise der Lohnarbeit', in G. Vobruba, (ed.), *Strukturwandel der Sozialpolitik*, Suhrkamp, Frankfurt.

Vobruba, G. (1997), *Autonomiegewinne*, Passagen, Wien.

Vobruba, G. (1998), 'Income-Mixes. Work and Income After Full Employment' in *Crime, Law and Social Change*, Vol. 29, No. 1, pp.67-78.

Vonderach, G. (1980), 'Die "neuen Selbständigen". 10 Thesen zur Soziologie eines unvermuteten Phänomens', in *MittAB* 2.

Vonderach, G. (1982), 'Eigeninitiativen, informelle Arbeit und Arbeitszeitflexibilität. Überlegungen zu einer wünschbaren Umstrukturierung der Arbeitsgesellschaft', in C. Offe, K. Hinrichs and H. Wiesenthal, (eds), *Arbeitszeitpolitik*, Campus, Frankfurt.

3 Social Exclusion and the Flexibility of Labour
A theoretical exploration

GERRIT VAN KOOTEN

Introduction

This chapter starts with a brief discussion of the developments that gave rise to the growth of flexibilization of the labour market. It concerns on the one hand government developments like deregulation and internationalization of policy, and on the other hand economic developments like globalization of production and competition relations and increasing individualization of needs on the part of consumers. Collectively these developments compel flexibilization of the supply of goods and services and therefore influence both the organizational structure of companies as well as the way labour is organized, resulting in 'the flexible firm'. The next section shows that flexibilization of labour can take several forms. Numerical flexibility refers to the ability of employers to alter the size of the work force. Functional flexibility refers to extending the range of tasks and skills in a job. The varying location of employees along the flexible - non-flexible continuum may cause a divergence of interests between different groups of employees. On the one hand there will be a group of highly educated, well-paid employees and on the other hand, a growing number of employees who, due to a lack of qualifications, are dependent on flexible labour in the low-qualified industries and the services sector. Then some recent trends with regard to different flexibility strategies in the Netherlands will be presented, followed by a discussion of the conceptual relation between labour market participation and social exclusion. The chapter ends with some concluding remarks concerning the consequences of these developments for the social exclusion of some groups in society.

The unemployment crisis and economic restructuring

The stagnation of economic growth in the early nineteen-eighties, accompanied by rising levels of inflation and unemployment, led to the broadly accepted conclusion that traditional Keynesian measures, stressing the stimulation of the demand side of the economy, were no longer effective. The lag in western European levels of job creation, as compared to the performance of Japan and the United States in this respect, was at least partly blamed on the lack of flexibility of the labour market. The functioning of the labour market was looked upon as rigid in terms of the price of labour and conditions of employment, as well as the quality and quantity of manpower. In turn these rigidities were supposed to be a consequence of such widespread phenomena as centralized bargaining and collective agreements between trade unions and employers' organizations, legislation, social policy and government guidelines. This gave rise to the idea that the existing institutional arrangements within organizations and the welfare state were strengthening the rigidities of the labour market. This idea was so widespread that it was labelled 'eurosclerosis' (Treu, 1992). For this reason in the international literature on the concept, flexibilization initially referred to labour *market* flexibility. In this period policy measures were focused on '...eliminating a variety of rules and regulations which made the labour market rigid, on the grounds that such rules prevented the labour market from, on the one hand, absorbing the labour supply and on the other, adapting to the requirements imposed by technological change and adjusting to external competition' (Lagos, 1994).

The globalization of the economy is leading to tight competition with industries especially in Japan and south east Asia. Given the substantially lower wage levels in that part of the world, the only way for western industries to stay in business is through a profound rationalization of production. This means a growing pressure on 'Fordism' as a basic characteristic of the industrial relations in the Western world. The key elements of Fordism are mass production, in order to keep costs per unit low, and a Taylorist organization of labour, leading to high levels of standardization and a far-reaching division of labour. These elements match very well with the production of large numbers of standardized products at relatively low costs, but lose their value when production shifts in the direction of custom made goods. The introduction of micro-electronics allows a more flexible production in order to meet rapidly changing consumer preferences and entails a great push towards the functional flexibilization of the labour force, to be discussed in the next section of this chapter. The accompanying management strategies are known as 'Total Quality Management', 'Human Resource Management' and 'Business Process Redesign' (Hofman, Steijn and Van der Laan, 1997).

In combination the developments mentioned above lead to the transition of industrial organizations in the direction of what Watson (1995) calls the flexible firm. Watson defines the flexible firm as 'a type of employing organization which divides its work force into core elements which are given security and high rewards in return for a willingness to adapt, innovate and take on new skills and peripheral elements who are given more specific tasks and less commitment of continuing employment and skill enhancement'. The concept of the dual labour market is reflected in this definition. Following Atkinson (1987), Watson distinguishes four categories of employees:

1. A core group of permanently employed primary labour market staff of skilled workers, managers, designers, technical sales staff and the like. These will share a single status (abolishing the work-staff distinction) and in return for their relatively advantageous work, reward and career conditions, will be flexible in the work they do and be willing to retrain and shift their careers within an internal labour market as required.
2. A first peripheral group of secondary labour market staff will also consist of full-time employees, but their security and their career potential will be less. They will do clerical, assembly, supervisory or testing jobs which can more easily be filled from external labour markets.
3. A second peripheral group will consist of part-timers, public subsidy trainees and people on short-term contracts or job-sharing arrangements.
4. In addition to these three categories of employees a range of specialized tasks like systems analysis and simple tasks like cleaning are 'put out' through the use of agency temps, subcontracting and other 'outsourcing' practices such as 'teleworking' or 'networking' whereby people work from home and are linked by computer into the organization.

At the same time the shift from an industrial to a service economy also has an enormous impact on the organization of labour. Unlike material goods, services, due to their nature cannot be produced at stock. They can only be produced at the same time they are consumed. This implies that labour must be available at the time of consumption, which gives another push towards flexibilization. The different forms of flexibilization will be discussed in more detail in the next section.

The flexibilization of labour

The flexibilization of labour may take several forms, depending on organizational goals, the level of skills involved and the period within which it occurs. The main distinction in this respect is between numerical and functional flexibility. Numerical flexibility refers to the ability of the employer to alter the level of productivity in response to variations in the level of demand. In order to do so the employer can follow two different strategies. The first one is just to decrease or increase the number of workers. Because this form of flexibility involves the exchange of workers between the organization and the external labour market it is known as external numerical flexibilization. The second strategy consists of increasing the flexibility of working time arrangements. This flexibilization of working time includes the reduction or restructuring of working time and working overtime and/or outside authorized hours - for example, during the weekend. This type of flexibilization is achieved with the existing work force and is hence labelled internal numerical flexibilization.

Functional flexibility involvesthe ability to use the work force in a more effective way by varying the tasks performed in response to changing workloads. Functional flexibilization involves such aspects such as multi-skilling, job rotation, retraining and upgrading (Lagos, 1994). By its nature functional flexibilization is a mainly internal phenomenon. Some authors, however, consider external advisers or workers sent on secondment, who are performing highly specialized tasks on a temporary basis, as examples of external functional flexibilization (De Haan, Vos and De Jong, 1994; Kleinknecht, Oostendorp and Pradhan, 1997).

In combination the distinctions between numerical and functional flexibility on the one hand, and between internal and external flexibility on the other, lead to the typology below (Kleinknecht, Oostendorp and Pradhan, 1997). Although it is analytically possible to distinguish the following four different categories of flexibility, the classification of the various forms is sometimes rather arbitrary.

Part-time jobs, for example, are most of the time considered as an internal numerical flexibilization strategy in the literature. As stated before these kind of strategies are aimed at adapting the level of production to variations in the level of demand. In practice, however, for regular part-time jobs the number of working hours is contractually fixed. The conversion from a full-time into a part-time job or the other way round may be a once-only adaptation, but does not mean flexibility in the sense of a permanent potential for the organization. The same argument holds for flexible retirement schemes. Besides, the demarcation lines between the categories are fading. Temporary agencies are used as recruitment channels for new employees, and fixed term contracts are often meant to cover a probationary period and thereby as a leg up to an indefinite labour contract (Tijdens, 1998). Before elaborating on the relationship between participation on the labour market and the concept of social exclusion, we will first discuss some recent trends concerning the different forms of flexibilization in the Netherlands in the following section.

Figure 3.1   Categories of Flexibilization

Internal numerical flexibilization	External numerical flexibilization
* working overtime * part-time jobs * stand-by contracts * flexible working hours * flexible retirement schemes	* fixed term contracts * temporary work * out-sourcing
Internal functional flexibilization	External functional flexibilization
* job rotation * job-enlargement * job-enrichment * multi-craft	* secondment * external advisers

Recent trends in flexibilization in the Netherlands

In this section some recent trends in the flexibilization of labour are presented. These will be illustrated with figures for the Netherlands, derived, together with their original sources, from an elegant overview by Tijdens (1998). The common denominator of functional flexibilization strategies is the idea that employees should be versatile. In the case of internal functional flexibilization this means that workers must be able to perform different tasks within the organization. In this way local peaks in production are easily met by shifting labour from one department to the other. Well-known types of this form of flexibilization are job rotation, job enlargement and job enrichment. It is clear that this kind of strategy is easier to adopt in the case of unskilled or low skilled labour. In the case of tasks requiring higher qualifications this strategy implies the development of skills and the breaking down of traditional barriers of craftsmanship. In 1996 in their opinion almost three quarters of all employees was qualified to perform different tasks within their organization (Kunnen *et al.*, 1997). There are no reliable figures, however, to indicate whether or not this strategy is adopted by employers to a growing degree. With regard to the topic of this chapter this is no problem, since in general it does not imply negative consequences for employees in terms of labour conditions or rewards. For this reason employees consider internal functional flexibilization to be an acceptable strategy. As stated earlier, sometimes external advisers or workers sent on secondment, who are performing highly specialised tasks on a temporary basis, are considered as examples of external functional flexibilization. These types of flexibilization are not only less widespread, but are also almost exclusively related to highly paid specialists. Consequently these are not very relevant to the relation between flexibilization and social exclusion. Therefore the remaining part of this section deals with numerical flexibilization.

Internal numerical flexibilization

As examples of varieties of internal numerical flexibilization we shall discuss working overtime, flexible working schedules, and stand-by contracts. For reasons already given in the previous section we will not discuss part-time jobs and flexible retirement schemes. Working overtime follows the business cycle and is easy to realise, but due to bonus agreements is a rather expensive strategy. Between 1987 and 1996 the number of paid hours working over time in the Netherlands fluctuated around one to two percent of total contractual working time. One should note, however, that the number of unpaid hours of overtime, as estimated by employees, at least equals the number of paid hours. So, on average the flexibility reached by the total number of hours of overtime is about two to four percent of the normal working time.

The main trade union strategy for combating unemployment in the early eighties concerned the introduction of a general reduction in working time, contractually laid down in collective agreements. As a consequence the number of working days was reduced on average by approximately three days on a yearly basis by the mid-eighties. Originally, these days could either be taken up as extra holidays by the employees or were scheduled by the employer. When markets were picking up in the early nineties, these days were used to meet the growing demand for labour. Nowadays in over half of the collective agreements the general reduction in working time (GRW) has resulted in a shorter standard workweek of less than forty hours, thereby more or less losing its flexible character. However, in the remaining 47 per cent of the private sector GRW is still a source of flexibility.

Flexible working schedules may be organised on a daily, weekly or yearly basis. In 1997 in 40 per cent of the collective agreements in the private sector there were possibilities to alter the number of working hours per day or per week within a certain range. In slightly less than a quarter of the companies under these agreements these possibilities were in fact implemented (De Jong and Van Bolhuis, 1997). This kind of flexibility allows the employer to vary the numbers of working hours according to the needs of the moment in order to improve productivity, and is most common in the agricultural and the public health sector. On the other hand employees in one out of every five enterprises are, within certain limits, free to choose the daily time to start and finish their job.

The most vulnerable type of employees on a flexible basis are those who are employed on a standby contract. In such a contract an employment relationship exists, but there is no arrangement with regard to the number of working hours. In the case of a so called min-max-contract, a minimum and a maximum number of hours is agreed upon. In some cases the minimum number of hours is equal to zero. This type of employment is more vulnerable because in 43 per cent of the companies with standby labour there is no written agreement between the employer and the employee (Massaar and Faas, 1996). In the Netherlands almost 30 per cent of all organizations employ workers on a standby contract. In these organizations workers on a standby contract count up to 17 per cent of the total labour force. As a consequence of the generally low number of working hours, however, this category is responsible for approximately three to four percent of total production in these organizations (Van Bolhuis, 1996). The main difference between temporary workers and standby workers lies in the nature of their role in the production process. Temporary workers are hired for incidental tasks, whereas standby workers are used to meet unforeseen peaks in regular production. In this regard standby work is comparable to working overtime. Both are short-term flexibility strategies.

External numerical flexibilization

The number of people working on a temporary basis is, like that of those working overtime, positively related to the business-cycle. This means in times of economic recession their numbers drop, in times of recovery they rise. In the beginning of 1998 temporary workers made up approximately three percent of the total work force (CBS, 1998a). They are mainly hired to take care of peaks in production, perform temporary tasks and, to a somewhat lesser degree, replace absent regular employees. Though the proportion of temporary workers in the Dutch work force is still growing, there are some institutional constraints. In almost half of the most important collective agreements, for example, the use of temporary workers is limited to specified circumstances. The main limitation, however, is the predominantly unskilled nature of the tasks temporary workers perform. The shrinking segment of unskilled labour is increasingly occupied by temporary workers. The further growth of temporary labour is expected to come about in specialized areas as automation, legal advice and secretarial support.

The number of workers on a fixed term contract seems to be much less dependent on the business cycle, as it has been constantly growing in recent years. In 1996 almost half a million people were working on a fixed-term contract. Four out of five of them did so on a contract lasting for less than one year. Together these workers made up six percent of the total work force in 1992, while the corresponding figure for 1996 amounted to nine percent (CBS, 1998b). This makes working on a fixed term contract the most widespread type of external flexibilization in the Netherlands. This conclusion requires some elaboration. In an important number of cases the fixed term contract serves to cover the preparatory stage preceding a permanent appointment with an indefinite contract (Van Bolhuis, 1996). In as far as the only difference from regular employees lies in the nature of their contract, these workers on a fixed-term contract in fact do not belong to the flexible work force. Tijdens assumes that the growing number of fixed term contracts is at least partly a consequence of the lengthening of probation periods. She gives two possible explanations for this phenomenon. First, as a result of demographic developments the annual proportion of new employees is decreasing. Therefore organizations attach greater importance to an optimal selection of employees and do so by lengthening the period preceding a permanent appointment. Second, since the economic recession of the early nineties, many organizations have adopted a risk-avoiding strategy. They are only willing to employ people on an indefinite contract if they are sure that there will be no reduction of the workforce in the near future (Tijdens, 1998, p. 6). Despite the foregoing, however, there is no doubt that the number of employees on a fixed-term contract, but not including a probationary period, has been rapidly growing in recent years. In order to be able to evaluate the implications of these trends in flexibilization for social exclusion in the last section, we will first elaborate on the relationship between this concept and labour market participation in general.

Labour market participation and social exclusion

At present the concept of social exclusion has come to hold a prominent place in the political discourse of all governments in the European Union and the European Commission itself. The recently announced campaign against social exclusion by the Blair government in the UK may serve as an example of the first category. Recommendation 1304 in 1996 by the Assembly of the European Union on the future of social policy may be regarded as an example of the second category. In this recommendation it is stated that:

> 1. The Assembly considers the combating of unemployment, and the different forms of exclusion it entails, to be a priority for the restoration of confidence in social cohesion; and,
> 2. Unemployment destroys those who are its victims, particularly young people, and entails difficulties of integration, increasing violence and insecurity in towns and cities where certain districts become veritable 'ghettos'.

The explicitly or implicitly formulated (causal) relationship between social exclusion on one hand and unemployment and poverty on the other seems to be typical for policy oriented discussion papers and conference contributions. For example in this year's annual report of the Committee of socio-economic experts, an advisory board to the Dutch government, the relation between economic dynamics and social exclusion is the central topic. In this report social exclusion is simply defined as long-term exclusion from the labour market. The conceptual relation is also far from clear in the academic debate. To illustrate the problematic character of this relation and some of the pitfalls, I shall briefly discuss the interpretations of Berting (1998), Heady (1997) and Kronauer (1998).

Berting starts his analysis with the statement that: 'on the political level, the debate on *social exclusion* (italics by Berting) has become quite popular, notwithstanding the incredible vagueness of the concept'. Despite this observation, Berting nevertheless does not explicitly define the concept of social exclusion either, but restricts himself to a general description of the socially excluded as 'those without stable social ties' (1998, p. 8). According to Berting the category of socially excluded individuals is very heterogeneous and unstable, and consists of: 'the (long term) unemployed with very different occupational backgrounds, those who are qualified as unfit to work under the present market conditions, young people who leave the educational system but who fail to find a job in spite of good educational qualifications, unskilled members of various ethnic minorities, those who retire from their professional life at a rather early age etc.' (1998, p.17). What catches the eye immediately in this list is the assumed direct relation between participation in the labour market and social exclusion. (Note in passing that 'unskilled members of various ethnic minorities' are unemployed by definition.) The simple equation of unemployment with social exclusion seems to become explicit when the list above is followed by the statement that '....many do eventually find jobs, while others join the ranks of the socially excluded for good'. In contrast to this conclusion however, Berting indicates further on in his analysis that this is a misrepresentation of reality, when he challenges the proposition that due to the individualization of society, individuals who lose their jobs will not be sufficiently supported by other social institutional groups or networks. 'If this statement were true, it would simply mean that anyone who is not gainfully employed is socially excluded, because society is so strongly individualized that it no longer offers an integrated framework' (1998, p. 19). To do justice to the complexity of the concept Berting proposes to approach social exclusion as a process and as a relative phenomenon. There are different degrees and types of social exclusion, and in order to arrive at *a clear definition* (italics mine) of the phenomenon the following elements have to be considered:

1. the market economy that produces (long term) unemployment, stress, and uncertainty;
2. the redistribution of income by the state (social security system) and by private insurance companies;
3. the non-monetary economy, that is, the production of commodities and services without financial inputs, such as direct exchange, self production, and voluntary activities;
4. the financial reserves acquired by inheritance and/or a person's own activities;
5. the system of family ties, networks of friends, etc. who can, to a certain degree, provide (financial) support and security;
6. the educational system providing qualifications for entry into the labour market.

According to Berting, with this list in mind it is now possible to distinguish between different types and degrees of social exclusion. He does so by contrasting two examples. The first is:

...a young person without formal qualifications (6) with only scant opportunities to enter the labour market (1), who has only a minimum of financial support, or none at all, as in the case of an illegal immigrant (3), who has no financial reserves (4), no access to the non-monetary economy (3), and does not have a family network which can provide some security (e.g., a wife who has a full-time job, parents who provide food and shelter) (5).

The second example is:

...a senior manager, 45 years of age, who becomes unemployed (1), but receives substantial financial compensation from his company (1), who is entitled to unemployment allowances for a few years (2), has accumulated considerable financial reserves (4) to which his wife also contributes (4,5), because she has a very well-paid supervisory function (1); both of them are very skilled participants in the non-monetary economy (3) and have good support networks to help him in his quest for a new position in the market economy as a manager or a consultant (5). If necessary, he can try to acquire new qualifications (6) in order to start a second career in another niche of the economy.

This comparison is then followed by the conclusion that these '...two examples illustrate that the degree of social exclusion is highly dependent on the individual's capacities and resources' (Berting, 1998, p. 19). But apart from the arbitrary labelling of some of the elements, the second example conflicts somewhat with the original description of the socially excluded as 'those without stable social ties'. For being a very skilled participant in the non-monetary economy and having good support networks, implies the presence of these ties. As a consequence this approach does not seem to lead to the promised clear definition of social exclusion, let alone to the clarification of the conceptual relation between the latter and unemployment. In fact, all that has happened is the replacement of the original dichotomous variable by one on an ordinal basis. Yet, despite the earlier denial, in this view the demarcation between the socially excluded and the socially included is still simply their formal position on the labour market.

In another important strand of research social exclusion is equated with poverty - again, however, without explicitly defining it as such. One example is the research project 'Family structure, labour market participation and the dynamics of social exclusion'. This project is part of the Targeted Socio-Economic Research Programme as funded by the European Union and includes researchers from the United Kingdom, Norway, Austria, Portugal and Greece. The project has four main objectives:

1. to increase the understanding of the processes of social exclusion and social reintegration in Europe by using an explicitly dynamic approach;
2. to examine and compare the extent and impact of social exclusion among men and women at transitional stages in the life course;
3. to establish the ways in which the policies of EU member states affect the risk of social exclusion during these transitions;
4. to explore the relationship between public and private solidarity in combating social exclusion associated with life course transitions.

Then, in explaining the way in which these objectives will be addressed, Heady (1997) states that '...taking a dynamic approach, looking at the way people become *socially excluded* or reintegrated ... is a fairly new approach to the study of *social deprivation*, but one that has already shown advantages...' (italics mine). So, Heady continues 'the methodology of our study naturally builds on recent work on the dynamics of social deprivation. In fact, most empirical studies of deprivation, have concentrated on the concept of *poverty*, rather than the broader concept of *social exclusion*' (italics mine). Despite this conclusion, in the research programme the concept of poverty is nevertheless used as the sole indicator for social exclusion.

One of the few exceptions who at least tries to clarify the conceptual relationship between the concepts of unemployment, poverty and social exclusion in a more systematic way is Kronauer (1998). Kronauer, discussing the situation in Western Germany, suggests a distinction between (1) the statistical category of long term unemployment, (2) the concept of exclusion from the labour market and (3) the concept of social exclusion. The statistical category 'long term unemployment' consists of those who are unemployed for longer than one year. Following Kronauer's argument, this is considered to be

> .... a first, important indicator of the problems people face re-entering employment. It is also an important indicator of financial hardships, since in Germany most unemployed people lose their eligibility for unemployment insurance benefits after one year, and their income declines to the even lower level of unemployment aid, given they do not lose their unemployment support altogether because of shared income with a spouse. However, this indicator does not make it clear how long unemployment actually lasts, and what happens afterwards, whether people are able to find gainful employment again or not. Long term unemployment does not necessarily mean definite exclusion from employment.

The concept of exclusion from the labour market is reserved by Kronauer for those social constellations in and by which people are definitely locked out of employment, or have only a slight chance of ever (re)gaining it. As a rough indicator Kronauer suggests extreme long-term unemployment, defined as unemployment lasting longer than two years. The reason for doing so is twofold. First, different studies reveal a sharp decrease in chances in the labour market after two years of unemployment. Second, as time goes by the intensity of searching for a new job decreases. Again, according to Kronauer, the two years of unemployment are an important turning point: 'most unemployed men at that point ceased their own search for a job, and only went to the employment agency because they had to do so in order to keep their benefits' (Kronauer *et al.*, 1993). At this point of the analysis the question is raised as to what happens to the people who are definitely excluded from employment. Kronauer, unlike

Berting, states that there is no one-to-one relation between exclusion from the labour market and social exclusion. Examples of individuals who are excluded from the labour market but not socially excluded are women who take on the role of housewife while their husbands earn enough money to meet family needs, and older unemployed people who manage to organize their circumstances as a kind of transitional stage into retirement. Next Kronauer continues: 'To be sure, whenever people are forced to retreat from employment against their will, they are victims of social inequality. But this does not in every case imply being and feeling excluded from society at large.' Observe that here Kronauer introduces in passing a distinction between an objective and a subjective variation of social exclusion. Clearly one can be socially excluded without feeling so and the other way around. According to Kronauer, social exclusion '... is a particular, extreme, form of social inequality, but not every kind of social decline and social inequality can be meaningfully termed social exclusion'. Kronauer concludes that exclusion from the labour market and social exclusion coincide for those people who are unemployed, who are bereft of status protection and are also confronted with particularly strong financial stress.

So far it is clear that there is a lot of confusion concerning the concept of 'social exclusion'. As we have seen, it is sometimes simply equated with either unemployment (Berting, 1997) or poverty (Heady, 1997), or described as a combination of long-term unemployment and poverty or, in Kronauer's (1997) terminology, 'particular financial stress'. In the remaining part of this section I will try to resolve this confusion.

First of all I agree with Atkinson (1997) that social exclusion is not simply poverty or unemployment. Atkinson argues subsequently that:

1. Unemployment causes social exclusion, but a job does not guarantee social inclusion. Jobs must be acceptably paid and hold out prospects for the future: dead-end jobs are not the answer.
2. Social exclusion is not the same as poverty: Continental Europe has seen a major rise in unemployment over the past two decades without this leading to mass poverty. The European welfare state has been remarkably successful in providing an effective safety net - unlike the UK, where the proportion of households with low incomes more than doubled in the Thatcher years. But European countries are right to be concerned that unemployment *may* lead to people being *excluded from participation in society* (italics mine).
3. People are excluded not just because they are currently without a job or income but because they have few prospects for the future.

Observe that this argument is not consistent in every respect. Under (1.) Atkinson postulates an unconditional relationship between unemployment and social exclusion. Under (2.) this relationship is obviously dependent on the level of social security benefits and in the meantime social exclusion is equated with exclusion from participation in society. Then under (3.) another necessary condition is explicitly introduced: the lack of prospects for the future. With this addition in mind it is easy to see why Berting's first example discussed above is, according to Atkinson, socially excluded, while the second example is not. In order to get a clear impression about the relation between participation in the labour market and social exclusion, consider the following figure:

Figure 3.2   Relationships to the Labour Market by Type

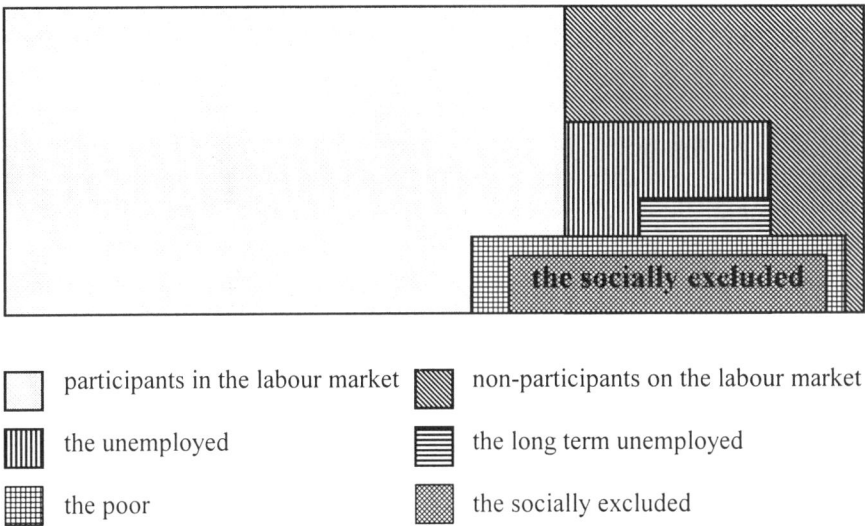

participants in the labour market	non-participants on the labour market
the unemployed	the long term unemployed
the poor	the socially excluded

In this figure the left side represents those who participate in the labour market and the right side, those who do not. The latter includes the unemployed and a rather heterogeneous category of, among others: housewives, students, old age pensioners and others who are released from labour for reasons concerning mental or physical health. In mathematical terms the long-term unemployed are a sub-set of the unemployed. As is clear from the figure 'the poor' as a category does not exclusively coincide with one of the former categories, but covers them all, albeit to differing degrees. This fits the interpretation by Atkinson that having a job without acceptable rewards may also lead to social exclusion. The degree to which each category is covered indicates the composition of 'the poor' as a category. According to this (fictional) figure the relatively highest concentration is found, consistent with Kronauer's view, among the long term unemployed. The sub-set of the poor who do not have prospects of improving their situation is, more or less in line with Heady's definition of the socially excluded. As presented here, however, the figure depicts a static situation. In reality there is a lot of movement between the different categories. Employed people may lose their job or retire. Students enter the labour market after graduation. Unemployed people either find a job, or will join the ranks of the long-term unemployed. The long-term unemployed may find employment or, when without alternative resources and future prospects, eventually become socially excluded. Finally, the retired with few or no pension claims may, after spending their savings, if any, become impoverished. To define the socially excluded as the poor without prospects for escaping poverty, seems to imply that becoming socially excluded is an irreversible process. However, prospects may change over time, so in some cases it is possible to reverse the process. At the same time to realise that these are exceptions to the rule, stresses the seriousness of the problem. In the concluding section of this chapter the trends described in the earlier section will be analysed in terms of their possible consequences for the dynamics between the different groups distinguished above.

The flexibility of labour and social exclusion

In this concluding section we will review the recent trends in the numerical flexibilization of labour in terms of their possible consequences for social exclusion. In order to do so we refer back to the figure presented in the previous section. In this figure the category of the socially excluded was depicted in its relation to categories of participants and non-participants in the labour market. The question to be answered now is in what ways the flexibilization of labour affects the intensity as well as the direction of the movement between the different categories. Therefore, we first recall the distinction made in the second section - between labour market flexibility on the one hand and the flexibilization of the labour force on the other. *Labour market* flexibility, defined as the elimination of rigidities through deregulation, is aimed at increasing the mobility between the categories of the non-participants and the participants in the direction of the latter.

According to neo-classical economists this is the recipe to combat high levels of structural unemployment. The flexibilization of the *labour force* is an employer strategy to adjust the labour force of an organization in a quantitative and/or qualitative way to the varying needs of its production processes. In other words: *labour market* flexibility leads, at least in theory, to a growing number of jobs; the flexibilization of the *labour force* leads to a growing variety in labour patterns.

The number of jobs in the Netherlands has been rapidly growing over the last decade. Whether this is the result of deregulation of the labour market, the recovery of the international economy or the Dutch policy of moderating wages, is a question hard to answer. When it comes to their nature the vast majority of these new jobs can be categorized under the heading of numerical flexibilization. This is because most of the time it concerns either temporary work or work on a fixed-term or stand-by contract. The fact is, however, that the number of participants in the labour market has gone up and the number of non-participants has gone down, though not to the same extent. An important proportion of the new jobs are taken by young people leaving school and entering the labour market for the first time. The remaining part is almost completely taken by students, working along with their studies, housewives with a working husband, and short-term unemployed re-entering the labour market. What does this mean for the relation between participation in the labour market and social exclusion? In a static way this relation, as depicted in the former section may be represented schematically as follows.

Figure 3.3   Labour Market Participation and Social Exclusion

	socially included	socially excluded
participating in the labour market	A	B
non-participating in the labour market	C	D

Category A consists of workers in the primary sector of the labour market and the majority of the numerically flexible labour force. Part of these flexible workers may have such low paid jobs that they are to be considered poor, but do have prospects for the future and so are not socially excluded. Category B contains the minority of the flexible working force. These workers are poor and have no prospects and thus are socially excluded by definition. Category C includes those who are not participating in the labour market but either have alternative resources, or if not, at least have future prospects to escape poverty. Examples of those with alternative resources are married women with a working husband, retired employees with an acceptable pension and unemployed people on social security benefits above minimum subsistence level. An example of the second sub-category are students without additional income to their grants. In category D, finally, we find the poor, mostly long-term, unemployed, poor single-parent families and impoverished old age pensioners, with a lack of prospects as a common denominator. As stated before this is the static situation. As a consequence, at least partly, of the flexibilization of the labour market, the mobility between the different categories has increased over the last decade. Although exchanges between any two categories are possible, some are, given the current circumstances, more likely than others. As made clear above, the bulk of the mobility taking place is from category C to A. Mobility out of category D is low by definition and, if any, it will be most likely to category B. This kind of mobility implies joining the ranks of the working poor by the (long term) unemployed or heads of single parent families, mostly women, without the prospect of escaping poverty. The main consequence in the light of the topic of this chapter is that these kinds of mobility do not affect the overall level of social exclusion. The same holds for the mobility from A to C and from B to D. The former type of mobility, at present, mainly concerns people retiring from the labour market. The latter type concerns people loosing their poorly paid temporary and/or flexible jobs. Given the growing number of these jobs, however, this type of mobility must be supposed to be rather low. So logically the only types of mobility affecting the overall level of social exclusion are either horizontal or diagonal in the scheme. By definition mobility from B or D in the direction of either A or B will be at a low level. As a consequence of the growing economy, mobility from A to B or D is rather unlikely. This means that the mobility from C to B or D are the only types which affect the number of socially excluded people. In fact, in the Netherlands there are indications that at present old age pensioners from minority groups, due to a lack of adequate pension provision, become impoverished step by step. Though a serious problem, this is not a consequence of the flexibilization of labour. All in all this leads to the conclusion that the flexibilization of labour does not lead, at least at present in the Netherlands, to social exclusion on a large scale. Favourable economic conditions and acceptable levels of social security, however, must be considered necessary conditions in this respect. When the business cycle turns downward the situation may change dramatically. To what extent is not a matter of theoretical debate, but, as ever in the social sciences, of empirical research. To avoid such a situation is a political assignment.

References

Atkinson, J. (1987), 'Flexibility or fragmentation? The UK labour market in the eighties', *Labour and Society*, 12(1): 87-105.

Atkinson, J. (1997), 'The economics of social exclusion – it's not simple poverty or unemployment', http://www.res.org.uk/media/atkinson1.htm.

Berting, J. (1998), 'Rise and fall of middle-class society? How the restructuring of economic and social life creates uncertainty, vulnerability, and social exclusion', in B. Steijn, J. Berting and M.J. de Jong, (eds), *Economic restructuring and the growing uncertainty of the middle class*, Kluwer Academic Publishers, pp. 7-24.

van Bolhuis, M. (1996), *Externe flexibilisering, een onderzoek bij bedrijven*, Den Haag, Ministerie van Sociale Zaken en Werkgelegenheid, Inspectiedienst SZW.

CBS (1998a), 'Uitzendbranche blijft groeien', in *Persberichten*, June 5th 1998.

CBS (1998b), 'Forse toename langlopende tijdelijke arbeidscontracten', in *Sociaal-economische maandstatistiek*, nr. 1, 21-22.

de Haan, E., P. Vos. and Ph. De Jong, (1994), *Flexibilisering van de arbeid; op zoek naar zekerheid*, Welboom, The Hague.

Heady, C. (1997), Household transitions and the dynamics of social exclusion, http://www-staff.lboro.ac.uk/-sssdm/cologne.htm.

Jong, F. de and M. van Bolhuis, (1997), *Flexibilisering van de arbeid. Een onderzoek naar aspecten van interne flexibilisering in bedrijven*), Den Haag, Ministerie van Sociale Zaken en Werkgelegenheid, Inspectiedienst SZW.

Kleinknecht, A.H., R.H. Oostendorp, and M.P Pradhan, (1997), *Patronen en economische effecten van flexibiliteit in de Nederlandse arbeidsverhoudingen*, Servicecentrum Uitgevers, The Hague.

Kronauer, M. (1998), 'Social exclusion and increasing uncertainty of the middle classes: the West German case', in B. Steijn, J. Berting and M.J. de Jong, (eds), *Economic restructuring and the growing uncertainty of the middle class*, Kluwer Academic Publishers, pp. 61-71.

Kunnen, R., W.C.M. Praat, A.M. de Voogd-Hamelink and C.M.M.P. Wetzels (1997), *Trendrapport Aanbod van arbeid 1997*, Den Haag, Organisatie voor Strategisch Arbeidsmarktonderzoek, OSA-rapport nr. 25.

Lagos, R.A. (1994), 'Labour market flexibility: what does it really mean?', *Cepal Review*, 54, pp. 81-95.

Massaar, J. and A. van Faas (1996), *De wet Informatie arbeidsverhouding. Een onderzoek naar de toepassing van artikel 1637f BW*, Den Haag, Ministerie van Sociale Zaken en Werkgelegenheid, Arbeidsinspectie.

Savage, M. (1998), 'Social exclusion and inclusion within the British middle classes, 1980-1995', in: B. Steijn, J. Berting and M.J. de Jong, (eds), *Economic restructuring and the growing uncertainty of the middle class*, Kluwer Academic Publishers, pp. 25-43.

Steijn, B, J. Berting and M.J. de Jong, (eds), *Economic restructuring and the growing uncertainty of the middle class*, Kluwer Academic Publishers.

Tijdens, K. (1998), 'Flexibilisering in het Nederlandse bedrijfsleven; ontwikkelingen in de jaren negentig', Paper presented at the WESWA-congress, November 25th, Rotterdam.

Treu, T. (1992), 'Labour flexibility in Europe', *International Labour Review*, 131, 4-5, pp. 497-512.

Watson, T.J. (1997), *Sociology, work and industry*, Routledge, London.

4 Paid Work: A Crucial Link Between Individuals and Society?

Some conclusions on the meaning of work for social integration

IGNACE GLORIEUX

Two different views on the meaning of work

In our society, work is both a crucial mechanism for social participation and a mechanism to distribute income. In addition, the welfare state guarantees that those who are excluded from work can count on a redistribution of the income from work. The massive unemployment that has afflicted most industrialized countries for more than two decades has lead to much pessimism about the viability of this type of society. It becomes more and more probable that a large number of people will be permanently excluded from work. Some observers argue that the period of full employment is over and that far-reaching processes of social change and adaptation are on their way (see Vobruba in this book). Consequently, questions are being increasingly posed about the future nature of a society once but no longer centred on work.

Some scholars are convinced that, together with the increased instrumentalization of work and the growing number of people who are frequently and for longer periods excluded from the labour market, industrial societies are witnessing a change of values. They argue that a subculture that is hostile towards the values and discipline of the work society is in the making (for example, Samuel, 1983; Offe, 1985; Dumazedier, 1988; Méda, 1993; Rifkin, 1995). In the eyes of these authors, this subculture is the herald of a new culture and society in which personal expression, freedom and autonomy - or the absence of the discipline and constraints inherent in work - will be the central values. The bearers of those values would no longer be ready to accept any job. If it is not possible to offer them meaningful work, then they probably will consciously opt for, or accept, a life without work. The authors who believe in this kind of scenario, and are in favour of it, are bidding farewell to the work society. They see a solution for the current crisis in a radical uncoupling of labour and income or the introduction of a system of basic income (see for instance, Van Parijs, 1992).

Others are much more pessimistic about the recent developments because they believe that work is (still) the only way to integrate large groups of people in a complex, pluralistic society (for example, Jahoda, 1982). They often turn to the work of Emile Durkheim, who argued more than one hundred years ago that the division of labour in industrial societies is an effective means to create solidarity on a large scale (Durkheim, 1986 [1893]). By doing their work and exchanging commodities, people get the feeling that they belong to, as well as contribute to, a larger entity, and thus become conscious of their mutual dependence. The social cohesion of industrial societies is, according to Durkheim, based on this complex and somewhat abstract and impersonal network of mutual interdependencies that arise out of work. The implication of this thesis is of course that large-scale unemployment is a threat to the solidarity and social cohesion of industrial societies. This leads to the conviction that the consequences of unemployment can only be solved by means of employment. The government is expected to contribute to the creation of jobs by means of stimulating economic growth and competition, public investments, taxing automation, reducing National Insurance contributions, reducing working time and redistributing work, introducing new types of employment contracts, service cheques, etc. In short, job creation is put forward as the first priority for policy.

These two reactions to the crisis of the work society imply two different views on the meaning of work. In the first model, work is considered to be a social mechanism to distribute material means and as a source of income for individuals. In the second model, work is much more than a mechanism of distribution. Work is considered as a means of attaching individuals to a collectivity - creating social cohesion and in so doing, giving the lives of individuals a social meaning.

The first model is based on the assumption that most of the employed are only weakly committed to their work, to the organization they work in, to the colleagues they work with, and to the people they work for. The authors who defend this thesis assume that paid work in our society is mainly considered as a necessary evil, as a means to earn money and to realise values outside work. In other words, it is assumed that people have an instrumental attitude towards work. If work plays a role in the integration of people in society, this role is restricted to the provision of the material means to participate in it.

The second model implies that work, besides being a source of income, is experienced as a pre-eminently social activity. In their work, individuals orient themselves toward others, forge social alliances, develop feelings of doing something useful for other people, of belonging to a collectivity, and as such they develop social orientations and attitudes. This view of work is adopted in most research on the consequences of unemployment and is used as an explanation for the social exclusion the unemployed experience.

In this chapter we develop some arguments in favour of the second model. On the basis of evidence from our studies on the meaning of work and the consequences of unemployment in Flanders, we argue that paid work is a key institution for the integration of individuals in society. Our chapter gives an overview of some of the findings and arguments that were more extensively reported in Glorieux (1995), Elchardus and Glorieux (1994, 1995) and Elchardus, Glorieux, Derks and Pelleriaux (1995, 1996). (Given the distinctiveness of some aspects of the Flemish social structure and its cultural formations, we of course recognise that our conclusions may be less applicable elsewhere, at least in their detail.) After a brief summary of our research methods, we discuss first the social meaning of work and then the consequences of unemployment. We argue that employment is essential for the development of social orientations and to connect individuals into the more abstract social networks that are fundamental for the solidarity and integration of large-scale societies. This argument is further developed in the next section, in which we look at the enduring consequences of unemployment after a longer period of re-employment. Our study of the formerly unemployed reveals that even after being re-employed the experience of unemployment leads to an enduring loss of self-confidence, mistrust of others and a loss of faith in social institutions and the collectivity. It emerges that the formerly unemployed feel damaged by a society that is not able to offer meaningful work for all of its citizens, and as a consequence become distrustful of such a society. Finally we consider some of the specific problems women face in the labour market. Women have often been neglected in discussions of the situation of 'full employment' in the fifties and sixties and in the debates on the consequences of the end of 'full employment'. We argue that traditional gender roles still to a large extent hinder women from exercising their rights to meaningful work and as such, act as a mechanism to exclude women from public life. (This theme is further developed in the chapter by Jönsson in this book.)

Research methods

In order to be able to evaluate both views on the meaning of work and to gain more insight into the role of paid work in the integration of society, we studied the meanings people give to their work activities. We did this by means of two time budget surveys among men and women between 20 and 40 years old in Flanders (TOR'84 and TOR'88*). The respondents of these surveys were asked to write down their time use respectively for one day (TOR'84) and three days (TOR'88) in a diary specially developed for this research. In this diary the respondents were asked to record all characteristics of the activities they did, such as their exact timing and duration, their location, and the other people involved in them. Besides this basic information, which is gathered in 'classical' time budget studies, our respondents also had to answer for each activity they recorded in their diary different questions concerning the meanings of the particular activity (for more detail see, Glorieux, 1995 and Elchardus and Glorieux, 1995). To do this, we distinguished seven different generalized meanings of time use based on a scheme developed by Elchardus (1983, 1991). Each meaning refers to a value (e.g., something that can motivate action or be used to evaluate the time spent) in terms of which activities can be given meaning. There is, of course, no need for an activity to have only one meaning. We left open the possibility that different meanings may be relevant to signify a single activity. The same activity can even be rendered meaningful in terms of apparently contradictory values.

The values or meanings used are: (1) time for physiological gratification; (2) time for personal gratification; (3) 'meaningless' time, spent to 'pass' or 'kill' time; (4) time spent as an obligation enforceable by others; (5) instrumental time, used as a means to an end; (6) time spent out of a sense of duty (which refers to internalized values); and (7) time spent to please others and maintain relationships (social alliance). On the basis of exploratory research, these seven meanings were translated into fourteen statements. Each pair of statements formulated the meaning as both a motivation, and as a criterion of evaluation. Time as duty, for instance, was formulated as 'I do this [activity] because I consider it my duty; should I not do it, I would feel guilty'; and then as 'the feeling that I did my duty, is important in evaluating this activity'. The respondents were asked to indicate on a 5 point Likert scale to what extent each of the seven motivations and seven criteria of evaluation applied to each of their activities. They were asked to rate their activities on these 14 items, immediately after registering them.

The TOR'84 time budget survey resulted in a file of 3653 activities for which the meanings were registered. The TOR'88 file contains 20598 activities for which we have the scores for meanings. A factor analysis (with the discriminating eigenvalue=.6) of those scores (for both surveys separately) yielded the seven proposed meanings. When the discriminating eigenvalue is rendered more conservative (put equal to 1), four distinct factors emerge (see Elchardus and Glorieux, 1988, 1991). One of these factors comprises the meanings 'time as duty', 'time as obligation', 'instrumental time' and 'time to please others (affectivity/solidarity)'. These four meanings appear as specifications of a more general social meaning. They constitute the uses of time that are motivated and/or explained as consequences of the participation in collectivities, henceforth called 'social meaning': time spent meeting the demands of living in society, whether these demands come under the form of obligation, sense of duty, instrumental use or sense of solidarity. Therefore, it can be argued that the social meanings point to the ways individuals orient themselves towards others or take others into consideration when acting (see Glorieux, 1993).

In our analyses below, we use factor scores as indicators for the meanings of activities. The factor scores for 'duty', 'obligation', 'instrumentality' and 'social alliance' are derived from the factor analyses using an eigenvalue of .6. The factor score for 'social meaning' points to the more general meaning that comprises all four social meanings and is derived from the factor analysis with an eigenvalue of 1. Factor scores are standardised scores with a mean (over all activities) of 0 and a standard deviation of 1; a positive value points to a score higher than average, a negative score to one lower than average.

The social meaning of work

From our diary data, as summarized in Table 4.1, it seems very clear that the men and women we investigated do not only consider their wage labour as a means to an end and as an obligation, but they also experience it as an important duty and as an activity in which they feel a social bond with other people.

Table 4.1 Factor Scores for the Social Meanings of Paid Work

	TOR'84 employed men	TOR'88 full-time employed men	TOR'88 full-time employed women	TOR'88 part-time employed women
Instrumentality	.61	.74	.75	.75
Obligation	.44	.89	.60	.79
Duty	.72	.80	.74	.71
Social Alliance	.23	.49	.40	.41
Global Social Meaning	.97	.88	.74	.78

Of course, people work because they receive money for it. They do something for someone else because they are paid for it (work in this sense is instrumental, or a means to an end). Work is also clearly associated with obligations that are amongst other things included in labour contracts, sales contracts, laws and different rules and regulations. Experiencing work as an obligation can in a sense be considered as a part of an instrumental attitude towards work: one is ready to accept the obligations because this is instrumental in attaining other goals. In accordance with those who advocate that work is experienced as a means to an end, we find no other activities in both our surveys scoring higher for 'instrumentality' or 'obligation' than paid work. For both men and women, full-time or part-time employed, paid work seems to be their first obligation, an obligation that is carried out in a highly instrumental way.

Waged work, however, is also considered to a great extent as valuable in itself. Whereas an 'obligation' refers to something that is enforced by others, a 'duty' is internalized and as such refers to values that actors *want* to implement. Waged work is considered as a duty, with respondents asserting that they would feel guilty if they did not work. The full-time employed men and women in both our samples consider paid work as their most important duty. Only the activities relating to children have factor scores for 'duty' coming close to those of paid work. For part-time working women, 'taking care of children' even scores higher on 'duty' (.88) than paid work (.71). Rather than pointing to an instrumental work attitude, the great extent to which work is viewed as a duty refers to the normative meaning of work or to a strong work ethic. Finally, social alliance also seems to be an important motivation to work. This meaning of work not only points to the alliance one feels when working together with others (as colleagues), but also with those whom one works for (as customers, clients, etc.). Although there are activities (such as educating children, socializing and going out) with higher scores for 'social alliance' than paid work, the score for this social meaning of work is still substantially above the average.

The four social meanings together give a unique meaning to paid work. In both our surveys, paid work is the only activity in the time budgets of the employed respondents that has positive factor scores for the four social meanings. In our samples, paid work is the only activity of the employed respondents in which the four social meanings together are considered as highly important to signify the activity. Therefore it is no surprise that work also has the highest score for our general indicator of social meaning. The only activity that comes near to it is 'educating children' (which includes playing, telling stories, helping with homework and so on), although for most groups the score for social meaning for this activity is below .5, which is much lower than that for paid work.

Our findings on the meaning of work contradict the view that reduces paid work to a necessary evil or an instrumental activity. In our view, the authors who only emphasize the instrumental and obligatory character of work commit a crucial mistake because they neglect the other meanings work has. Paid work clearly gives people the feeling that they act in conformity with a number of important values and that they do their duty, as well as giving their social alliance with others a concrete shape. The specificity of work, however, lies not so much in these meanings as such, but in the coupling of the different meanings: in joining the domains of necessity and values. Work is the activity that at one and the same time is instrumental in acquiring material resources and social security, has an obligatory character, links one with other people and gives a sense of doing one's duty. We called this coupling of different meanings the social meaning of work. As indicated earlier, all four meanings point to a different manner in which individuals co-ordinate or orient their actions towards others.

The consequences of unemployment

The finding that paid work has a very high social meaning for individuals is consistent with an assumption often made in the literature on unemployment. In this literature it is often assumed that paid work is the only social institution in our society that is able to integrate individuals into the larger society (see Jahoda, 1979, 1981, 1982, 1984, who was the main source of inspiration for research on the consequences of unemployment). In doing their work, individuals have to orient themselves towards others, and they have to take the wants of others into consideration and have to moderate their individual preferences. Because in the sphere of paid work one needs to co-ordinate one's behaviour with that of other individuals (mostly people with whom one has no affectionate relationship or even people that one does not know personally), it is assumed that this experience is important for the development of generalized social attitudes. Proceeding from this view, it is predicted that feelings of social alliance and social attitudes are diminishing among the unemployed.

Since we had a substantive sample of unemployed men in our TOR'84-data, we were able to test this hypothesis by comparing the meanings employed and unemployed men give to their activities. From this comparison, it emerged that the hypothesis that unemployed people attach less social meaning to their activities is only partly true. We found that the unemployed respondents in our sample try to compensate for the deficit of social meaning caused by the absence of the activity with the highest social meaning (paid work). They do this in two ways. First, by changing the meaning of activities. We found that a number of activities have much more social meaning for the unemployed than for the employed. Most striking in this shift of meaning was that a number of activities were considered more as a 'duty' for the unemployed, as compared to the employed. This redefinition was especially clear for household work, and to a lesser extent for chores, errands and caring for children.

We can clearly see in Table 4.2 below that household work for the unemployed is considered as a duty, and for the long-term unemployed it is even considered as an 'obligation' to do household work. As a result of this change in the meaning of household work, the unemployed generally give much more social meaning to household work than do employed men. This trend increases with the duration of unemployment. Among the long-term unemployed, the social meaning of household work (expect for the low score for instrumentality) comes rather close to the social meaning of paid work for the employed. Also for household chores, errands and caring for

Table 4.2   Factor Scores for the Social Meanings of Household Work for Employed, Short-Term and Long-Term Unemployed Men (TOR'84)

		Employed men	Short-term unemployed men	Long-term unemployed men
Household work	Instrumentality	.00	.06	.06
	Obligation	.05	.02	.29
	Duty	.07	.42	.55
	Social Alliance	.27	.21	.24
	Global Social Meaning	.18	.37	.61
Chores	Instrumentality	.35	.04	.29
	Obligation	-.02	-.33	.10
	Duty	.05	.00	.38
	Social Alliance	-.33	-.65	-.37
	Global Social Meaning	-.04	-.47	.19
Errands	Instrumentality	.18	-.08	.14
	Obligation	.16	.20	.35
	Duty	-.08	.04	.13
	Social Alliance	-.00	.11	-.12
	Global Social Meaning	.11	.17	.31
Caring children	Instrumentality	.25	-.09	.19
	Obligation	-.10	-.06	-.03
	Duty	.51	.83	.88
	Social Alliance	.42	.18	.37
	Global Social Meaning	.47	.49	.71

children, the shift in social meanings is most clear among the long-term unemployed. These activities are considered more as duties and (to a lesser extent) obligations by the long-term unemployed than by the employed. Because of the resemblance of these activities to the meaning paid work has for the employed, we call them 'substitute activities for work'.

The deficit of social meaning, however, is not only compensated for at the level of meanings of activities. We also found that the unemployed spend relatively more time on these 'substitute activities for work'. Of the extra time they have because of having no paid work (which is about 8 hours a day), short-term unemployed men spend about 2¼ hours, and long-term unemployed men about 3¼ hours, on what can be called 'substitute activities for work'.

The consequence of these compensating mechanisms is that in general these activities for the long-term unemployed have more social meaning than they do for those in employment. For the short-term unemployed the situation is somewhat different. They clearly have more problems filling up their time in a meaningful way. A great deal of the activities and routines that in the past derived meaning from the context of employment become meaningless after becoming unemployed. The first period of unemployment clearly is period of confusion and transition. It is not clear yet whether the situation of unemployment will last or whether a new job will be found soon. This situation is not favourable for the development of new activity patterns. It takes some time before the unemployed adapt to their situation and develop new routines and give their activities new meanings. After a while, however, it seems that the engagement in different household activities gives their lives a new social sense. This finding could be interpreted as an argument against the Durkheimian thesis that paid work is a crucial institution in developing social meaning and for the integration of individuals in society. This interpretation could, however, be misleading for several reasons.

First of all, we should not be too optimistic about the compensation mechanisms we detected among the unemployed. Clearly, they do not resolve all negative consequences of unemployment. Even the long-term unemployed still complain of boredom and spend a lot of time in front of television. The 'substitute activities for work' only fill part of the time that became free after they lost their job. For most of the unemployed men, the redefinition and the performance of different household activities are only an attempt to take up a role and to earn a status as a replacement for paid work. Most of them are very conscious, however, that such a strategy - at least for men - can never be a real success. It always remains as a surrogate for what they really want, a full-time job.

The restricted context in which these 'substitute activities for work' take place - mainly the household with its small scale and concrete relationships - points to another danger. A drastic uncoupling of work and income probably would not affect social alliance in general, but it seems that it would reduce the scale of social alliance drastically and, as such, also affect the kind of social ties. The remaining social bonds would be more personal. By this, the meaningful experience of larger, impersonal ties could be undermined. These impersonal, larger bonds and more abstract solidarity are, however, vital factors for the redistribution mechanisms on which the basic income is dependent.

On the basis of our finding that paid work has a very high social meaning, and the reactions we found among the unemployed, we are very sceptical about all solutions for unemployment that are restricted to the relief of the loss of wages. Creating jobs for the long-term unemployed in subsidized work, as is witnessed in a lot of European countries, could be a step in the right direction. The danger exists, however, that these kinds of jobs - because they are restricted to unemployed people and because of unfavourable contracts - are not perceived as proper jobs by the workers themselves. If these jobs are viewed by those who are employed in subsidized work as an obligation rather than as an intrinsically meaningful activity, then it is very probable that these measures will not be very effective in integrating them into the larger society.

Enduring consequences of unemployment

In 1993 we had the chance to re-interview 177 of the respondents of TOR'84. One of the main objectives of this study (extensively reported in Elchardus, Glorieux, Derks and Pelleriaux, 1995, 1996) was to see whether the former experience of unemployment has consequences that endure after re-integration into the labour market.

Among the 177 respondents we were able to interview in 1993 for a second time, 91 had been unemployed when we interviewed them in 1984. Apart from the structured interview we had with all of these respondents, 20 of them were selected for an in-depth interview. To study the enduring consequences of unemployment (on the basis of the structured interviews), we selected those respondents who had not been unemployed in the period of one year before the interview in 1993. Thirty-two respondents thus were omitted from our analyses either because they were unemployed at the time of the interview, or because they had been unemployed during the year before the interview. The 145 respondents we selected can be considered as being either integrated or reintegrated into the labour market in a relatively stable way. We divided these respondents into two groups. One group consisted of 57 respondents whose total unemployment experience since they left school did not exceed 12 months. The other group of 88 respondents had been unemployed for at least 12 months since they left school. By comparing both groups, we wanted to find out whether a substantial unemployment experience leaves traces, even after a longer period of re-employment.

We compared both research groups for an array of indicators, and at first glance it seemed that all of the consequences of unemployment we detected among the unemployed we studied in 1984 disappeared after a longer period of re-employment. Some of the negative consequences we found among the unemployed in 1984 were: difficulties with time use and structuring time, the shortening of future horizons, a decrease (albeit small) in social participation and a lower sense of well-being. All these differences vanish in the comparative groups of those employed with and without a substantial experience of unemployment. So it seems that unemployment leaves no permanent traces; after re-employment one seems to recover and to resume one's former life. Yet such a conclusion would be premature since both research groups differ from each other in other important respects. These differences, however, come to the fore only after re-employment. It is only then that the formerly unemployed fully realise the damage they suffered.

As compared to those who did not go through a longer period of unemployment, the formerly unemployed have become more distrustful towards their fellow-men and society at large, and they suffer from a loss of self-confidence. The formerly unemployed see themselves as more 'unsuccessful', 'lacking responsibility', 'unstable', 'uncertain' and 'passive'. They are more pessimistic about the future and feel they have no control over their own future. Some of them have lost faith in being able to count on others, and a lot of them have lost their faith in public institutions such as the labour unions and the government, and in traditional political parties and their leaders. This last point became very clear when we analysed their voting behaviour in the parliamentary elections in 1991. Among the respondents who did not suffer from unemployment, 7 per cent had voted for one of the two protest parties in Flanders, the right-wing party 'Vlaams Blok' and the pseudo-anarchist party 'ROSSEM'. Of the formerly unemployed no fewer than 22 per cent gave a protest vote.

Our study clearly suggests that the social consequences of unemployment do not disappear with re-employment. In a society in which a great number of people are confronted with unemployment during the course of their lives, a growing part of the population expresses feelings of uncertainty and powerlessness. These people have a negative picture of the self, relatively little self-confidence and little faith in public institutions. The magnitude of this group is not a function of the number of unemployed at a certain moment in time, but of the number of people who have been confronted with unemployment in the past. An increase in the number of people who have experienced unemployment influences the cultural climate, since these people are looking for an explanation for their unemployment: they are searching for new grounds for self-respect, for possibilities to get a grip on their lives, for future prospects, and for institutions and social agencies in which they can put their faith. In the in-depth interviews we had with some of the respondents in 1993, only one coherent discourse on unemployment emerged. It was the discourse which offers self-esteem in terms of national or ethnic identity, which blames the 'immigrants' for the high unemployment rates, which seeks solutions in 'sending back the foreigners', and which considers the right-wing parties ('Vlaams Blok' in Flanders) as the key agency promoting this kind of solution. The combination of a damaged self-esteem and self-confidence, the feeling of loss of control over the future and the distrust in society and its institutions, will all probably further promote this kind of ideological development. Societies with high unemployment rates are clearly not only confronted with socio-economic, but also with cultural and ideological challenges.

Women and paid work: the myth of the double workload

Our analysis of the consequences of unemployment in the sections above is based exclusively on a sample of relatively young men who have families to support. We can expect them to experience high social expectations, and social pressure to be active in the labour market. It is very clear from our results that the work role is the most central role in their life. It is only when they cannot meet the expectations of this role, that they engage themselves fully in the household. But even then, the engagement in the household is still only a substitute for what they really want: a full-time job.

The situation for women is very different. Most women in contemporary industrial societies are socialized to participate in the labour market. In Belgium about 75 per cent of women between the ages of 20 and 40 are effectively employed. This does not mean, however, that the traditional gender roles have disappeared. Women are still, despite their high labour market participation, primarily responsible for domestic tasks and child-care, while men are primarily responsible for paid work and for the more durable maintenance work that is performed (largely in the form of 'odd jobs' and do-it-yourself activities). For women in our society it is much more difficult to withdraw from a commitment to the household. Women in paid work are still expected, much more so than men, to fulfil their duties and obligations in the home. So it is not so surprising that we find that even full-time employed women in our sample spend on average about eight hours per week more on household work than full-time employed men. Sometimes findings such as this are cited in order to argue that working women have a double workload - one in and one outside the household - while the work of men is mainly restricted to their job. The double workload of women is often misunderstood to imply that they work much longer hours than men. We found no evidence for this. The total workload for men and women hardly differs, mainly because of certain social mechanisms that limit the extent to which women perform paid work.

In many cases, women with a heavy family burden, mostly women with young or many children, switch to a part-time job or even give up their job to be able to fulfil their duties in the household. In our sample of women between 20 and 40, 70 per cent of those working part-time and 80 per cent of those without employment had children, while only 43 per cent of the full-time working women were mothers. Seventy three per cent of the women without children had a full-time job, while only 41 per cent of the mothers in our sample worked full-time. It is clear that household duties are an important factor for women in making decisions about labour market participation. Most men do not take these options into consideration; they do not even think of adapting their labour market participation to the needs of their family. Almost all working men in Belgium are full-time employed and they seldom drop out of the labour market by choice.

Taking a part-time job or staying at home are not the only strategies women adopt in order to be able to fulfil their household duties. Full-time employed women also seem to adapt their job commitment to the demands of their families. More often than men, they opt for less demanding jobs or jobs with less overtime, more time off, less travel time and so on. In general, women work more often in sectors, occupational groups and jobs which, for both men and women, entail shorter working hours (such as in the public sector or teaching). As a result of this, we found that women with full-time jobs on average spend about 8 hours a week less at their jobs than full-time employed men. These kinds of mechanisms of adjustment make it possible for the total workload of employed women to remain within certain limits. We thus find that the total workload (the time spent on paid work, household work and children) of full-time employed men and women and part-time employed women is, on average, more or less the same. As Table 3 indicates, the total workload for full-time employed women in our sample is on average about 56½ hours a week. For full-time employed men it is on average just over 56 hours, and for part-time employed women the average total workload is just over 54 hours.

Table 4.3 Time Devoted to Paid Work, Domestic Work and Child Care, for Full-Time Employed Men, Full-Time and Part-Time Employed Women, and Housewives, in Hours and Minutes per Week (TOR'88)

	Full-time employed men	Full-time employed women	Part-time employed women	Unemployed women/ Houseviwes
Paid work	41h51'	33h58'	28h37'	4h18'
Domestic work	11h56'	19h42'	19h51'	31h39'
child care	2h19'	2h45'	5h40'	11h12'
TOTAL	56h06'	56h25'	54h08'	47h09'

It is therefore an exaggeration to speak of a double workload for employed women. Women in full-time employment do not have a double workload but they definitely carry a double responsibility. It is this double responsibility that weakens their position in the labour market. Because they have to adapt their commitments in paid work to their household demands, women more often have jobs with lower pay, less job security and fewer chances to pursue a career. In almost all industrial societies unemployment rates are much higher among women than men and, even in societies with only slight differences in the education levels between men and women (as in Belgium), women are greatly underrepresented in the more favourable positions in the labour market.

Work and social meaning for women: an unsteady balance

Just as for employed men, paid work for employed women is the activity with the highest social meaning, as can be seen in Table 4.1 above. For women too, the four dimensions of instrumentality, obligation, duty and social alliance are all important in giving meaning to paid work. Among women without employment we find, in accordance with what we found among unemployed men, that they derive a lot of social meaning out of their labour in the household. Women without employment give much more social meaning to their household work than employed women do.

In the light of what we concluded concerning the unemployed men, our conclusions here support the stress that most sections of the women's movement have placed on the importance of the labour market participation for women. Housewives also run the risk that the limited scale of their engagement, however valuable in itself, reduces their commitment to large scale and more abstract community relations. Consequently, we consider demands that paid work for women should be discouraged in order to reduce the supply in the labour market, to be socially unfair.

All this does not mean, however, that the labour market participation of women is without problems. An indication of this is our finding that, in general, the activities of full-time employed women have less social meaning than the activities of full-time employed men, and women who are part-time employed or unemployed. This rather surprising conclusion could be partly explained through the finding that for women in particular, family relationships play an important part in generating social meaning. Women who spend little time together with their family - and these are obviously to a great extent women with full-time jobs - seem to orient their activities less towards the world outside the home. For men, the time spent with members of the household seems to be less essential in stimulating social meaning. This clearly reflects the continuing differences in the orientation of men and women in our culture. Women, even if they are full-time employed, are still much more family-oriented than are men. Consequently, it is much more difficult for women to combine a full-time job with the demands it makes on their family life. This is not because of the double workload of working women; as already indicated, this is a myth. Rather, the strong family orientation of women in general, together with the difficulties faced by full-time working women in reaching the standards they set for their family life, entail that the social meaning of full-time working women is not of the same level as that of full-time working men. Having enough time to be together with the other members of the family seems to be crucial for most women to generate social meaning. In accordance with our findings among unemployed men, this points to the importance of the context of the household, besides the social context of paid work, in the development of a social orientation. Women in our culture seem to have difficulty in finding a balance between the social involvement in concrete family relations and the engagement in the broader and more abstract working sphere. Part-time work for women seems to be optimal in this sense. Among part-time working women, the participation in the world of paid work (which is crucial for the development of a more abstract and more general social orientation) does not lead to a deterioration of social meaning because there is still enough time left for family relationships. This does not mean, however, that we want to argue against full-time employment for women. We simply want to record that, given our cultural context, for a lot of women it is difficult to combine a full-time job with the demands of the household. These demands are not only a matter of the responsibility of women for most of the domestic work, but are also connected to the importance of the more concrete family relationships in the lives of women.

Conclusions

We started this chapter by summarizing two contrasting views on the current crisis facing the work society. One of these views is based on a somewhat materialistic conception of work. It conceives of paid work mainly as a means to an end, as a necessary evil to provide one's material needs. Consequently, at the societal level work is mainly considered as an institution that distributes income and material resources. The other view embraces a more idealistic vision of work. In this view paid work is a means of attaching individuals to a collectivity, to create social cohesion and to give the lives of individuals a social meaning. As such, paid work is seen as fundamental for the development and maintenance of solidarity in large-scale societies. Because we highlighted the contrast, it is clear that our representation of both these views is rather one-sided. Thus it should not be surprising that our findings do not fully fit in with either of the models. Our respondents associate their work activities with both necessities and values. Work is instrumental for earning money and it has an obligatory character; but it also gives people the feeling of realizing important values and of being tied to other people and broader society. Moreover, our findings suggest that paid work is the only institution in our type of society where the domains of necessity, values and social alliance come together. As such unemployment not only leads to material deprivation, but it is also very difficult for the unemployed to maintain their orientation to the broader society. This is not only clear from our analysis of the meanings unemployed men give to their activities and the way they use their time, but it also came also to the fore in our analysis of the enduring consequences of unemployment. Most striking in the latter analysis was the finding that the formerly unemployed men we studied had become more distrustful of their fellow men and the wider society. Findings such as this support the view that paid work is a key institution for integrating individuals into society at large. Performing paid work seems to be crucial for widening one's social horizons beyond the restricted context of primary relationships. It is also crucial for the development of social orientations towards, and feelings of belonging to, a wider community. On the basis of these findings, we want to support the maintenance of the work society.

We have found no evidence that having a paid job is less important for women than for men. It is clear, however, that traditional gender roles still have an important influence on the sexual division of labour. Women are still more family oriented, while men take up more public roles. The responsibilities of women in the household set limits to their chances in the labour market and as such have a negative influence on the development of social orientations and the performance of public roles.

If we believe that women are equally entitled to participate in the labour market and to take their places in public life, then it is rather painful to see that the cultural mandate of women makes it very difficult to exercise this right. Cultural patterns, however, are not laws of nature. Therefore, it seems to us that a profound change of mentality is essential if we are to achieve the equality of men and women in the labour market. Nevertheless, we have to realise that a cultural change is not possible in the short term. In most cases this is a process of generations. In the meantime it seems appropriate to reduce the working time of men significantly. We would even argue for the extension of part-time work for men. To the extent that this leads to a more equal division of household labour and paid work between the sexes, it would support the breakdown of traditional role patterns. It is not very probable that a reduction in the working time of men would be at the expense of their social orientation. It is expected, however, that the increased availability of the husband in the household, as a result of the reduction of the working time, would have a positive influence on the social meaning of the activities of the working wife. Given our finding that for most people paid work as well as the family are the pillars of a meaningful life, it seems anyhow desirable to reduce the tension between both these spheres of life. Parental leave for men, as negotiated on a European level, is a very modest step in this direction. Obligatory parental leave (for female employees maternity leave is an obligation as well) and more drastic forms of reduction of working time would seem to be more appropriate. Moreover, it would be a welcome bonus if the reduction of working time were to lead to the creation of more jobs. It is probably quite unrealistic, however, to expect spectacular effects from a reduction of working time on the level of employment. To reduce the unemployment rates drastically, new jobs have to be created. In our view this should not be done artificially, for instance by slowing down the automation of work. We do not expect much impact from either economic growth or the increase in consumption. These kinds of measures seem too artificial to us because they treat the creation of work as a means in itself and, as such, they do not necessarily lead to meaningful work. There is no need to create jobs in frenetic way because there is already enough work to be done in our society. Just consider all those public services that function defectively because of a lack of personnel. We have overcrowded school classes, public transport systems that are neglected or cut back, museums that cannot deal with their collections or exhibit them, and nursing staff who are overworked and have to restrict themselves to the most basic level of care. Legal cases are delayed for years or are just dismissed because of a lack of personnel, our inner cities and many public monuments have become run down, and so on and so on. While millions of people yearn for work, a lot of socially meaningful activities are not performed because this is not cost-effective in an economic sense. Maybe we have to question the economic standards of a society that permits itself to ignore the talents and commitment of millions of people. We are aware that this is not an easy task, that there are no ready-made solutions. However, we think it is necessary and urgent to reflect in a creative way on the cultural foundations of our society and our economy, and also to explore new forms of organization that can bring together the demand and supply of labour in a meaningful way.

* The first survey (TOR'84) took place in 1984 among a sample of 95 employed (8 of them were part-time employed), 56 short-term unemployed (less than one year) and 55 long-term unemployed (more than one year). All subjects in this sample were men between 24 and 37 years old, married or living together with a partner and having at least one child at home. The second survey (TOR'88) was held in 1988 among a random sample of 466 Flemish men and women between 20 and 40 years old. Due to disproportional sampling of women, we had 256 time budgets from women and 210 from men. In our analyses we corrected for the disproportional sampling by weighting our data, so that the results can be interpreted like those of a proportionally stratified sample. After weighting our sample consists of 233 men and 233 women. For the analyses reported in this chapter we mostly compared the full time employed men (n=196), the full time employed women (n=121), the part time employed women (n=45) and the non-employed women (n=57) of our sample. TOR refers to the name of our Research Group: 'Tempus Omnia Revelat'.

References

Dumazedier, J. (1988), *Révolution Culturelle du Temps Libre 1968-1988*, Méridiens Klincksieck, Paris.

Durkheim, E. (1986 [1893]), *De la Division du Travail Social*, Presses Universitaires de France, Paris.

Elchardus, M. (1983), 'De Ethiek van de Dualistische Conceptie van de Tijd', *Vrije Tijd en Samenleving*, 1, 4, pp. 343-373.

Elchardus, M. (1991), 'Rationality and the Specialization of Meaning: A sociological approach to the allocation of time', in G. Antonides, W. Arts, and W.F. Van Raaij (eds), *The Consumption of Time and the Timing of Consumption: Towards a new behavioral and socio-economics*, Amsterdam, North-Holland, pp. 69-86.

Elchardus, M. and I. Glorieux (1988), *The Generalized Meanings of the Use of Time*, Paper presented at the International Meeting on Studies of Time Use, Budapest, Hungary, June 14-16, 1988, Centrum voor Sociologie, VUB Press, Brussels.

Elchardus, M. and I. Glorieux (1989), 'The Generalized Meanings of the Use of Time: Replication and progress report', in J. Gershuny, *et al.* (eds), *Time Use Studies World Wide: A collection of papers presented at the 1989 Varna conference of the International Association for Time Use Research*, Sofia, Socioconsult, pp. 209-229.

Elchardus, M. and I. Glorieux (1994), 'The Search for the Invisible 8 Hours: The gendered use of time in a society with a high labour force participation of women', *Time and Society*, 3, 1, pp. 5-27.

Elchardus, M. and I. Glorieux (1994), 'The Search for the Invisible 8 Hours: The gendered use of time in a society with a high labour force participation of women', *Time and Society*, 3, 1, pp. 5-27.

Elchardus, M. and I. Glorieux (1995), *Niet aan de Arbeid Voorbij: De werkloosheidservaring als reflectie over arbeid, solidariteit en sociale cohesie*, Koning Boudewijnstichting / VUB Press, Brussels.

Elchardus, M.; I. Glorieux; A. Derks and K. Pelleriaux (1995), *Werkloosheid ... wordt vervolgd: De reïntegratie van landurig werklozen, een longitudinale analyse*, Federale Diensten voor Wetenschappelijke, Technische en Culturele Aangelegenheden, Brussels.

Elchardus, M.; I. Glorieux; A. Derks and K. Pelleriaux (1996), Voorspelbaar Ongeluk: Over letsels die werkloosheid nalaat bij mannen en hun kinderen, VUB Press, Brussels.

Glorieux, I. (1993), 'Social Interaction and Social Meanings of Action: A time-budget approach', *Social Indicators Research*, 3, pp. 157-181.

Glorieux, I. (1995), *Arbeid als Zingever: Een onderzoek naar de betekenis van arbeid in het leven van mannen en vrouwen*, VUB Press, Brussels.

Jahoda, M. (1979), 'The Impact of Unemployment in the 1930s and the 1970s', *Bulletin of the British Psychological Society*, 32, pp. 309-314.

Jahoda, M. (1981), 'Work, Employment and Unemployment: Values, theories and approaches in social research', *American Psychologist*, February, pp. 184-191.

Jahoda, M. (1982), *Employment and Unemployment: A social-pychological analysis*, Cambridge University Press, Cambridge.

Jahoda, M. (1984), 'Social Institutions and Human Needs: A comment on Fryer and Payne', *Leisure Studies*, 3, pp. 297-299.

Méda, D. (1995), *Le Travail: Une valeur en voie de disparition*, Aubier, Paris.

Offe, C. (1985), *Disorganized Capitalism: Contemporary transformations of work and politics,* Polity Press, Cambridge.

Rifkin, J. (1995), *The End of Work,* Putnam's Sons, New York.

Samuel, N. (1983), 'Loisir, Valeurs et Structure Symbolique des Temps Sociaux', *Loisir et Société/Society and Leisure*, 5, 2, pp. 321-338.

Van Parijs (ed.) (1992), *Arguing for Basic Income,* Verso, London/New York.

5 The 'Underclass': A Misleading Concept and a Scientific Myth?

Poverty and social exclusion as challenges to theories of class and social structure

SEBASTIAN HERKOMMER and MAX KOCH

Introduction

With the manifest return of pauperization, brought about by increasing mass unemployment and constantly less preventive social welfare policy, European social scientists are confronted with a debate which first started in media reports in the USA in the 1970s, and then led to a broad range of empirical research, mostly in black urban ghettos. The so-called underclass debate has been comprehensively covered in books and reviews (e.g. Devine and Wright, 1993; Gebhardt, 1995; Katz, 1993; Andersen and Larsen, 1995); therefore we do not need to repeat or summarize them in all their aspects and complexity. Rather, we are going to concentrate on three questions.

First, is the emergence of what is arguably a new underclass an exclusively American phenomenon, or do we have to recognize it as a general feature in developed capitalist societies undergoing severe friction in the process of transformation towards 'post-industrialism'? Will European welfare societies be better prepared than the USA to cope with social marginalization and the exclusion of an impoverished 'class' at the fringe or bottom of society? (Schmitter-Heisler, 1991).

Second, is the concept of class or underclass useful at all when we try to analyse the new social structures emerging with the ongoing processes of polarization, social exclusion and segregation? Do the new paupers, the long-term unemployed, the socially isolated and sometimes also spatially concentrated poor in our society constitute a distinct social class with common interests of its own and with a common mentality?

Third, is there a 'class analysis of poverty'? Whether one considers the 'underclass' a strong or a weak concept, the consequences of mass unemployment constitute a serious challenge to the theory of class and social stratification for the following reason. Since the sociology of social inequality - be it milieu-sociology or class-theory - is mostly oriented towards the 'economically active', people who do not form part of the occupational system are not objects of observation. We therefore would like to raise the question as to whether the 'excluded' can be integrated within a modern conception of social class.

Among those who try to answer these questions we find quite contradictory approaches. In addition, on the one hand not everbody who lays stress upon the uniqueness of the phenomenon in the USA would like to use the concept of an underclass to describe it, while on the other hand those who speak of social exclusion as a general trend in all capitalist metropoli do not altogether agree on the usefulness of the concept.

We shall demonstrate this with two examples. First, we consider the work of Ralf Dahrendorf who, like a number of other liberal sociologists (Andersen and Larsen, Esping-Andersen, Gans, Paugam, Schmitter-Heisler, Wilson), is not convinced that there is a strong similarity between American and European trends in social structure. Then we turn to the conservative Charles Murray and the socialist Martin Kronauer, who both assert the convergence of modern industrial and welfare societies in the process of 'Americanization' and propose the idea of a coherent class or stratum distinguished by and excluded from those who are 'in' society.

Dahrendorf, Kronauer and Murray

In Dahrendorf's view (1988), the underclass is the specifically American aspect of a wider social problem which he describes as a paradox: modern societies are still fundamentally based on the work ethic, and the social chances of their members primarily depend on their employment and their position within the occupation system; but at the same time work is becoming less and less available for all. But whereas in European countries the number out of work is perpetually rising, to about or clearly above 10 per cent, in the USA millions of new but essentially low paid jobs are being created. A great number of 'working poor' and a high level of persistent poverty are, in Dahrendorf's opinion, the American equivalent of long-term and persistent unemployment in Europe. It is a particularly concentrated and therefore visible pauperism, with cumulative 'social pathologies' which, in his eyes, validates the use of the term underclass: these people are unqualified, they live together in distinct areas (urban ghettos), very often in incomplete families, they belong to racial and ethnic minorities, and they are conspicuous by a peculiar and sometimes offensive, deviant and aberrant behaviour. Their life is determined by a vicious circle of deepening deprivation, and they become more and more socially isolated from the majority. Although some of these phenomena could perhaps also be observed in some areas of Great Britain, on the whole the European social map is, in Dahrendorf's view, quite different from the American. If the term underclass is to make any sense, it should denote an identifiable category of people in a common social position and with distinct social and political behaviour. Dahrendorf does not see sufficient indications of this in European societies. Here the long term unemployed are widely dispersed and do not constitute a visible pauperism. As they are unable to organize their social interests politically, they are just part of all the socially excluded, of the useless and superfluous residual population, 'those whom the full citizens of the society do not need' (Dahrendorf, 1985, p. 104), - 'in sociological terms, it is a lumpen-proletariat' (*ibid.*, p. 106).

Regarding the situation in Germany, Kronauer (1993, 1995) makes three assertions. First, as in the USA, there is a new gap emerging between those who are participants in the labour market and those who are more or less permanently excluded from it; second, the unemployed are less visible than in other countries, but nevertheless there are signs of the emergence of a new class of long-term jobless, whose members are tied together by their common life conditions and by a distinct consciousness, as well as by common patterns of behaviour; third, if the 'Americanization' of welfare policies in Germany is effective, the social cleavages could quickly be transformed into political ones, and this could be dangerous for democracy.

The essential difference between Kronauer's position and that of Dahrendorf and others is his conviction that the long-term jobless constitute a class or stratum of their own and who, on the basis of their lack of future prospects, develop a specific class mentality. Like the American underclass, he claims, the German class of unemployed and excluded people, however dispersed, shares a feeling of no longer belonging to society at all. Combined with the fear of social insecurity increasingly experienced by sections of the middle classes, this would lead to severe conflicts between the 'included' and 'excluded' parts of the population.

This in a sense resembles Murray's view. He also speaks of a distinct underclass, and he also argues that north America was the forerunner of the emergence of an underclass in European welfare societies. However, as well as contrasts in their use of language - for example, Murray uses such words as 'plague' and 'cancer' in characterizing the spreading disease and threat of modern welfare societies - the intentions of these authors are quite different. Murray is blaming members of the underclass themselves, and above all the welfare policies which, in his eyes, offer 'perverse incentives' which have made it profitable for the poor to behave in the short term 'in ways which were destructive in the long term'. In the words of two European experts:

> Murray did not identify the underclass by the degree or persistence of poverty - unlike most of his British colleagues - but stuck to his previous approach defining the underclass by a distinct type of poverty linked with pathological behaviour. The underclass was defined not by its socio-economic conditions but by their deplorable behaviour in response to their condition, e. g. unwillingness to take the jobs that are available... Murray identified the British underclass primarily by the same three phenomena that have turned out to be early warning signals in the United States: illegitimate births, violent crime and dropping-out of the labour force (Andersen and Larsen, 1995, p. 166).

Murray argues, in a perversion of Oscar Lewis's culture of poverty thesis, that social policy has created a 'dependency culture'. He defines the underclass in European countries, like that of the United States, not by socio-economic conditions but primarily by deviant and pathological behaviour; their members are not victims of economic disruption but rather of the generosity of welfare spending. In order to reinforce a feeling of responsibility, the poor would best be served by cutting social provision and by strengthening the family and other traditional values.

Defining the underclass

In order to learn from this confrontation between observers who are in favour of the convergence thesis, and those who are against it, it is necessary to look more closely at their definitions of the underclass. What are the fundamental or core criteria by which this specific class or stratum is distinguished from the rest of society, respectively from other classes and strata? Only a few social scientists fail to refer to Marx's famous denotation of a *lumpenproletariat* (see among others: Mann, 1992, p. 130ff.; Devine and Wright, 1993, p. 79ff.; Pugliese, 1995, p. 217), either to draw an analogy, or to distinguish between the underclass of early capitalism and the new, 'post-industrial' underclass. Those who tend to draw the analogy use a rather formal sociological perspective leading to a *universal* definition of underclass as the residual population - the very heterogeneous stratum of the poor, the marginalized, declassified, excluded, superfluous and useless, often seen as the 'scum', both politically and morally. On the other hand, definitions of a 'new', post-industrial underclass point to the *distinct* phenomena of the actual emergence and formation of a socially and culturally isolated class which, by spatial concentration and racial or ethnic homogeneity, is visible as such, and which is located in the black ghettos of the big cities of the United States.

> Although relatively small in numbers, the so-called underclass has recently become the most visible and widely discussed segment of the contemporary poverty population. As might be expected, the term is used by different authors in a variety of ways to demarcate different aspects of the poverty situation, but in the most common rendition, it refers to chronic, concentrated, innercity, minority impoverishment accompanied by extreme social isolation and exceptionally high rates of social pathology of all sorts. The underclass is *not* just the poorest stratum among the poor, but rather that subgroup of the poverty population most resistant to successful intervention (Devine and Wright, 1993, p. XXI).

Wilson, in his very thorough field research in *The Truly Disadvantaged* (1987) and *The Ghetto Underclass* (1993), concentrated on the specifically American phenomenon of urban, inner-city class formations among the poorest within the African-American and Latino minorities. Contrasting his research with that of authors of the Right, he argues that the so-called culture of poverty is the *answer* to restrictions in the conditions of life; it has to be seen as the *consequence* of crisis, not its *cause*. The key notion cannot be culture of poverty, he claims, but social isolation. Social isolation is seen as the result of two processes reinforcing each other: race segregation and class division. Social isolation of the mostly black minorities living in neighbourhoods marked by urban poverty was completed after members of the middle class and qualified working class left these areas and, benefiting from their long fought for access to civil rights and formal equality, moved to other districts with better living conditions.

This is because the most disadvantaged minority group members, who have been crippled or victimized by the cumulative effects of both race and class subordination..., are disproportionately represented among that segment of the total population that lacks the resources to compete effectively in a free and open market (Wilson, 1987, p. 113). Increasing joblessness has its most devastating effect in the most highly concentrated poverty areas... I believe that the exodus of middle- and working-class families from many ghetto neighborhoods removes an important 'social buffer' that could deflect the full impact of the kind of prolonged and increasing joblessness that plagued inner-city neighborhoods in the 1970s and early 1980s, joblessness created by uneven economic growth and periodic recessions (*ibid.*, p. 55-56).

Since then the consequences of out-migration of the qualified members of minorities have become even worse, under conditions of rapidly increasing unemployment, as the latest book by Wilson shows (Wilson, 1996). Therefore, the solution earlier proposed seems to be even more urgent:

If the life chances of the ghetto underclass are largely untouched by programs of preferential treatment based on race, the gap between the haves and have-nots in the black community will widen, and the disproportionate concentration of blacks within the most impoverished segments of our population will remain... The hidden agenda is to improve the life chances of groups such as the ghetto underclass by emphasizing programs in which the more advantaged groups of all races can positively relate (Wilson, 1987, pp. 17-120).

That is to say, better than laws against discrimination are political programmes for economic development and employment.

Wilson's efforts to formulate a comprehensive concept of underclass have become landmarks in public as well as academic debates. He lays stress on the combined effects of race segregation and class division, and then relates these to economic change in the society as a whole, including change in certain branches of industry, regions and cities. This has been systematized, among others, by Devine and Wright. They state that:

an adequate definition and understanding of the underclass requires some attention to (1) structural and economic factors, (2) social-psychological components, (3) behavioral phenomena and (4) spatial-ecological factors. None of these considered in isolation from the others proves sufficient (Devine and Wright, 1993, p. 81). We prefer a definition of 'the' underclass as persons living in urban, central city neighborhoods or communities with high and increasing rates of poverty, especially chronic poverty, high and increasing levels of social isolation, hopelessness, and anomie, and high levels of characteristically antisocial or dysfunctional behavior patterns. No one factor is sufficient to create an underclass; all must be simultaneously present (*ibid.*, pp. 87-88).

This rather formal definition does not include race and ethnicity, nor class position, nor the gender problematic, but if taken as a tool in empirical research, it will fairly soon be seen that, in the poorest neigbourhoods in American cities, ethnic minorities and black working-class families, unqualified men and women, single mothers, young drop-outs and elderly homeless, etc., dominate the scene. Actually, most authors perceive the new character of the contemporary underclass to be black (and perhaps Hispanic) and concentrated in the most devastated slum districts (Anderson, 1990; Wilson, 1987, 1996; Mollenkopf and Castells, 1992; Marcuse, 1996; Wacquant, 1995, 1996).

Finally, we come to a more comprehensive definition which lays stress mainly on the access to or exclusion from citizenship rights.

The case of the underclass is characterized by the correlation of extreme economic marginality and the existence of significant structural barriers and obstacles that together act to separate and exclude this population from economic, social and political institutions. Long-term institutional exclusion most likely also involves spatial segregation and concentration... Although race (and to a lesser extent ethnicity) adds salience to the boundary creating processes, it is by no means necessary to that process. More important than race is the political power of lower socio-economic groups to expand citizenship rights and to keep their erosion in check (Schmitter-Heisler, 1991, pp. 475-476).

Looking at the ambiguities of these definitions, we should accept the warning given by the French author of *L'Exclusion*.

On questions as socially and politically sensitive as poverty and exclusion, sociologists must first of all recognize the impossibility of finding exhaustive definitions. These concepts are relative, and vary according to time and circumstance. It is unreasonable to expect to find a fair and objective definition, which is distinct from social debate, without falling into the trap of putting unclearly defined populations into clumsily defined categories. Defining the 'poor' and the 'excluded' according to precise long-term criteria leads almost to a reification of new social groups, or ones that are similar to the current categories, and gives the impression that the study of poverty and exclusion is an exact science which can divorce them from their social and cultural context' (Paugam, 1996, p. 4).

The 'underclass' in Europe

Having clarified the scope and contents of the term underclass, however unclearly defined and however much its meaning varies from one author to another, we can now answer our first question. With a few exceptions in some areas of the United Kingdom and France, and perhaps the Netherlands, there does not (at least yet) exist an underclass in the sense of an economically, socially and culturally isolated social group of the poorest, most hopeless and most anomic persons, concentrated in distinct urban communities and predominantly constituted by racial and/or ethnic minorities. Similar conditions of spatial concentration to those which are predominant in the United States, only exist - if at all - to a clearly smaller degree, in places where mostly coloured immigrants from former colonies are living together. In general terms, we agree with the conclusion reached by Schmitter-Heisler:

> Whether the emergence of an underclass is a strictly American phenomenon or an emergent characteristic shared by all advanced industrial societies is an empirical question that can only be fully addressed by systematic comparative research (Schmitter-Heisler, 1991, p. 475).

Drawing on empirical comparisons made by Wacquant (1992), Paugam concludes that:

> the general use of the term 'ghetto' as a label for the French suburbs is inappropriate. It does not help resolve the problems to be found there which sustain a collective sense of insecurity in the face of possible 'social upheaval'. Of course, it is not a matter of denying the existence of deprived communities, where a large proportion of the unemployed are to be found, or of minimising the social effects which result. Rather, it is to encourage a rigorous analysis of the facts. This term 'ghetto' is at the root of many misunderstandings. To equate the poorer parts of the Paris suburbs with the ghettos of Chicago and New York demonstrates a serious misunderstanding of the American situation (Wacquant, 1992). French suburban areas, including the most hemmed-in ones, are rarely completely sealed off as they are in the United States, due to their geographic positions. Their ethnic composition is highly diverse, and their levels of poverty, the degradation of the quality of

life, and the extent of criminality, are incomparable with the American ghettos (Paugam, 1996, p. 3).

This present state of less developed features in areas of European poverty as compared to the United States may change, of course. If the economic crisis with continued and ever growing mass unemployment deepens, if at the same time cuts in welfare spending increase, and if social policy in the European welfare societies is further 'Americanized', then there will be a growth in the conditions of isolation and perhaps even spatial concentration of the poor in European big cities and other areas of poverty as well. As the American case shows, there is no future in creating more precarious and low-paid jobs, and the eradication of slums and scum will depend not on less public spending but more. Welfare societies will best be prepared to cope with the spreading 'diseases' of poverty and long-term unemployment when they are able to develop economic and political incentives which block further polarization. Wealth and also work, which has become a rare resource, must be redistributed in a way which guarantees full civil, political *and* social citizenship rights for everybody (Offe, 1996; Habermas, 1998).

The 'function' of the underclass

The second question to be discussed is the following: does the concept of underclass in any way meet the needs of an analysis which intends systematically to describe and explain the trends of the impoverishment and social exclusion of distinct sections of the population? Or is it possible that the term underclass plays a functional role in the justification of existing inequalities, thus impeding or preventing necessary measures of public intervention? Scruples about and objections to the term have often been uttered in the American debate. Most of these objections can be understood as a reaction to the conceptual hegemony of the neo-conservatives and the corresponding identification of poverty with immorality, laziness, apathy, etc. Stigmatism, blaming the victims, racism, latent or manifest association with unworthiness and threat, or even with 'scum' and the 'scrap-heap of society', are the major reasons why the term is seen as pejorative and destructive (Wilson, 1987, p 3ff.; Crompton, 1993, p. 147 ff.; Katz, 1993, pp. 4, 23; Andersen and Larsen, 1995, p. 170ff.).

As a consequence, some participants in the debate suggest using the term underclass as a metaphor only (Devine and Wright, Katz), whereas others, more strictly and plausibly, would like to avoid it altogether and use instead more specific terms like the poor, the socially excluded and marginalized, the long-term unemployed, etc.

> Like most critics of the term underclass we suggest that social scientists should avoid using the concept 'underclass', because it overwhelmingly tends to focus on behavioural aspects of the poor and has a more or less explicit agenda, the intent of dividing the poor into deserving and undeserving according to their 'good' or 'bad' behaviour (Andersen and Larsen, 1995, p. 173).

But even when one refers to the behavioural aspects, including values and political consciousness, there is little evidence of a common identity by which an underclass could be classified as distinct from the rest of society or from other social classes. As to a specific mentality, which Kronauer *et al.* (1993) thought was emerging among the long-term unemployed, Andersen and Larsen point to divergent findings:

> Many studies show that the long-term unemployed and other socially excluded individuals, contrary to the presuppositions of the arguments of the right wing, in spite of their social exclusion continue to orient themselves towards and hold 'mainstream' norms and values (Andersen and Larsen, 1995, p. 175).

Indeed, the Danish authors cite empirical studies by Alcock in Britain and by Moore in the Netherlands, which show that poor people do not refer to themselves as a class, and that they have similar hopes and values to those who are better off.

Some would simply go no further than to use the term in a sense of statistical groups or social categories, not of class.

> Since the underclass lacks any meaningful market position, it is best conceptualized as a social category, not a class. The term 'underclass' implies some sort of class position, but it may be more appropriate to locate the underclass outside the class structure. While members of the underclass live in a politically defined territory and are thus bodily present, they are not included in ongoing economic, social, and political life. Ultimately I would agree with Dahrendorf that the underclass is best conceptualized in terms of its superfluousness and uselessness (Schmitter-Heisler, 1991, p. 476).

For Procacci too the concept itself is superfluous and useless. Underclass is in her eyes a 'pseudo-scientific concept'. 'The notion of underclass has always under-estimated decisive factors such as institutional barriers, or constant discrimination in the labour-market (in relation to blacks as well as women, and even more so black women) or the weight of urban renewal policies. The theoretical weakness of the concept is not abated by recourse to the terminology of social classes'. And she adds that neither Marx nor Weber made the definition of class dependent on behaviour. Behaviour, she claims, is never specific enough for a distinction to be made between classes. And she continues,

> Even more serious is the fact that the concept of underclass does not refer to any theory of social division. Nor does it even try to construct one. On the contrary, it designates a class outside the social class structure which is defined by itself, not *vis-à-vis* other classes and is thus bereft of any relational dimension. ... The underclass is a scientific myth that transforms a number of partial truths into a collection of middle class ideological beliefs. Its result is to renew the conviction that was always at the very heart of the notion of the undeserving poor: goods must be earned through work and/or good behaviour (Procacci, 1996, p. 6-8).

Bagguley and Mann also argue that the concept of underclass is the ideology of the dominant upper and middle classes. Whether one stresses the uselessness of those excluded (Dahrendorf), or the positive function they have for the dominant majority (Galbraith, Gans), in either case there seems to exist an inherent need for justification by those who are included and who are able to live up to the middle-class norms. 'The term underclass is a symbolic manifestation of socially constructed definition of failure', assert Andersen and Larsen, and they continue by quoting Bagguley and Mann: it is the expression of a '"desperate need for the middle classes to justify their relatively privileged place in society by pointing to the failings of the poor..."' (Andersen and Larsen, 1995, p.171).

This desperate need will rise rather than fade away, as sections of the middle classes increasingly fear for their relative privileges, and as their 'culture of contentment' (Galbraith, 1992) comes under increasing pressure. This is because 'the comfort and economic well-being of the contented majority was being supported and enhanced by the presence in the modern economy of a large, highly useful, even essential class that does not share in the agreeable existence of the favored community' (Galbraith, 1992, p. 29). Therefore one could even speak of the 'functional underclass' (in Galbraith's terms); that is, the ideological function of the underclass follows the same pattern as that in Durkheim's analysis of crime. According to his theory, crime and criminals enforce by their deviancy the dominant norms of society and thus strengthen the degree of social cohesion. It is likewise 'functional' for the *status quo* of society, and for the middle classes, insofar as an excluded group of 'failing' people demonstrate to the majority the value of being in line with the norms of individual efficiency and success, moral decency, family-orientation, etc. It is part of the ideology of neo-liberalism.

The 'underclass' and class analysis

Now we turn to answer our third question, to what degree the 'excluded' can be integrated into the conception of social class. So far, we can summarize: the social category denoted as 'underclass' is not a class in the classic sense of the term, either in the Marxian or in the Weberian sense. Neither is it defined by its common position in the relations of production (like capitalists, the working-class and the various fractions of the middle classes), nor does it constitute a 'social' class with a distinct market position, shared objective living conditions and a corresponding pattern of *Lebensführung* and mental orientation. We agree with Ralf Dahrendorf's statement, 'If the term "underclass" is to make any sense, it has to describe an identifiable category of social position and behaviour' (Dahrendorf, 1988, p. 151). More generally, as Marx stated in his class analysis in 'The 18th Brumaire of Louis Bonaparte':

> In so far as millions of families live under conditions of existence that separate their mode of life, their interests and their culture from those of other classes and put them in hostile opposition to the latter, they form a class. In so far as there is merely a local inter-connection ... and their interests beget no community, no national bond, no political organization among them, they do not form a class (Marx, 1969, p. 278).

As a new phenomenon in highly developed industrial societies, emerging from the dynamics of capitalism and mediated by the modern welfare state, this social category cannot be called a *lumpenproletariat* either, as long as this term is used to circumscribe the rotting away of the old society, including the 'passive putrefaction of the lowest strata of the old society' (Marx and Engels in *The Communist Manifesto* of 1848); that is, remnants of a social order which has gone, eradicated by the bourgeois order. Most convincing seems to be a purely negative conceptualization which is nevertheless related to contemporary capitalist welfare society: the excluded and superfluous part of population, in itself highly heterogeneous, is distinguished from all other classes and social strata by negative characteristics - lack of any meaningful market position, more or less complete exclusion from social citizenship rights, and exclusion from the economic and cultural standards achieved by the majority. It refers, in Bourdieu's terms (Bourdieu, 1983), to those who have no economic capital, no cultural capital and no social capital which would provide them with a positive identity. Their negative identity is ascribed to them from outside - as a stigma.

This does not mean that there does not exist any structural relationship between the class structure of contemporary capitalist society and the (relatively) superfluous population it produces. It was again Marx who identified as a general law of capitalist accumulation the 'progressive production of a relative surplus population or industrial reserve army' (*Capital*, vol.1, pp. 781-794). In his analysis, a surplus population does - or at least did - exist in several forms. Each worker belongs to it as long as he or she is working part-time or is altogether out of work; but Marx also distinguished the floating, the latent and the stagnant forms of surplus population, according to the rhythm of repulsion and attraction by capital, to the temporal length of exclusion from work and to different economic sectors. The stagnant group 'is characterized by a maximum of working time and a minimum of wages... It is constantly recruited from workers in large scale industry and agriculture who have become redundant, and especially from those decaying branches of industry where handicraft is giving way to manufacture, and manufacture to machinery... (It) forms at the same time a self-reproducing and self-perpetuating element of the working class...' (*ibid.*, pp. 796-797).

So far the different elements of the so-called industrial reserve army have been conceived of as parts of the working class. The facts that they are temporarily out of work, that the value of their qualifications are destroyed from time to time, and that their low wages make them poor, do not exclude them from their class relation with capital. Therefore, their interests and their culture are, in an objective sense, close to those of the employed members of the working class. But Marx then introduces a fourth element of the relatively surplus population, one which is less tied to the industrial reserve army, but rather serves as its 'dead weight': this 'lowest sediment ... dwells in the sphere of pauperism' and consists of the vagabonds and criminals - the *lumpenproletariat* - the jobless, pauper children and those unable to work - 'the demoralized, the ragged, the victims of industry, the mutilated, the sickly, the widows, etc.' (*ibid.*, p. 797).

However far-reaching Marx's original analysis might be, French structuralists - Louis Althusser and Nicos Poulantzas in particular - remind us that the general theory of capitalism as a mode of production, as presented in Marx's *Capital*, is located at a fairly high level of abstraction. While this general theory of capitalism and its development provides us with an abstract map of class relations applicable to every capitalist society - the class antagonism of capitalists and wage labourers in contrast to other historical types of class antagonisms such as between serfs and lords - it is simply impossible to derive the entire social structure of a given society from it. Or, put more simply, 'The "capitalist mode of production" does not exist' (Lipietz, 1983, p. 18). Historical reality exists as unique social formations within the epoch of capitalism, such as the France of Louis Bonaparte, the Germany of Bismarck at the end of nineteenth century, or the welfare state capitalism of the various nations of contemporary Europe. Since Marx's theory of the capitalist 'mode of production', and of the class relations within capitalism as a 'social formation', was not applied (for obvious reasons) to the actual social structures of advanced capitalist societies, we must seek elsewhere for such an application which incorporates recognition of contemporary manifestations of the 'dead weight'.

The class theory of Erik Olin Wright provides such an attempt, and is useful for considering systematically the 'excluded' in actual class analysis. For Wright poverty is an inherent feature of a society which in its economic structure is grounded in class and exploitation. Much more clearly than other contemporary social scientists, he claims that there are powerful and privileged actors in modern capitalism who are interested in maintaining poverty: 'It is not just that poverty is an unfortunate consequence of their pursuit of material interests; it is an essential condition for the realization of their interests. To put it bluntly, capitalists and other exploiting classes benefit from poverty' (Wright, 1994, p. 38). In order to understand Wright's argument adequately one has to distinguish between two concepts: 'economic oppression' and 'exploitation'. This distinction is of special significance for class analysis. Economic oppression denotes a situation in which the material benefits of one group are acquired at the expense of another, and morally indictable coercive exclusion from resources is an essential part of this process. We can regard exploitation as a specific form of economic oppression: 'In exploitation, the material well-being of exploiters causally depends upon their ability to appropriate the fruits of labor of the exploited' (ibid., p. 40). Therefore, the welfare of the exploiter depends on the effort of the exploited, whereas in non-exploitative economic oppression there is no labour transfer from the oppressed to the oppressor. The welfare of the latter is due to exclusion of the oppressed from access to certain societal resources, but not to their effort.

Thus, the crucial difference between exploitation and non-exploitative oppression is that the exploiter needs the exploited, whereas in the case of non-exploitative oppression, the oppressors might sometimes even be content if the oppressed simply disappeared. Historically, genocide has been a potential strategy for non-exploitative oppressors, but it could never be an option for exploiters. Wright observes 'that it is not an accident' that American settlers used to say, 'the only good Indian is a dead Indian', but not 'the only good worker is a dead worker'. A comparison of the colonization of South Africa and of north America might illustrate this. In north America indigenous people were coercively displaced from the land in the first place; in South Africa, in contrast, the settlers heavily depended upon African labour power, hence genocide was not an option for them. Drawing on Wright's argument we suggest considering the problem of poverty within a class analysis in the way illustrated in figure 5.1 below.

The dependency of the exploiter on the exploited gives the exploited a certain form of power, insofar as human beings retain at least some minimal control over their own expenditure of effort. Control over the work process based exclusively on repression is costly and normally does not lead to optimal outputs. Hence, exploitation should be regarded as a social relationship in which the exploiter tends to moderate his or her domination. In most cases s/he prefers a mode of regulation in which the exploited establish some degree of autonomy and identification with their concrete work. Therefore, the basis of power and collective bargaining for the exploited lies in the constraint on the exploiter to gain some level of cooperation.

Political representation of the interests of those oppressed who are not exploited is generally more difficult than representation of exploited workers. Since there is no economic constraint for the oppressors to cooperate with the former, resistance historically was often reduced to physical defence. This does not mean that there have not been strong political movements of unemployed people: for example, the point of contact for the strongest opposition against the dictatorship of Pinochet

Figure 5.1   Exclusion and Exploitation (elaborated from Wright's concept of 'economic oppression')

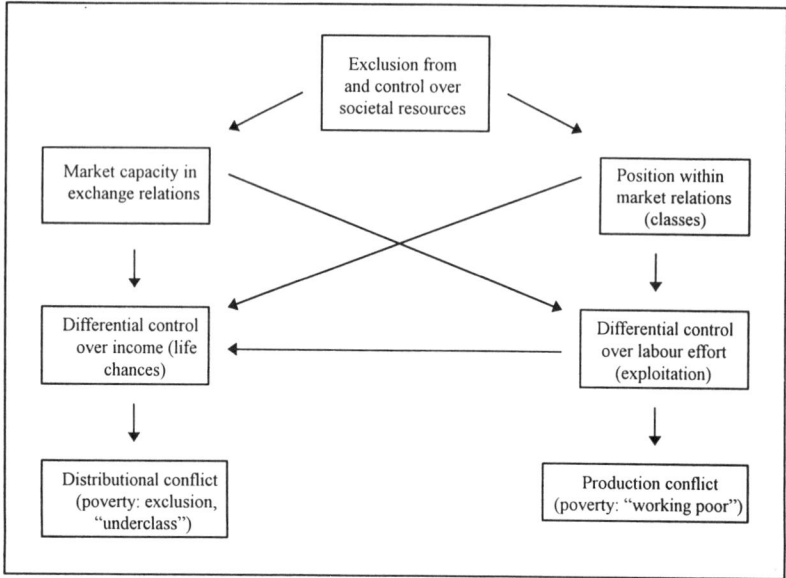

in Chile were the *barrios*, the urban districts of the poor, and not the capitalist firm (Koch, 1998). More recently the movement of the unemployed in France seems to have been influential. But since the 'excluded' are abundant from the capitalist point of view, there is no economic reason for cooperation, and therefore violent confrontation is more likely than in the case of the exploited workers. It is true that concepts of both exploitation and non-exploitative oppression involve certain moral arrangements. The abundance of the non-exploited oppressed from the capitalist perspective made murderous repression always an attractive solution but today, unlike in the nineteenth century, the moral and political forces are such that genocide is no longer a viable strategy. The modern American alternative is rather to build prisons and to isolate the neighbourhoods of big cities where the marginalized and poor people, the so called underclass, live.

If we now try to relate this argument to class analysis, the concepts of both simple material oppression and of exploitation underly the general idea that there are various kinds of material and non-material resources which are necessary for human welfare and to which certain groups in society manage to exclude others from access. We may call 'economic oppression' any process whereby one group illegitimately excludes another from access to these resources. Wright notes that the qualification 'illegitimate' is necessary since there may be circumstances 'in which the exclusive use of a resource by one group may be justified' (Wright, 1994, p. 43). 'Exploitation', by contrast, occurs when such exclusion from resources also gives the owners of the resource the capacity to appropriate the fruits of the labour done by others.

Class theory - at least in the Marxian tradition - is closely tied to the concept of exploitation, although it also encompasses other forms of structuration such as qualification or amount of 'cultural capital', and organizational assets in the production process. We agree with Wright that the notion of poverty within class theory needs to be broken down into two sub-problems: poverty generated inside exploitative relations, and poverty generated by non-exploitative oppression. The former corresponds to what in contemporary political discourse is called 'the working poor', and the latter corresponds to the 'excluded'.

The existence of the working poor is the result of two social facts: first, many firms have low levels of productivity and in order to compete they can only offer low wages; second, many workers have low levels of skill or only very limited possibilities of geographical mobility and are thus constrained to take poorly paid jobs. Within a class analysis the existence of a sizeable population of the working poor can be viewed as one of the consequences of a weak, fragmented, and relatively conservative labour movement. On the other hand, a strong, solidaristic labour movement is more likely to prevent large wage inequalities within the working class. When such a movement is closely linked to a political party in power - as used to be the case in Sweden - the eradication of a category of impoverished employed workers is ever more likely.

Conclusion

In the light of the analysis above, we are now able to define the theoretical status of the 'excluded' more precisely than was possible at the start of the chapter. If we regard them in the context of both relations of exploitation and simple material oppression, it is clear that, first of all, the excluded are excluded from exploitation. What the heterogeneous social category of the excluded has in common is that it is economically oppressed but not at the same time exploited. Capitalist society abolished slavery, and everyone who does not dispose of capital goods, man and woman alike, is supposed to own a 'unit of labor-power' (Wright), and is free to sell it to capital owners. Now the crucial point for the 'excluded' is that they do not dispose of labour power which could productively be used by a capitalist. Their situation is, in a sense, similar to that of a capitalist who owns nothing but outmoded machines: 'While the capitalist physically controls these pieces of machinery, they cease to be "capital" - a productive resource - if they cannot be deployed within a capitalist production process profitably. In the case of labour-power, a person can physically control his or her own labouring capacity, but that capacity can cease to have economic value in capitalism if it cannot be deployed productively' (*ibid.*, p. 48). The excluded are not exploited but oppressed because they are denied access to various kinds of productive resources, above all the necessary means to acquire the skills needed to offer their labour power for sale.

Future research

From the foregoing analysis it is clear that there is much scope for a further exploration of contemporary pauperization, and we want to end this chapter with a proposal. On the basis of the distinction drawn between mode of production and social formation by Althusser and Poulantzas, we encourage further research which would interpret the phenomena of 'new poverty', 'exclusion' and 'underclass' in the context of the transformation of regimes of accumulation in Europe. This entails starting with a critical reflection on the 'school of regulation', which was developed in France by Aglietta, Lipietz and others. A critical elaboration of the elements of this approach is in any case necessary, since Lipietz self-critically concedes that it brought forth a consistent 'theory of Fordism' but not a theory of its transformation (Lipietz, 1994, p. 78). Since this theoretical discussion is not as yet very advanced, we would like to conclude with some remarks which might also serve as provisional hypotheses for further research.

It is clear that the relationship between capital accumulation and various forms of relative surplus population has become more mediated as a result of social policy in modern welfare states. At the same time, however, it can be argued that political institutions and representatives of the welfare state in the recent period of economic crisis are no longer willing or no longer able to act against market forces, i.e., the general laws of capital accumulation. As a consequence particularly of neoliberalism, long-term exclusion from work and declining public action against poverty together lead to new cleavages which overlap with class conflict and make it difficult to include the poorest members of the population in activities of the unions and other political movements opposing fundamentally the ongoing processes of deprivation and polarization.

In order to make this more concrete, one must examine national and regional realities, as Paugam has proposed. He indicates the existence of a close relation between levels of economic development, family cohesion and perceptions of poverty within different capitalist societies:

> It is evident that poverty is perceived differently according to the degree of economic development. Collective representations thus partially account for national contrasts found in statistical evidence. In those regions where the level of poverty is high, 'the poor' or the unemployed are not heavily stigmatised. Social integration seems to be founded principally on belonging to the family unit. Those who are most economically disadvantaged do not lose this security, as is often the case, for example, in France and Great Britain. In the statistical analysis ... we could observe a lack of correlation between low standards of living and weakened family cohesion in Spain and in Italy ... In these countries, results obtained from other indicators, such as private aid networks, were similar: even those who were poorest economically were not deprived of contacts or the possibility of help if needed (Paugam, 1996, pp. 10-11).

The following general conclusions to our discussion might make further research easier:

1. The new quality of exclusion and segregation of 'superfluous' and 'surplus' parts of population in modern capitalism is not a direct consequence of capitalist production and the corresponding principal distribution of wealth between the classes, but is mediated by social policy. Different types of welfare societies (Esping-Andersen) will show typical forms of redistribution of wealth and therefore will produce different degrees of inequality. Fiscal as well as social policy cannot only have levelling effects; it can also accelerate trends of polarization and segregation by discriminating against social groups with little power.

2. Under these circumstances it becomes more important than ever to look at the contents and institutional forms of politics in the various contested terrains. An asymmetric division of power should be understood as a consequence of capital accumulation, and the central social conflicts therefore as being primarily grounded in the industrial

relations between capital and labour. But the fields of contest are multifold and include the shop floor as well as social policies at state level and in local communities (Kreckel, 1990).

3. The possibilities of combining and organizing heterogeneous interests of the various groups of excluded will depend on temporal aspects such as the length of joblessness and the duration of poor living conditions. Therefore contemporary research in pauperism is right in distinguishing between periodic and permanent poverty (Leibfried *et al.*, 1995).

4. The same is valid regarding spatial aspects of exclusion (Lynn and McGeary, 1990; Marcuse, 1996; Mollenkopf and Castells, 1992). Poverty and social isolation are not necessarily connected with their local concentration, but it is always situated in a specific, historically grounded social space. Dispersion and concentration, respectively, of poverty make it more or less visible/invisible to the public and to the impoverished themselves, which may have consequences for the development of a specific mentality or even a 'culture of poverty'.

5. Traditional class analysis was reluctant to consider the relevance of race, ethnicity, gender and structure of the family (Frerichs, 1997). The underclass debate has provided an incentive to rectify this. On the other hand, however, research in the fields of social segregation and exclusion isolate these variables from class analysis of society as a whole. (Castel, 1991; Frerichs 1997; Herkommer, 1996b).

6. Thanks to Bourdieu, recent analysis of social stratification and class structuration is now taking into account the symbolic dimension of inequality and its reproduction (Koch, 1996). Social closure and exclusion works *via* stigmatizing denotations, by non-verbal communication of prejudice and by signs of distinction in the form of the aesthetics of everday life.

References

Andersen, J. and J.E Larsen (1995), 'The Underclass Debate - a Spreading Disease?' in Mortensen, N. (ed.), *Social Integration and Marginalisation*, Frederiksberg.

Anderson, E. (1990*)*, *Streetwise: Race, Class, and Change in an Urban Community*, Chicago, London.

Bagguley, P. and K. Mann (1992), 'Idle Thieving Bastards? Scholarly Representation of the "Underclass"', *Work, Employment and Society*, vol. 6, no. 1.

Bourdieu, P. (1979), *La distinction*, Paris.

Bourdieu, P. (1983), 'Ökonomisches Kapital, kulturelles Kapital, soziales Kapital', in: R. Kreckel (ed.), *Soziale Ungleichheiten. Soziale Welt*, Sonderband 2, Göttingen.

Bourdieu, P. *et al.* (1993), *La misère du monde*, Paris.

Castel, R. (1991), 'De l'indigence à l'exclusion, la désaffiliation', in: J. Danzelot (ed.), *Face à l'exclusion. Le modèle francais*, Paris.

Crompton, R. (1993), *Class and Stratification. An Introduction to Current Debates*, Cambridge.

Dahrendorf, R. (1985), *Law and Order*, Boulder, Colorado.

Dahrendorf, R. (1988), *The Modern Social Conflict*, London.

Devine, J. A. and J.D Wright, (1993), *The Greatest of Evils. Urban Poverty and the American Underclass*, New York.

Esping-Andersen, G. (1993), (ed.), *Changing Classes*, London.

Frerichs, P. (1997): *Klasse und Geschlecht: Arbeit, Macht, Anerkennung, Interessen*, Opladen.

Galbraith, J. K. (1992), *The Culture of Contentment*, Boston, New York, London.

Gans, H. (1992), 'Über die positiven Funktionen der unwürdigen Armen', in S. Leibfried and W. Voges, (eds), *Armut im modernen Wohlfahrtsstaat, Kölner Zeitschrift für Soziologie und Sozialpsychologie*, Sonderheft 32.

Gebhardt, T. (1995), 'Die "underclass" als neues Phänomen im US-amerikanischen Armutsdiskurs', in *Berliner Debatte/Initial*, H. 1.

Habermas, J. (1998), *Die postnationale Konstellation und die Zukunft der Demokratie*, Frankfurt/Main.

Herkommer, S. (1996a*)*, *Veränderungen in der Klassenstruktur Europas, Sozialismus* (Supplement), H. 4.

Herkommer, S. (1996b), 'Das Konzept der "Underclass" - brauchbar für die Klassenanalyse oder ideologieverdächtig?', in Z. - *Zeitschrift für marxistische Erneuerung*, no. 26.

Herkommer, S. (1997), 'Die feinen und die krassen Unterschiede', in J. Klages and P. Strutynski (eds), *Kapitalismus am Ende des zwanzigsten Jahrhunderts, Hamburg.*

Katz, M. B., (ed.), (1993), *The 'Underclass' Debate*, Princeton, N. J.

Koch, M. (1996), 'Class and Taste. Bourdieu's Contribution to the Analysis of Social Structure and Social Space', in *International Journal of Contemporary Sociology*, 33, no. 2.

Koch, M. (1998), *Unternehmen Transformation. Sozialstruktur und gesellschaftlicher Wandel in Chile*, Frankfurt/Main.

Kreckel, R. (1990), 'Klassenbegriff und Ungleichheitsforschung', in Berger and Hradil (eds), *Lebenslagen, Lebensläufe, Lebensstile*, Soziale Welt, Sonderband 7, Göttingen.

Kronauer, M. (1995), 'Massenarbeitslosigkeit in Westeuropa: Die Entstehung einer neuen "Underclass"?' in *Soziologisches Forschungsinstitut,* Göttingen (SOFI), Im Zeichen des Umbruchs, Opladen.

Kronauer, M. (1997), 'Soziale Ausgrenzung und Underclass: Über neue Formen der gesellschaftlichen Spaltung', *Leviathan* 1/97.

Kronauer, M., B. Vogel and F. Gerlach (1993), *Im Schatten der Arbeitsgesellschaft. Arbeitslose und die Dynamik sozialer Ausgrenzung,* Frankfurt/Main, New York.

Leibfried, S., L. Leisering and P. Buhr, (1995), *Zeit der Armut. Lebensläufe im Sozialstaat,* Frankfurt/Main.

Lipietz, A. (1983), *The Enchanted World. Inflation, Credit and the World Crisis,* London.

Lipietz, A. (1994), 'De l'approche de la régulation à l'écologie politique: une mise en perspective historique', in: Aglietta *et al.*, *École de la régulation et critique de la raison économique,* Paris.

Lynn, L. E. and M. McGeary (1990) (eds), *Inner-City Poverty in the United States,* Washington D.C.

Mann, K. (1992), *The Making of an English 'Underclass'? The Social Divisions of Welfare and Labour,* Open University Press.

Marcuse, P. (1996), 'Space and Race in the Post-Fordist City', in: Mingione (ed.), *Urban Poverty and the Underclass,* Oxford.

Marx, K. and F. Engels (1956 onwards): Werke (MEW), Berlin.

Mingione, E., (ed.), (1996), *Urban Poverty and the Underclass,* London.

Mollenkopf, J.H. and M. Castells (1992) (eds), *Dual City,* New York.

Murray, C. (1984), *Losing Ground. American Social Policy 1950-1980,* New York.

Murray, C. (1990), *The Emerging British Underclass,* London.

Murray, C. (1994), *Underclass: The Crisis Deepens,* London.

Offe, C. (1996): Moderne 'Barbarei', in Miller and Soeffner, *Modernität und Barbarei,* Frankfurt/Main.

Paugam, S., (ed.), (1996a), *L'exclusion, l'état des savoirs,* Paris.

Paugam, S. (1996b), *A New Social Contract? Poverty and Social Exclusion,* Working Paper European University Institute, Florence.

Procacci, G. (1996), 'A New Social Contract? Against Exclusion: The Poor and the Social Sciences', in *European University Institute Working Papers,* RSC No. 96/41. Badia Fiesolana, San Domenico (FI).

Pugliese, E. (1995), 'Die Entstehung einer neuen "Underclass"?' In: SOFI, *Im Zeichen des Umbruchs,* Opladen.

Schmitter-Heisler, B. (1991), 'A Comparative Perspective on the Underclass. Questions of Urban Poverty, Race and Citizenship', in *Theory and Society,* 20, no. 4.

Wacquant, L. (1992), 'Banlieues francaises et ghetto noir américain: de l'amalgame à la comparaison', in *French Politics and Society,* 10, no. 4.

Wilson, W. J. (1987), *The Truly Disadvantaged. The Inner City, the Underclass and Public Policy,* Chicago.

Wilson, W. J. (1993), *The Ghetto Underclass*, Social Science Perspectives, Newbury Park.

Wilson, W. J. (1996), *When Work Disappears. The World of the New Urban Poor,* New York.

Wright, E.O. (1994), *Interrogating Inequality. Essays on Class Analysis, Socialism and Marxism*, London, New York.

6 Women, Work and Welfare

INGRID JÖNSSON

Introduction

The complex relationship between paid work, unpaid work and welfare is of special importance to women. All over the world, women do most of the household and care work. It is mostly done as unpaid work in the family but can also be organized by the state or through the market. Work has primarily been discussed in relation to the labour market. The concept was broadened by feminist researchers who included unpaid work in the analysis. Mainstream welfare research neglects gender and very little attention is paid to women's position in the welfare system. The point of departure is the full-time male worker. The relation between paid work, unpaid work and welfare is linked to the sexual division of labour. This implies a hierachical power relation between women and men and between the work done in the private and public sphere respectively. Irrespective of the organization of household and care work, the main part is done by women. The access to many social benefits is connected to paid labour but entitlement can also be based on citizenship, as mothers or as wives. If gender is incorporated, women's and men's different structural positions will point to how differently they in practice are included in or excluded from full membership in society. Social inclusion and social exclusion are closely linked to the concept of citizenship.

According to Roche (1997), social exclusion in a narrow sense, refers to the problem of poverty and unemployment and social inclusion to the policies trying to tackle such problems. In a broader sense it refers to all forms of discrimination and barriers to social inclusion, including the political, civil and cultural exclusion of racism and ethnic discrimination. A mainstream view understands social exclusion as a deprivation of social rights and access to the public sphere and thus of social citizenship and of citizenship more generally.

In this chapter, I will start by exploring how a gender aspect is neglected in writings about citizenship and how women are excluded from

113

public life through history. By getting access to the public sphere, women gain some aspects of citizenship. Their role as unpaid providers of welfare will be discussed in relation to welfare regimes. The sexual division of labour in society and in families is important to women's inclusion in public life. The construction of public support for women's labour market participation is also important and large variations are found between different welfare regimes. Women's inclusion as citizens in the public sphere will be considered in relation to paid and unpaid work. Women are not a universal category and large variations are found between groups of women depending on their social and educational background. Finally, I will relate present trends in the contemporary European society to the issue of inclusion and exclusion of women from the public sphere.

Three elements of citizenship

Marshall's article on 'Citizenship and Social Class' (1950) is a common point of departure when discussing citizenship, nowadays often from a critical point of view. Marshall focuses on citizenship as membership in a given community. Nationality, age of majority and full legal agency were crucial to citizen's rights. The contemporary discussion of citizenship takes place in a different social and historical context. The transformation of the nation state and the insecure future of the capitalist welfare state are new conditions. Vogel and Moran (1991) discuss the influence on citizenship of changing outer limits along a number of dimensions - territorial, temporal, social, political and behavioural. The nation state plays a less important role in a world with growing international economic relations constituted by cross-sector actors, supranational institutions and with huge movements of population across frontiers. Citizenship is discussed in relation to adults but adulthood is perceived as insufficient to encompass the possible boundaries of citizenship. In addition to class and capitalism, the social rights of, for example, women, children and the elderly must be included. Such an approach leads to a debate about policy measures: to whom such measures are to be extended and what is expected from citizens in order to get access to policy measures. In recent debates, a 'duty discourse' has gained salience. Entitlements are discussed in relation to obligations to perform in return.

Citizenship as rights derives from the three aspects of citizenship discussed by Marshall. According to Marshall, citizenship embraces civil, political and social rights.

The civil element is composed of the rights necessary for individual freedom - liberty of the person, freedom of speech and thought and faith, the right to own property and to conclude valid contracts, and the right to justice. By the political element I mean the right to participate in the exercise of political power, as a member of a body invested with political authority or as an elector of the members of such a body... By the social element I meant the whole range from the right to a modicum of economic welfare and security to the right to share to the full in the social heritage and to live the life of a civilised being according to the standards prevailing in the society (Marshall, 1950, pp. 10-11).

Marshall saw the three kinds of rights as being steadily built up. Social citizenship was the last stage of full citizenship following the acquisition of civil and political rights. Civil rights were established in the eighteenth century through the establishment of institutions like the courts of justice. Political rights were achieved by the franchise in the nineteenth century and through the establishment of institutions such as parliaments and councils of local governments. Finally, social rights were achieved in the twentieth century through the expansion of the welfare state.

Marshall is primarily concerned about the relationship of social class to social integration and like many other more contemporary writers on citizenship, he underestimates the significance of gender, race and ethnicity. The omission of gender is especially stressed by feminist researchers (e.g. Lister, 1990, 1997; Walby, 1994, 1997). Women gained access to all three rights at a later stage than men. There are also large variations between countries. By including gender, the claim that there has been a steady development from civil and political to social citizenship rights falls into disarray. In most western countries, women did not achieve political rights at the same time as men. Women's suffrage was not won until the twentieth century. Women's civil rights are often achieved later than political rights. Even in the late twentieth century, women still do not have the full right in all countries to control their bodies, e.g. to decide about contraceptives or abortion. Their rights to property and to countersign valid contracts were not reached until the late nineteenth century or the beginning of the twentieth century. Until then, women lost the basic entitlements to citizen's status when they got married. Neither did they have access to the right of justice or the right to avoid the physical coercion of their husbands or to refuse them sexual intercourse (Vogel, 1991; Walby, 1997). Marshall's evolutionism is contested when gender is included and citizenship as a universalistic phenomenon is being questioned. Feminist researchers have made 'visible the female non-citizen who stood outside it and reveal the male citizen lurking behind it' (Lister, 1997). The abolition of overt discrimination against women does not mean that women will attain the same kind of citizenship as men. Women's different structural positions and experiences weaken their claims to full citizenship when such rights are primarily based on participation in the public sphere (Lister, 1990, 1997; O'Conner, 1993, 1996; Walby, 1994, 1997).

Sainsbury (1996) claims that Marshall's conception of social citizenship is laden with patriarchal implications upholding a division between the public and private spheres. Political and social rights stem from participation in and contributions to the public sphere. Women were long restricted in their participation in paid work and confined to domestic duties. They were not allowed to make public speeches and were often physically threatened when appearing unaccompanied. It is by gaining access to the public sphere that women gain some aspects of citizenship (Walby, 1994). Having formal and legal rights does not, however, mean a participation on equal terms.

Welfare state typologies

Different models or typologies have been worked out in the attempts to describe and understand differences between social welfare systems. One of the most referred to in recent debates is that elaborated by Esping-Andersen (1990). The notion of regime refers to the qualitatively different arrangements between the state, the market and the family, but Esping-Andersen focuses mainly on the relation between the state and the market. He makes clusters of western welfare states into liberal, conservative and social-democratic welfare regimes. One crucial point of departure is the extent to which human needs are satisfied by public social policy measures or by the market, how the social relations are constructed within each welfare regime and the basis for access to social benefits. Of special interest to Esping-Andersen is the degree of decommodification - i.e. 'the degree to which individuals, or families, can uphold a socially acceptable standard of living independently of market participation' (*ibid.*, p. 37). As a consequence, it is of importance whether social benefits are reached through citizenship or are related to labour market participation. In opposition to functionalist analyses which treat economic development as primary, Esping-Andersen identifies the importance of political and ideological circumstances, i.e. politics matter. He argues that the size of the left-wing and conservative catholic parties, and the relative strength of authoritarian traditions, are of significance.

The Liberal welfare regime

The Liberal welfare regime has been present in countries such as the USA, Australia, Canada and the UK since the 1970s. In these countries, working class mobilization is weak. There is also weak support for conservative catholic parties and no tradition of absolutism. The role of the state is limited while the market has a strong position. Private market solutions are preferred. Only in exceptional cases is public support given to the citizens. The support is dominated by means-tested benefits and some insurance schemes exist. Welfare is to a large extent organized by voluntary organisations.

The Conservative welfare regime

The Conservative welfare regime is found in countries with strong conservative catholic parties and historically strong totalitarian tendencies. The welfare organization is tied to type of employment and position on the labour market, which determine status and class relations. Consequently, redistribution of resources is limited. The principle of subsidiarity plays an important role and the main responsibility for social security rests on the family. This welfare regime is found in Germany, France and southern Europe.

The Social-democratic welfare regime

In the third welfare regime, which is found in the Scandinavian countries, social benefits are tax-based and access is to a larger extent based on citizenship. The state plays an active role and the welfare state is extensive. Family policy is closely linked to labour market policy. Each adult individual is expected to have a paid job. Politically, these countries are characterized by large left-wing parties in coalition with other political parties. No authoritarian traditions are found.

Liebfried (1992) claims that Esping-Andersen does not properly identify the situation in the 'Latin Rim', i.e. Greece, Italy, Portugal and Spain, and suggests the addition of a fourth welfare regime. Ferrera (1996) more generally finds that comparative social policy literature fails to consider the situation of the southern European countries systematically.

Trifiletti (1995) questions whether the Italian welfare state can be described as rudimentary and belonging to the conservative welfare regime. She claims that the influence of the traditions of statism and corporatism has been far greater than that of the Catholic Church.

Women's position in different welfare systems

Esping-Andersen's typology has been widely criticized by feminist researchers for its lack of a gender perspective (e.g. Borchorst, 1994; Daly, 1994; Orloff, 1993; O'Conner 1993, 1996; Lewis, 1993). The typology of welfare regimes concerns primarily the distribution of responsibilities between the state and the market and neglects the role of the family as provider of welfare and services. The theory is nevertheless useful as it makes a link between work and welfare. Decommodification is seen as necessary for political mobilization, but as is pointed out in Lewis (1993), this also depends on unpaid female household labour. Women are only included in Esping-Andersen's analysis if they enter the paid labour market. Research shows that tending to children, the elderly, the sick and disabled in private households is done by women. The inclusion of gender will point to the fact that all three kinds of welfare regimes rest on female labour, although in different forms. In all welfare systems, women's rights to welfare have historically been indirect, a function of their presumed dependence on a male bread-winner. Women's access to first-class social benefits has always been connected to labour market participation. Women's inferior labour market positions means that women are disadvantaged when benefits reflect work-related inequalities (Orloff, 1993). Social benefits related to motherhood and marriage imply lower rates than work-related social benefits (Lewis, 1993; Orloff, 1993; Sainsbury, 1994, 1996).

... in the Conservative welfare regime

The Catholic social doctrine is the foundation for the Christian Democratic parties which hold strong positions in countries with conservative welfare regimes It is reflected in a traditional support for the housewife-breadwinner family model. It is among other things characterized by tax relief for dependants and child allowances. The state is involved only modestly in the provision of care for the sick, the elderly and children. The influence from the Church has become weaker. Married women are dependent on the husband's social insurance for access to social benefits. The rate is lower than for men which leads to a vulnerable situation for divorced women. The Catholic Church exerts a larger impact on the political culture in Germany than in France. The family is often the unit for family policy measures in Germany while family policy in France to a larger extent addresses the individual (Borchorst, 1994). The parents (i.e. mothers) are supposed to provide for their small children. The idea is supported by long parental leave and by lack of public provision for children under the age of three. The provision for older children is better organised. Seventy nine per cent of the age group from three to six is attending public child care arrangements, although only 12 per cent attend establishments open during the whole day (Lohkamp-Himmighofen, 1994). The service is mostly being offered during a limited number of hours and at odds with full-time employment, which makes it complicated for women to combine work and family life.

... in the Liberal welfare regime

In the UK, which since the 1970s is classified as a liberal welfare state, very few public incentives are taken to encourage married women's labour market participation. Maternity rights introduced in the 1970s became less favourable in the 1980s. Only women with two years of continuous employment are entitled, which means that only 54 per cent of working pregnant women in 1990 qualified for maternity leave (EU Commission 1990). In relation to the number of working women, the public provision of child care is very modest. There is no statutory obligation at central or local level to provide child care facilities for children under five. Mothers leave the labour force when their children are small. In spite of the fact that part-time work among mothers is encouraged there is no or only little protection for part-time workers. There are also modest family transfers as the family members are expected to be provided for by the male family wage or in case of needs by welfare benefits. The child benefit is very low relative to much of Europe.

... in the Social-democratic welfare regime

In the Social-democratic welfare regime, market forces are modified. Care work has gone public to a larger extent than in the other welfare regimes (Hernes, 1987). The family is ascribed a less prominent role as provider of care for children, elderly and disabled. The Scandinavian model as a single regime is, however, questioned (Leira, 1992; Borchorst, 1994, Ellingseter, 1998). Sweden and Denmark are very secularized states while religion continues to have a larger impact on the Norwegian society where traditional norms are more persistent. The production of social services in Sweden and Denmark involved a different partnership between women and the state supporting women's economic independence from that in Norway. The dominant strategy to achieve gender equality was through education and integration into the labour market (Borchorst, 1994). Separate taxation introduced in the beginning of the 1970s supported such a development. Swedish and Danish women entered the labour market in large numbers during that period; at the same time as the public sector and public child care facilities were expanded. The Norwegian welfare state developed later; when Norwegian women entered the labour market in larger numbers in the 1980s, the provision of public child care was not very extensive (Ellingsaeter, 1998).

Female labour market participation

The possibility of exerting political power increases with the independence of the worker, i.e. by the degree of decommodification. Decommodification refers to paid work, which limits its applicability to the situation for women. There is, however, a general trend in contemporary Europe of rising female labour market participation, but large differences are still found between countries. The participation rates amount to 70 per cent or more in the Scandinavian countries, 60-70 per cent in the Anglo-Saxon countries and between 52-57 per cent in continental Europe (SCB, 1992; O'Conner, 1996). The rise is mainly due to increased activity rates among women in the 25-49 age group. A division between activity rates in the north and south of Europe is still found but recent developments point to an eventual blurring of the divide. The rate of female market participation is probably higher in several countries, especially in southern Europe, partly due to the way statistics are kept but also due to the widespread existence of informal work. In Spain, this group is estimated at about 1.5 to 2.0 million, mostly women (Valiente, 1990). Also in Italy, women work to a large extent in the informal sector and/or in agriculture, and are thereby left out from official statistics (Trifiletti, 1995).

Men's activity rates are either falling (e.g. in the ex-German Democratic Republic, Belgium, Spain, France, the UK, Greece, Ireland, Italy and Portugal) or increasing less than women's (Germany, Denmark,

Luxembourg and the Netherlands) (Meulders *et al.*, 1993). In comparison to men, women are lower paid, have jobs of lower status and work shorter hours in paid jobs.

Part-time work

Part-time work may be voluntary and regarded as the first step into the labour market. Women with and without children work part-time to a varying extent. In Sweden, working mothers with young children are entitled to reduced working hours until the child is eight years old. This facilitates mothers with small children staying in contact with the labour market (Sundström, 1997b). The opposite situation is found in Germany where mothers exit from the labour market when the children are small. Part-time work can also be non-voluntary and function as a trap for women. Statistics from France and Finland show that part-time working women do so because they cannot find full-time employment (Eurostat, 1996 quoted in Hantrais and Letablier, 1997). Consequently, the function of part-time work in different countries and for different groups of women should be problematized (Nätti, 1994).

There are large variations in rates of female part-time work and in the number of hours worked. Such variations have implications for the qualification for social benefits and women's autonomy. The number of 'geringfügig Beschäftigte' in Germany amounts to about 7 million. Most of them are held by women. The employed do not pay tax for income which does not exceed 600 DM per month or on jobs which last for fewer than 19 hours per week. In return they do not qualify for social benefits (Fölster, 1996). Part-time work is most frequent in the Netherlands (67.2 per cent), UK (44.3 per cent), Sweden (41.2 per cent), Denmark (35.5 per cent) and Germany (35.5 per cent). The lowest rates are found in southern Europe (Spain 16.6 per cent, Italy 12.7 per cent, Portugal 11. 6 per cent). In all 15 EU member states, the male average amounts to 7.7 per cent compared to 31.3 per cent among employed women (the figures on part-time work and weekly hours refer to the year of 1995, Eurostat 1996 quoted in Hantrais and Letablier, 1997).

Fifty-eight per cent of the part-time working women in Sweden work more than 25 hours a week. Also in Denmark and Finland, part-time means long hours for almost half of the females working part-time. Short part-time (less than 10 hours per week) is most frequent in the Netherlands (27.2 per cent) and in the UK (22.5 per cent). The average difference of weekly hours worked by men and women in the EU member states amounted to 7.4 hours. Modest differences were found in Finland (2.5 hours) and Greece (3.1 hours) while they were considerable in the Netherlands (11.1 hours) and the UK (12.9 hours). The large difference in the UK is the result of a non-interventionist policy in reducing working hours. The opposite strategy has been applied in other countries such as Germany.

Education and work

A comparative European study of attitudes to different types of family models revealed a declining support for the traditional bread-winner family model in the period from 1970 to 1985. Large differences are still found between countries; an equal family model was supported to the largest extent in Denmark, while the opposite opinion was more frequent in Germany, Ireland and Luxembourg (Kiernan, 1992, quoted in Landgren-Möller and Uhlén, 1994). Results from other studies indicate growing positive attitudes to female labour market participation. Young men and women above all are more opposed to traditional gender roles (Sundström, 1997a).

In spite of such changes in attitudes, there are still large differences in female labour market participation in European countries. There are significant differences between groups of women due to class and educational background. In Scandinavia, with the exception of Norway, women work to almost the same extent as men. There are only minor differences due to educational background. In most other European countries, labour market participation is much higher among men and the difference is especially pronounced among the less educated. In Sweden, the labour market participation rate among less educated women has slightly decreased in later years. As a consequence, the level of education of the total labour force increased. It should nevertheless be noted that less educated women still exist but outside the labour force. The labour markets in all European countries are sex-segregated. At a first glance, the Swedish labour market seems to be more sex-segregated than in the rest or Europe. One should, however, keep in mind that part of the service and care work done by Swedish women as paid jobs in the public sector is provided unpaid by home-working women in other European countries (Stark, 1996). A comparative study of seven countries including home-working women supports Stark's arguments. Nermo (1997) finds greater similarities than dissimilarities between the countries.

Many of the educational systems in Europe were reformed during the post-war period. The level of qualification beyond basic schooling has risen over the last 25-30 years, but there are still large variations between countries. The expansion lead to increased generational differences. With few exceptions and to some extent depending on educational level, women outnumber men in the educational system. In spite of the abolition of formal obstacles to women's participation in education, differences in the traditions, cultures and organisation of the educational systems affect their participation rates at different levels and in the choice of study programmes. Female and male preferences in education still follow very traditional patterns which lead them to different sectors of the labour market (Eurostat, 1996; Jönsson, 1997). The level of education is an important factor for women's labour market participation. The level of education among working women is on average higher than that of men with the exception of Germany and Luxembourg (Eurostat, 1995). In all European countries, labour market participation is more frequent among more than less qualified women. The activity rate is more similar among highly educated women irrespective of country than that of less educated women. With the exception of Sweden, Denmark and Finland, less educated women's participation rate is lower than other educational groups and lower than comparable groups of men (OECD, 1996). Qualification levels also influence the activity cycles. Highly educated women pursue more often uninterrupted careers than women with lower levels of education (Meulders *et al.*, 1993).

Possibilities for and hindrances to female labour market participation

Policy differences

Large variations are found in support for women's labour market participation and public services to facilitate women working outside the home. A comparative study of policies in 12 EU member states (Gornick *et al.*, 1997) describes the pattern of female labour market participation in the late 1980s in the following way. In the Scandinavian countries female labour market participation was similar to that of men, i.e. increasing participation rates and a smooth decline with age (an inverted U-curve). In Germany and the Netherlands, women's labour market participation was highest in their mid-twenties and then fell steadily from that point, i.e. a labour market participation pattern which differs sharply from that of men.

In the UK, women's labour market participation fell in their late twenties and increased later on. Their labour market pattern was similar to an M-curve and also differed from that of men. Measures to facilitate women to combining full-time work with caring for children below school-age were only taken in Belgium, Denmark, Finland, France and Sweden These countries offered the most developed policy packages containing job protection and wage replacement at the time of childbirth, provision for the care of infants through extended leave and/or publicly subsidized child care, and support for the care of children over three in the form of public child care and/or early enrolment in public school. In other European countries the policy measures were modest or lacking. In e.g. Germany, the lack of public child care provision hampers women's return to work after a relatively generous maternity leave period. They are left with few options and women are expected to accommodate their family responsibilities by reducing their hours of employment or by leaving employment altogether until the children become older. The M-curve pattern of the labour market participation among women in UK implies that women with small children leave the labour market temporarily as a result of low job protection and few public measures to facilitate the combination of family and employment.

Pay differentials

Women's economic gain from paid labour is below that of men in all OECD countries. In 1988, the female-to-male hourly earnings ratios were 90 per cent in Sweden, 78 per cent in the Netherlands, 75 per cent in Belgium, 68 per cent in UK and 73 per cent in Germany (O'Conner, 1996, table 5:3). Meulders *et al.* (1993) report on the persistence and worsening of pay disparities between women and men. The gap has widened in Italy, Denmark and Portugal, due to changes in their economies. In the UK, the gender gap is not increasing. Instead, differences are growing within the female labour force. A polarization has taken place between the wages of highly paid women and the wages of women having jobs at the other end of the wage scale, which are remaining static or are declining (Maruani, 1993 quoted in O'Conner, 1996). An increase in the pay gap is found between full-time and part-time work. The economic policy pursued in the 1980s emphasizing decentralization is seen as one explanation. Since then wages are negotiated at the local level without any national guidelines. The effect of the breakdown of the national bargaining system is found to be larger on small firms and on the weakest groups (Humphries and Rubery, 1991, quoted in Meulders *et al.*, 1993).

Male support in the household

Women's entrance to the labour market happens at the same time as a new pattern of economic production and social reproduction is emerging. Employment becomes less stable and few jobs pay sufficiently to support a family on one salary (Frazer, 1997). The old forms of welfare states built on the assumption of male-headed families with stable jobs are becoming obsolete. At the same time as women are entering the labour market, men's working hours are decreasing. Such changes have only marginal effects on men's participation in domestic and care work in the household. Nor do they adjust their working hours to a changed family situation. In Sweden, the labour market participation among women fluctuates with the life cycle while just marginal fluctuations (Rydenstam, 1992) or none at all (Hörnqvist, 1997) are found among men, notwithstanding having small children. Among couples, irrespective of having children or not, women spend more time on domestic work. Lister's review of literature on changes in the allocation to women of the unpaid tasks of housework and childcare when entering the labour market, points to a persistent sexual division of labour (Lister, 1997, pp. 130-133). The situation is similar, although with some national differences in details, in countries in the First, Second and Third world. Researchers in western Europe and the USA report on 'some movement but without any significant disturbance of the traditional skewed pattern of responsibilities in the domestic spheres' (*ibid.*, p. 131). A Eurobarometer survey shows that according to the spouses two thirds of men in the EU do not do any domestic work. The increased input of domestic work by men was modest even in Denmark where women work full-time to a large extent. In most other countries, males' increased share of the domestic work is a result of a reduction in the time spent by women.

Paternal leave

All EU member states now offer some kind of paternity leave, male access to parental leave or leave to care for sick children with the exception of Britain, Ireland and Luxembourg. Countries with high rates of female labour market participation have developed more father-sensitive benefit leave systems. O'Brien (1995) claims further that politico-cultural factors are also of importance in explaining the differences in the provision of social benefits to parents. The governments in the UK and Ireland have historically emphasized private rather than public responsibilities for dependants. The role of the father was brought into the debate by a statement made by the EU Council of Ministers on childcare which encouraged more male participation in the rearing of children. Both fathers and mothers are beginning to be recognized as having family responsibilities. The official UK response was negative and the EU proposal on parental leave was rejected (O'Brien, 1995). In contrast, the Danish reaction was positive and led to policy changes. Previous benefits were extended. Fathers' take-up rates of paternity leave vary widely between the EU member states: 52 per cent in Denmark (compared to 3 per cent taking parental leave) 34 per cent in Finland (3 per cent parental leave). Parental leave benefits were used by 1.5 per cent of the eligible cases in Germany, 14 per cent in Spain (shared with the mother) and 2 per cent in France (Carlsen, 1994; Lohkamp-Himmighofen, 1994; Tobio, 1994, Barbier, 1994 quoted in O'Brien, 1995). Nearly three per cent of Swedish men used their parental insurance rights when this option first was introduced in 1974. The take-up rate had increased to 31.1 per cent in 1996. The introduction of one month's paternity leave introduced in 1995 has so far had little impact on the take-up rate. Men are, however, using only 10.6 per cent of days available. This means about 40 days on average. For shorter options such as 'daddy days' in connection to the birth of the child, time for leave when the children are ill and days available for contacts with e.g day care centres and schools, the take-up rates were higher (79, 40 and 30 per cent respectively). Fathers who took parental leave for at least one month had to a larger extent jobs within the public sector, worked in female dominated work-places and were better educated than those not using this possibility (Sundqvist and Dufvander, 1988). The importance of women's education was also found by Näsman (1992) and Hoem (1995).

Paid and unpaid work

Lister (1997) refers to several studies on working hours showing that when unpaid work is added to paid work, women have longer working hours than men (UNDP, 1995; Bryson *et al.*, 1994; Lewis and Åström, 1992; Einhorn, 1993; Piachaud, 1984). That women carry a double work load is contradicted by time-budget studies (e.g. Elchardus and Glorieux, 1994; Rydenstam, 1992) which claim that women and men work about the same number of hours per week. Davies (1994, 1998) suggests that this may be true in a narrow sense and claims that there is an inbuilt problem with the methodology of time-budget studies. It is problematic to quantify and pinpoint certain care activities as well as to include activities carried out simultaneously, to separate work from leisure, and to take account of the planning and mental work that goes into running a home and maintaining social relations. When men are doing household work they do not take the full responsibilities but often just assist and cream off the more enjoyable tasks. Women's spare time is more fragmented than men's and it is more often interrupted by urgent tasks, often in the form of household work. The time, energy and responsibilities they devote to the household are often open-ended with implications for their health and for their freedom to act as citizens in the public sphere (Lister, 1997). However, time-budget studies showing that women spend more hours per week on unpaid work compared to men who instead spend more hours on paid work neglect the long term consequences for women. The level of social benefits related to paid work will be affected. Men are reinforcing their privileged position in the public citizenship sphere.

(In)dependence of work and family

The proportion of unpaid work done by women affects their degree of (in)dependence. Economic dependence among women decreases with rising labour market participation. It should, however, be pointed out that at present only a small proportion of European women are economically independent (Hobson, 1990, 1994). Lister (1990, 1997) argues that interdependence is only possible when involuntary economic dependence is absent. (In)dependence has also been discussed in relation to the state. Scandinavian women rely to a large extent on the state as provider of jobs within the public sector. They also rely on the state as consumers of services. Hernes (1987) argues that such dependence differs qualitatively from being dependent on the state as a client, which is more common in the UK and USA. Pateman (1988) claims that paid work has replaced military service as the key to citizenship. Paid work also has other qualities. It is often valued by women as the locus of social participation as well as a source of self-esteem, which is important for the fulfilment of women's potential as citizens (Lister, 1997).

Orloff (1993) warns of a one-sided emphasis on women's labour market participation in relation to women's autonomy. A relevant point of discussion for those being responsible for care and domestic work - mainly women - would be their possibilities of forming and maintaining autonomous households, i.e. to reach independence from market and marriage. Orloff suggests that the dimension of decommodification should be subsumed under a more generic dimension measuring independence or autonomy. Public services offered on the basis of citizenship support women's autonomy to a larger extent than rights based on income and/or on need (O'Conner, 1993; Sainsbury, 1994, 1996). In all welfare regimes, women are disproportionately represented in mean-tested benefits while men are over-represented in work-related benefits. Decommodification is associated with entitlements and social rights which protect individuals, irrespective of gender, from total dependence on the labour market. The concept, however, is still not applicable to large numbers of European women as their work is not yet commodified (Daly, 1994). Most overt labour market discrimination is abolished but access to the labour market might be limited by caring responsibilities. O'Conner (1993) further claims that the theory of decommodification must be supplemented by the concept of personal autonomy or insulation from dependence, in the sense of both personal dependence on family members and/or public dependence on the state agencies (p. 514). Defamilialization may be as important as decommodification.

Entitlements to social rights

There are various ways of gaining access to social rights in European countries. They can be obtained on the basis of labour market participation, citizenship or residence, need, or eligibility on the basis of a family member's labour market participation. Even though European welfare systems include elements from all kinds of entitlement systems, there are national variations due to differences in historical, cultural, economic, political and social backgrounds. The social security of the individual is related to the organization of the welfare system. The basis for entitlement to social benefits plays a crucial role for women's autonomy and independence. In Esping-Andersen's typology, eligibility varies between the three welfare regimes. In the liberal welfare regime the entitlement is primarily based on need while labour market status is the most crucial factor in the conservative welfare regime. In the Social-democratic welfare regime, the entitlement is citizenship and to a growing extent residence. As Sainsbury (1994, 1996) and other feminists have underlined, these criteria do not exhaust the bases for entitlement of women. The main part of women's entitlements derives from their status as mothers and as wives.

Of special significance for women's autonomy and independence is the extent to which married women's entitlement to social benefits is through husbands or is influenced by the husband's income. Sainsbury (1996) underlines the significance of entitlements based on citizenship or residence for women's autonomy and independence. She argues that they have a special impact on family relationships and a stronger defamilialization potential than other principles of eligibility.

Access to universal citizen's rights neutralizes the influence of marriage; the benefits are not differentiated between wife and husband and they are reached irrespective of civil status. Neither do they differentiate between paid and unpaid work which means that the gender impact is decreased. Entitlements based on paid work are transferred onto the gendered division of labour. The principles of care and maintenance stem directly from the traditional division of labour. Entitlements based on other principles overlook unpaid work, primarily done by women.

Concluding remarks

In this chapter, I have been primarily concerned with how conditions at different levels of society affect women as citizens. In contemporary Europe, paid employment is still the key to full citizenship. All over Europe, increasing numbers of women are entering paid work. Yet, women's growing labour market participation has not led to fundamental changes in the sexual division of labour or to changes in time use and responsibilities between women and men. Men still do not share domestic tasks and care for children on an equal basis with women. Neither do women and men share the same working life conditions; women are lower paid, have more often low status jobs and work shorter hours. There are also, however, large variations among different groups of women in their labour market participation related to their social and educational backgrounds. In all European countries, irrespective of welfare tradition, highly educated women work outside the home to a larger extent than less qualified women. Women with higher education participate in paid work to about the same extent all over Europe while there are considerable differences between less qualified women. The narrowest gap is found in countries classified as belonging to the social-democratic welfare regime.

The issue of unpaid care work will be of crucial importance in the future due to e.g. demographic changes, new family forms, changed labour relations and uncertainty of the welfare state. Lewis (1997) questions a too one-sided emphasis on paid labour but building on evidence from present care-giving, she also claims that it is impossible to separate the study of unpaid work and caring regimes from the position women hold in relation to paid work. An analysis of women's relations to unpaid and paid work has to consider their positions in their families, their formal and informal rights and duties, and their right to choose whether they want to be committed to unpaid and/or paid labour.

In times of retrenchment of the welfare state, of changing labour relations and of demographic change, the issue the exclusion of women from the public sphere takes on a heightened importance.

References

Ahrne, G. and I. Persson (1997), (eds), *Familj, makt och jämställdhet*, SOU 1997: 138, Arbetsmarknadsdepartmentet, Stockholm.

Barbier, J-C. (1994), 'European Comparisons of Unemployment Categories and Parental Leave', in L. Hantrais and M.T. Letablier, (eds), pp. 48-55.

Borchorst, A. (1994), 'Welfare State Regimes, Womens Interests and the EC', in D. Sainsbury, (ed.), pp. 26-45.

Bryson, V. and R. Lister (1994), *Women, Citizenship and Social Policy*, University of Bradford, Joseph Rowntree Foundation, Bradford.

Carlsen, S. (1994), *When Men have Children. On men's use of parental leave.* Presentation at the 'Men's families' Conference, Copenhagen, October 1994.

Daly, M. (1994), 'Comparing Welfare States: Towards a Gender Friendly Approach', in D. Sainsbury (ed.), pp. 101-118.

Davies, K. (1994), 'The Tension between Process Time and Clock-Time in Care Work: The Example of Day Nurseries', *Time and Society*, 3(3), pp. 277-303.

Davies, K. (1998), 'New Times at the Workplace - Opportunity or Angst? The Example of Hospital Work', paper presented at the Tenth International Conference of the International Society for the Study of Time, Tutzing, 5-11 July 1998.

Einhorn, B. (1993), *Cinderella Goes to Market,* Verso, London.

Elchardus, M. and I. Glorieux (1994), 'The Search for the Invisible 8 hours: The Gendered Use of Time in a Society with High Labour Force Participation of Women', *Time and Society*, 3(1), pp. 5-27.

Ellingsaeter, A.L. (1998), 'Dual Breadwinner Societies: Provider Models in the Scandinavian Welfare States', *Acta Sociologica*, 41 (1), pp. 59-73.

Esping-Andersen, G. (1990) *The Three Worlds of Welfare Capitalism*, Polity Press Cambridge, Cambridge.

EU-Commission (1990), *Families and Policies. Evolutions and Trends in 1988-1989*, Euopean Observatory of National Policies, EC Commission (DG V), Brussels.

Eurostat (1995), *Employment in Europe*, Eurostat, Luxembourg.

Eurostat (1996), *Education Across the European Unit*, Statistics and Indicators, Eurostat, Luxembourg.

Ferrera, M. (1996), 'The 'Southern Model' of Welfare in Social Europe', *Journal of European Social Policy* , 6 (1), pp. 17-37.

Fölster, K. (1996), *Barn och äldreomsorg i Tyskland och Sverige. Tysklandsdelen,* Fakta/Kunskaper Nr 4, Socialdepartementet, Stockholm.

Frazer, N. (1997), 'After the Family Wage: A Postindustrial Thought Experiment', in B. Hobson and A.M. Berggren (eds), *Crossing Borders. Gender and Citizenship in Transition*, FRN, Stockholm.

Gornick, J.C., M.K. Meyers and J.E Ross (1997), 'Supporting the Employment of Mothers: Policy Variations Across Fourteen Welfare States', *Journal of European Social Policy*, 7(1), pp. 45-70.

Hantrais, L. and M-T. Letablier (eds), (1994), *The Family-Employment Relationship*, Cross National Research Papers, No.2, Fourth Series: Concepts and Contexts in International Comparisons of Family Policies in Europe, Loughborough University, Loughborough.

Hantrais, L. and M-T. Letablier (1997), The Gender of Paid and Unpaid Work Time: a European problem, *Time and Society*, 2/3 (6) pp. 131-151.

Hernes, H. (1987), *Welfare State and Women Power*, Norwegian University Press, Oslo.

Hobson, B. (1990), 'No Exit, No Voice. Women's Economic Dependency in the Welfare State', *Acta Sociologica*, 33 (3), pp. 235-250.

Hobson, B. (1994), 'Solo Mothers. Social Policy Regimes and the Logics of Gender', in D. Sainsbury (ed.), pp. 170-187.

Hoem, B. (1995), *Kvinnor och mäns liv. Del 1. Sysselsättning från 17 års ålder,* Statistiska Centralbyrån, Stockholm.

Hörnqvist, M. (1997), 'Familjeliv och arbetsmarknad för män och kvinnor', in G. Ahrne and I. Persson (eds), *op cit.*

Humphries, J. and J. Rubery (1991), *La Position des Femmes sur le Marché du Travail au Royaume Uni, Evolution entre 1983 et 1989,* Report for the Equal Opportunities Unit of the European Commission, Brussels.

Jönsson, I. (1997), *Female Participation in Education in Some European Countries*, paper presented at the Third Conference of ESA, Essex August 1997.

Kiernan, K. (1992), 'The roles of men and women in tomorrow's Europe', *Empoyment Gazette,* October 1992.

Landgren-Möller, E. and M. Uhlén (1994), *Att klara av ... arbete-barn-familj,* Demografi med barn och familj 1994: 1, Statistiska Centralbyrån, Stockholm.

Leira, A. (1992), Welfare States and Working Mothers. The Scandinavian Experience, Cambridge University Press, Cambridge.

Lewis, J. (ed.), (1993), *Women and Social Policies in Europe. Work, Family and the State*, Edward Elgar Publishing Limited, Aldershot.

Lewis, J. and G. Åström (1992), 'Equality, Difference and State Welfare: Labour Market and Welfare Policies in Sweden', *Feminist Studies,* 18(1), pp. 59-87.

Lewis, J. (1997), 'Gender and Welfare Regimes: Further Thoughts', *Social Politics*, Summer.

Liebfried, S. (1992), 'Towards a European Welfare State? On the Integration Potentials of Poverty Regimes in the European Community', in C. Jones (ed.), *New Perspectives on the Welfare State in Europe,* Routledge, London and New York, pp. 133-156.

Lister, R. (1990), 'Women, Economic Dependency and Citizenship', *Journal of Social Policy*, 19 (4), pp. 445-467.

Lister, R. (1997), *Citizenship. Feminist Perspective*, Macmillan, London.

Lohkamp-Himmighofen, M. (1994), 'The institutional dimension of the family-employment relationship in Germany, in L. Hantrais and M-T. Letablier (eds), pp. 55-58.

Marshall, T.H. (1950), *Citizenship and Social Class*, Cambridge University Press, Cambridge.

Maruani, M. (1992), 'The Position of Women in the Labour Market. Trends and Development in the Twelve Member States of the European Community 1983-1990', *Women of Europe,* Supplement No. 36, Commission of the European Union, Brussels.

Meulders, D., R. Plasman and A. Vander Stricht (1993), *Position of Women on the Labour Market in the European Community*, Dartmouth Publishing Company Ltd, Aldershot.

Nätti, J. (1993), 'Temporary Employment in the Nordic Countries. A "Trap" or a "Bridge"?', *Work, Employment and Society,* 7(3), pp. 451-463.

Näsman, E. (1992), 'Parental Leave in Sweden - a Work Place Issue?', *Stockholm Research Papers in Demography*, No. 73, Demografiska Avdelningen, Stockholms Universitet, Stockholm.

Nermo, M. (1997), 'Yrkessegregering efter kön - ett internationellt perspektiv', in I. Persson and W. Wadensjö (eds), *Glastak och glasväggar. Den könssegregerade arbetsmarknaden,* SOU 1997: 137, Arbetsmarknadsdepartmentet, Stockholm, pp. 82-108.

O'Brien, M. (1995), 'Fatherhood and Family policies in Europe', in L. Hantrais and M-T. Letablier (eds), *The Family in Social Policy and Family Policy.* Cross National Research Papers, no. 3, Fourth Series: Concepts and Contexts in International Comparisons of 'Family Policies in Europe, Loughborough University, Loughborough, pp. 48-56.

O'Conner, J.S. (1993), 'Welfare State Regimes: Theoretical and Methodological Issues', *British Journal of Sociology*, 44 (3), pp. 501-518.

O'Conner, J.S. (1996), 'From Women in the Welfare State to Genderng Welfare State Regimes', in *Current Sociology*, 44 (2) , Summer.

OECD (1996), *Education at a Glance,* OECD, Paris.

Orloff, A.S. (1993), 'Gender and the Social Rights of Citizenship', *American Sociologial Review*, 58 (3), June, pp. 303-328.

Pateman, C. (1988), *The Sexual Contract*, Cambridge Univesity Press, Cambridge.

Persson, I. and E. Wadensjö (eds), *Glastak och glasväggar? Den könssegregeradearbetsmarknaden* SOU 1997:137, Arbetsmarknadsdepartementet, Stockholm.

Piachaud, D. (1984), *Round about 50 Hours a Week*, Child Poverty Action Group, London.

Roche, M. (1997), 'Citizenship and Exclusion: Reconstructing the European Union', in Roche, M. and Van Berkel, R. (eds), *European Citizenship and Social Exclusion*, Ashgate Publising Ltd, Aldershot.

Rydenstam, k. (1992), *I tid och otid. En undersökning om kvinnors och mäns tidsanvänding 1990/91*, Levnadsförhållanden, Rappor nr 79, Statistiska Centralbyrån, Stockholm.

Sainsbury, D. (ed.) (1994), *Gendering Welfare States*, Sage Publications, London.

Sainsbury, D. (1996), *Gender Equality and Welfare States*, Cambridge University Press, Cambridge.

SCB (1992), *Om kvinnor och män i Sverige och EG. Fakta om jämställdheten*, Statistiska Centralbyrån, Stockholm.

Stark, A. (1996), 'Arbete och arbetsmarknad i ett könsperspektiv på Sverige', in A-M. Berggren (ed.), *Kvinnorna och välfärden*, FRN, Stockholm, pp. 105-113.

Sundström. E. (1997a), 'Bör kvinnor förvärvsarbeta? Attityder till kvinnors förvärvsarbete i Sverige, Tyskland och Italien', in G. Ahrne and I. Persson, (eds), pp. 7-30.

Sundström, M. (1997b), 'Managing Work and Children: Part-Time Work and the Family Cycle of Swedish Women', in H-P. Blossfeld and C. Hakim (eds), *Between Equalization and Marginalization. Women Working Part-Time in Europe and the United States of America*, Oxford University Press, Oxford, pp. 272-288.

Sundström, M. and A-S. Duvander (1998), 'Föräldraförsäkringen och jämställdhet mellan kvinnor och män', in I. Persson and E. Wadensjö (eds), *Välfärdens genusansikte*, SOU 1998: 3, Arbetsmarknadsdepartementet, Stockholm.

Tobio, C. (1994), 'The Family-Employment Relationship in Spain', in L. Hantrais and M-T. Letablier (eds), pp. 41-47.

Trifiletti, R. (1995), 'Family Obligations in Italy', in J. Millar and A. Warman (eds), *Defining Family Obligations in Europe*, Bath Social Papers, No. 23, University of Bath, Bath, pp. 177-205.

UNDP (1995), *Human Development Report 1995*, Oxford University Press, New York and Oxford.

Valiente, C. (1996), 'Women in Segmented Labour Markets and Continental Welfare States: the Case of Spain', in L. Hantrais and M-T. Letablier (eds), *The Family in Social Policy and Family Policy*. Cross National Research Papers, no. 4, Fourth Series: Concepts and Contexts in International

Comparisons of 'Family Policies in Europe', Loughborough University, Loughborough, pp. 86-93.

Vogel, U. (1991), 'Is Citizenship Gender-Specific?', in Vogel, U. and Moran, M. (eds), pp. 58-85.

Vogel, U. and M. Moran (eds), *The Frontiers of Citizenship*, Macmillan:London.

Walby, S. (1994), 'Is Citizenship Gendered?' in *Sociology*, 28 (2), May, pp. 379-395.

Walby, S. (1997), *Gender Transformations*, Routledge, London and New York.

7 Ideas of Social Justice in the Welfare State in Germany and the Netherlands

ROSWITHA PIOCH

Introduction

Social Justice is not an easy term to discuss in sociology. Nevertheless it is an important topic. Ideas of social justice are as relevant to the legitimation of social exclusion as they are to the creation of social inclusion in the welfare state (Offe, 1990). Whether or not modern societies share the nationally produced wealth in such a way that none of their citizens is materially excluded from society depends on the arrangements of distribution and redistribution provided by the welfare state. Whether a society accepts or is concerned about social exclusion depends on existing ideas of social justice. In this chapter I shall discuss the diverse images of social justice in the welfare states of Germany and the Netherlands.

Presently in all developed welfare states of western Europe we can observe on-going debates over reforms to and the future of the welfare state. I suggest the key issue in these debates is the question of how to solve problems of distributive justice in times of continuous mass unemployment. Historically evolved arrangements between the labour market as the primary source of income and social benefits are also becoming problematic because of incessant mass unemployment. Thus, established arrangements between the labour market and social security have to be reorganized as the labour market does not provide jobs for all citizens (Pioch, 1996).

At the end of the twentieth century something has become obvious which nobody could have foreseen at the time of industrialization and the introduction of workers' social insurance: mass unemployment turns out to be a structural problem of highly industrialized societies instead of being just a cyclical phenomenon. It is still an open question as to which policies can help to bring about improved employment opportunities in the labour market. In Europe all unemployment figures indicate that the small countries like the Netherlands and Denmark have performed best in job creation - at least much better than their big neighbour Germany. In the Netherlands the unemployment rate fell to a level of about 6 per cent, while at the same time in Germany it rose to almost 10 per cent (OECD, 1996). The differences in unemployment rates indicate that labour market policies matter. However, the unemployment rates also provide evidence of the fact that since the oil crisis in the mid-seventies, in all European countries, the labour markets have failed to provide full employment. Even in countries like the Netherlands we see that job creation policies obviously reach their limits of success at a level around 5 to 6 per cent of remaining unemployment.

European welfare states are faced with a situation in which one can no longer take for granted that everybody looking for a job will get one. In consequence the general idea of social justice in the welfare state, that everybody who asks for social security should contribute to society in return by equivalent labour market participation, can no longer be realized. The question of legitimizing social exclusion in the welfare state becomes relevant again. On the one hand the old idea of reciprocity becomes a promise which people cannot fulfil due to lack of jobs in the labour market. On the other hand even more people are in need of social benefits. As long as reciprocity is a norm they cannot attain, they have to fear social exclusion not only from the labour market but, because of insufficient benefits, also from participation in social life in general. Thus today in all European countries the question that debates about social reform must find an answer to is: according to which principles of social justice should social security be organized, when the labour market does not offer the opportunity of reciprocity for those who claim benefits? According to which principles of social justice should the welfare state provide a social minimum in order to avoid social exclusion even in times of mass unemployment?

Social justice as a sociological issue

Among classical sociologists it was Émile Durkheim who in his work devoted most attention to the issue of social justice. At the very beginning of his major work, *The Social Division of Labour*, he asks for a sociological approach for observing morality as a social fact, just like any other empirical phenomenon, which we as sociologists are duty-bound to observe (Durkheim, 1992, p. 76). In this manner Durkheim himself started out to describe the changes from mechanic to organic solidarity for modern societies. In the end, however, when he came to investigate the morality of professional groups, he left us with a far more normative plea for justice and solidarity rather than merely providing empirical evidence for his assumption that professional groups fulfil this normative function (Durkheim, 1991). It is well known that - contrary to Durkheim - Max Weber avoided the issue of social justice in his work in order to avoid making value judgements. While classical sociologists in general kept rather quiet on the issue of social justice, we find an intensive debate about it in social philosophy. It seems that sociologists focused on social inequality and left the issue of social justice up to the philosophers (Müller, 1995).

As much as liberal and communitarian ideas about social justice may differ in the social philosophical debate (Rawls, 1972, 1994; Walzer, 1983), what they have in common is that - even if they claim to be reconstructive - they address the issue of social justice in a normative rather than an empirical way. The problem with this is that in a modern society a debate over purely normative conceptions has lost its epistemic grounds. In a traditional society norms could be legitimized through an authoritarian structure - as for instance by reference to the one religion shared by everyone in that society. Because of the development of functional differentiation in modern societies, however, there no longer exists any epistemic point from which one could convincingly supply normative arguments as to why one idea of social justice should be more appropriate than others (Pioch, 1998a). Thus today the legitimacy of any idea of social justice has become an empirical question. For this reason, it seems to me, sociological and empirical investigations into the diversity of interpretations of social justice gain relevance.

In the following I will present results of such an empirical study of ideas of social justice in the welfare state (Pioch, 1998a, 1999). I investigated the images of social justice held by social policy experts who are actively involved in on-going reform processes concerning the future of the welfare state. I conducted my empirical research in Germany and in the Netherlands. First, I will briefly sketch out my research design. I will explore the idea that images of social justice held by social policy experts always refer to some extent to established welfare institutions. Therefore secondly, I will point out significant similarities and differences between the Dutch and German social security system. I will proceed by sketching out some empirical findings of experts' images of social justice. I will demonstrate that in all reform proposals the level of social benefits is highly dependent on established standards in each country. Then I will show that any further criteria for eligibility to social benefits in a reform proposal differ according to diverse ideas of social justice. I will demonstrate that images of social justice held by the social policy experts who argue over reform proposals do not only refer to one principle but take different principles of social justice into account. I will conclude by interpreting my findings on different ideas of social justice held by policy experts in Germany and in the Netherlands according to the different welfare institutions in the social security systems of each country. I will give special consideration to the degree to which the principle of solidarity has been institutionalized in each of the welfare systems.

Research design

In this chapter I refer to an empirical study which is based on thirty qualitative interviews gathered among high ranking social policy experts in Germany and the Netherlands. I conducted interviews with representatives of the political parties, labour unions, and employer associations. I especially contacted politicians who were known to have formulated a social policy reform proposal themselves, and introduced it into the political discussion. I focused my investigation on reform proposals concerning the 'bottom line' of the welfare state in order to provide a social minimum for its citizens. I concentrated my research on reform ideas about how to design minimum provisions of social assistance in Germany or *algemene bijstand* as it is called in the Netherlands. In Germany I also included proposals aimed at providing a basic pension scheme, which in the Netherlands was already established in 1957.

For interviewing I used the method of narrative interviews (Schütze, 1976). The interviews lasted about an hour or more, which meant a relatively high time commitment by the experts - especially given the tight time schedule politicians have in general. All politicians I addressed in both countries showed great co-operation in giving an interview for this study. The overwhelmingly positive response of the interviewees can be seen to indicate clearly that politicians involved in social policy take social justice as a serious issue.

I evaluated the transcribed interviews by using a reconstructive method of intensive text interpretation (Oevermann *et al.*, 1979). Methodologically an open, narrative interview as well as the reconstructive method of evaluation is the only way to reconstruct, when the experts themselves refer to principles of social justice within their talks. Using this method one avoids direct questions which would only allow the interviewer to learn what general knowledge experts have about theories of social justice, and not to what extent this knowledge is of any relevance for the politician involved in designing the reform proposal.

The research was done as a comparative study in Germany and the Netherlands. Why is it worthwhile to compare social policy reforms in these particular countries? Both countries have in common highly developed welfare states. Thus, any comparative study crossing national borders could broaden the view for the whole range of possible interpretations of social justice in advanced welfare states. However, there is another reason as to why it is worthwhile comparing precisely these two countries. It is that the institutional structure of the Dutch and German welfare state differs in respect of the way both countries have institutionalized a social minimum as a 'bottom line' of the welfare state.

Similar, but different: the Dutch and German welfare states

The German welfare state is considered as the prototype of a Bismarckian social security system. It is based on social insurance. It is a categorical system, which means that the right to claim for benefit depends on the claimant belonging to a specific group, like workers, employees or civil servants. The German social security system, which historically was the first to be founded, is strongly centred on waged work. Actually, there are three conditions, ensuring the primacy of the labour market in relation to social security (Vobruba, 1990). The first one can be illustrated by the biblical proverb: 'First you work, then you eat.' Social benefits are intended only for those who have made their contribution to society. Second, receipt of benefit is conditional upon no adequate job being available, and only lasts until such a job becomes available again. The primacy of the labour market is guaranteed because receipt of welfare benefits is meant to be the exception. Third, the level and duration of benefits depend on your income while in the labour market. Income differences in the labour market are extended into the area of social benefits through the principle of equivalence. Wage centred social insurance constitutes the main part of the social security system in Germany. In addition there exists a means-tested social assistance, provided to those who neither have a sufficient income from the labour market nor social insurance benefits (Lampert, 1996).

In the Dutch welfare state one also finds workers' insurance. There is a significant institutional difference, however, between the Dutch and the German social security systems. In addition to workers' insurance, the Dutch welfare state provides flat rate public insurance to which all inhabitants have access independently of their prior labour market participation. For this reason the Dutch welfare state is classified as an admixture of the German and the British welfare states (Esping-Andersen, 1990).

One can explain the specific Dutch mixture of wage centered and flat rate welfare institutions by the historical development of the Dutch welfare state. Compared to Germany, the Dutch welfare state came into existence rather late. This is due to a later industrialization of the Netherlands and due to the religious fragmentation of Dutch society called *verzuiling* or 'pillarization'(De Swaan, 1988; Cox, 1993).

Table 7.1   Date   of   Introduction   of   Social   Insurance   in   the Netherlands and other European countries

	Accident	Old Age/ Invalidity	Unemployment	Sickness
Netherlands	1901	1913/1919*	1917/1952*	1913/1930*
Germany	1871	1889	1927	1883
Austria	1887	1927	1920	1888
Great Britain	1887	1908	1911	1911
France	1898	1895	1905	1898

* The first date refers to the year of initiative for legislation, the second date shows the effective year of legislation.

At the start of its formation before the Second World War, the Dutch welfare state was closely modelled on the already established German social insurance system. Worker's insurance was also introduced. In its further development after the Second World War the Dutch welfare state was developed along the lines of the British welfare state and the influential Beveridge report. Public insurance (*Volksverzekeringen*) was introduced in order to provide a minimum provision of social insurance to which every citizen is eligible. In the Dutch welfare state, in addition to workers' and public insurance, there also exists a means tested social assistance, called *algemene bijstand.*

In the Netherlands the level of social assistance for a couple together amounts to 100 per cent of the net minimum wage, and for a single person, it is 70 per cent of the net minimum wage. This level is the same for the social minimum in the public insurance sector. In this way, in contrast to the German welfare state, the Dutch welfare state provides a '*bottom line*' of welfare provision, not just in addition to social insurance, but within the social insurance sector (see table 7.1 below). Thus the growing phenomenon in Germany - that pensions tend to be so low that many elderly people, especially women because of their lower wages in the labour market, have to claim for additional means tested social assistance - is in the Netherlands prevented by a well established and institutionally ensured 'bottom line' within the insurance sector of the Dutch welfare state. According to my hypothesis that images of social justice held by social policy experts are formed in reference to their institutional background, I suggest that the different degree of institutionalizing a basic provision in the German and Dutch welfare states affects the interpretations of social justice as much as the legitimation of social exclusion in each country.

Defining the level of the 'bottom line' of the welfare state

As a first result of my research I will show that the empirical material I collected tells us the following: in social policy reform proposals the 'bottom line' of the welfare state is defined in close connection with the established standard of minimum provision in each country. The level of the proposed provision is set with strong reference to the existing minimum level. This feature we find in all reform proposals regardless of their general political orientations.

In order to demonstrate my findings briefly I cite an extract from an interview with a member of parliament of the Green party in Germany. The Greens presented a reform proposal of means tested public assistance with a level of 800 DM for a single person:

Table 7.2   Social Security in the Netherlands

	Social Insurance									Social Assistance
	Workers' Insurance				Public Insurance					Public Assistance
	Ziektewet	Zieken-fondswet	Werkloos-heidswet	Wet op de Arbeidsonge-schiktheids-verzekering	Algemene Ouderdoms-wet	Algemene Weduwen-en Wezenwet	Algemene Kinder-bijslagwet	Algemene Wet Bijzondere Ziektekosten	Algemene Arbeids-ongeschikt-heidswet	Algemene Bijstandswet
	ZW	ZFW	WW	WAO	AOW	AWW	AKW	AWBZ	AAW	ABW
	Sickness Act	Illness Fund Decree	Unemploy-ment Act	Disability Security Act	Public Retirement Pensions Act	Public Widows and Orphans Act	Public Children Allowance Act	Public Exceptional Medical Expenses Act	Public Disability Act	Public Assistance Act
	1930	1942	1952	1967	1957	1959	1963	1968	1976	1965
	Workers	Workers	Workers	Workers	Citizens	Citizens	Citizens	Citizens	Citizens	Citizens
	Equivalence				Solidarity					Subsidiarity

Well, we began with the statistical model used in social assistance today. We accept that. When we wrote the proposal there was an estimate by a German welfare association (Deutscher Verein) they raised the present level by about eight per cent. This would be the level if one had continued to use the statistical model. We looked for the regular grants in social assistance and special funds, which were really given to people. This is 664 DM plus eight per cent. We added another 5 per cent, because we thought people need some more for their own disposition, if we want to give general payments. Well, that's 750 DM. Then, everybody was saying: Oh, that's not enough. So, we said 800 DM for a single person. At the end it is a political decision. (My translation, R. P.)

As pointed out by the interviewee, the Greens chose as a starting point for formulating their reform proposal the existing method of calculating social assistance. Only at the very end of the discussion did they decide to increase the present level of social assistance for political reasons.

If one looks at the opposite end of the political spectrum one finds in the Netherlands the *VVD*, the Dutch Liberal Party, who are generally considered to be a conservative-liberal party. They suggest a 'mini-system' by privatizing workers' insurance while keeping a social minimum level.

Suppose you don't have an income, [...] then you can have an income from what we call the *algemene bijstandswet*, that is a law for general, well, *bijstand*. Well, that is a social minimum, that's the social minimum. I think, we can restrict all social security benefits to that level, and that's the social minimum.

The quoted representative of the VVD explains his reform proposal by first referring to the given social assistance act. The present social minimum level obviously is the 'bottom line' of the welfare state even in the eyes of the conservative VVD.

A Dutch proponent of the idea of an unconditional basic income explained that you calculate the volume spent on basic income as a part of national welfare in which everybody has a right to participate. Practically, however, he also defined the level in respect of the established social minimum:

I think, if you decide something like that, you will use the present minimum level as a kind of reference point [...]. So, in practice, I think we will take the present system as starting point; and calculate which part of national income is needed to guarantee everyone that particular level of social income. From that moment on you can say, well, in the future we will always spend that particular percentage of national income on basic income.

All in all, then, the level of any reform proposal covered by my research depends in one way or another on the present level of social assistance, regardless of whether it comes from the left or the right. However, if one compares the amount of money people get in social assistance in Germany and the Netherlands, it turns out that social policy experts in the Netherlands have a higher level in mind than the German experts.

Table 7.3   Regular Rates in Social Assistance Comparing the Netherlands and Germany (accounted for in DM)

	The Netherlands		Germany	
	Algemene Bijstand (ABW) (1. 3. 1996)[a]	Algemene Bijstand (ABW) (1. 1. 1998)[b]	Sozialhilfe (HLU) Regelsätze (1. 7. 97) Hamburg[i]	Sozialhilfe (HLU) monthly gross average rate[e] 1994[f]
Couple[c] over 21 years old	1736 DM[d]	1806 DM	970 DM from full age on	1053 DM
Single Person over 21 years old	868 DM up to 1215 DM	903 DM up to 1264DM	539 DM	618 DM
Single parent	1215 DM	1264 DM	755 DM[h]	1038 DM[g]
Couple under 21	600 DM	624 DM	-	-
Single Person under 21	300 DM (without extra)	312 DM (without extra)	-	-

[a]   Source: Ministerie van Soziale Zaken en Werkgelegenheid, info516/jan./mar. 1996/5289, eigene DM-Berechnung (Kurs nach Auskunft Devisenabt. Deutsche Bank: 1996: 100 HFL=89,427 DM; 1998: 100 HFL=88,831 DM, Pfennigbeträge gerundet)

[b]   Source: Voorlichtingscentrum Sociale Verzekering, http: //home.pi.net/*vsv/cifjers.htm, eigene DM-Berechnung

[c]   This category counts also for unmarried couples sharing a household.

[d]   All rates inclusive a monthly rate for vacation subsidary of 5.2 per cent.

[e]   Monthly gross-average rate (regular rates plus special allowances, without housing subsidy)

[f]   Source: Statistisches Bundesamt, Datenreport 1997

g   Single parent with one child

h   Special allowances for single parents with one child under 7 years or two to three children under 16 years accounts 40 per cent of the regular rate (539 DM plus 215,60 DM).

i   Regular rates in social assistance differ between West and former East Germany. In East-Germany the regular rate was (1. 7. 97): 514 DM (Source: Sozialamt Leipzig). The average of special allowances differs regionally. The average rate of all cities for special allowances for one person a year was 1091 DM, about 90 DM monthly. (Source: Landessozialamt Hamburg: Benchmarking Sozialhilfe, 1996)

I conclude from this that for both countries there is a common conception of the level of the 'bottom line' of the welfare state. In other words: in each country there is a shared understanding about when social exclusion starts in relation to material living conditions. However, the numbers above showing the different regular rates in social assistance indicate that the experts obviously refer to different amounts of money, if in both countries they refer to given standards in their reform proposals.

Defining eligibility criteria for a basic provision

Proposals concerning the social assistance sector in the welfare state differ markedly in the eligibility criteria they set up for having the right to claim benefits. The eligibility criteria determine who belongs to the inner circle of materially secure citizens and who is excluded from receiving welfare benefits. They can be treated systematically in four ways (Mitschke, 1997):

1.   Willingness to work. This criterion defines whether and to what extent a benefit claimant has to show their willingness to participate in the labour market.
2.   Neediness. This criterion defines special needs which should be acknowledged - for instance, special needs of families, special needs of disabled people.
3.   Family maintenance. This criterion defines to what extent the claimant has to look for family support before asking for state provision.
4.   Means testing. This criterion defines whether and to what extent a claimant needs to live on their private means before being eligible for social benefits.

The empirical findings of my research indicate that the different criteria for eligibility for social benefits are highly dependent on the images of justice held by those who formulate or represent a particular reform proposal.

In addition, we learn that images of justice do not contain just one principle of social justice like *either* achievement *or* the principle of neediness. Rather, experts combine different principles in their images of justice. I call such combinations, configurations of social justice. My empirical investigation shows the configurations of social justice held by the social policy experts are derived from their interpretations of first, the principle of reciprocity, second, the idea of solidarity, third the idea of subsidiarity, and fourth the interpretation of individuality.

The definition of the first eligibility criterion concerning the willingness to work of the welfare recipient depends on the idea of *reciprocity*. Whenever an expert interprets reciprocity in a strong sense, then willingness to work means: any simple job that is there has to be taken by anyone who is healthy enough to do the job. If one interprets reciprocity in a more general sense of equivalence between the individual and society, then the meaning of willingness to work depends on what someone counts as equivalent activities done by the benefit recipient - like, for instance, child care. The definition of neediness as a second eligibility criterion depends on someone's interpretation of *solidarity*. Should one acknowledge the neediness of anybody claiming for benefits, or does solidarity depend on special criteria for defining those who deserve solidarity, like the family or workers in the labour market? The two criteria, of family maintenance and means testing, vary with the experts' interpretations of *subsidiarity* and *individuality*.

In the following I will outline how differences in the reform proposals go along with divergent images of social justice. I will do this by presenting contrasting cases from my Dutch sample. Then in the next section I shed light on differences between Germany and the Netherlands.

First I take into consideration proposals aimed at re-shaping the welfare state. What these proposals have in common is that in one way or another they aim to extend the rights to social benefits to certain groups and to strengthen the guaranteed social benefits. However, the question remains: what are the criteria being used to identify those who should be in the inner circle of those who are entitled to receive benefits?

The first case I refer to is a representative of the *Voedingsbond*, the Dutch Union for food branches. Among the unions the *Voedingsbond* is the one which has been in favour of the basic income idea for years.

However, the interviewee, who is working as researcher and advisor in the *Voedingsbond*, is proposing a different idea: the so called 'cappuccino model'.

> I was already saying three years ago that for a basic income really there is too little support from the public.

The Cappuccino model consists of three parts: the first part is the 'coffee'. It contains basic benefits of 900 guilders per month for each individual. This is the area where rights for social benefits will be extended to certain groups. The second part of the model is the 'milk'. This is the part where social insurance should be transferred from state responsibility to the responsibility of collective bargaining between the social partners. Third we have the 'chocolate' sprinkled on top of the milk. This is a small part of additional private insurance. If we look at the part concerning the 'bottom line' of welfare state activities, this proposal expands the inner circle of benefit receivers but with the strict condition of labour market orientation:

> Well, it is an individual right to nine hundred guilders, but you can only earn the right by labour market orientation. But the advantages are: it is for individuals, thus it is no longer family oriented, but for individuals, it also guarantees a minimum for people doing flexible work. If the flexi-job is over, there are always the nine hundred guilders.

This reform proposal represents an attempt to change the social security provision from family orientation to individual rights. Nine hundred guilders are paid individually. The group of people who would be advantaged by this system would be women who until now are economically dependent on their husbands, and flexi-workers. In this proposal the principle of individuality is of major importance. The idea of justice presented by this reform proposal can be described as a mixture of solidarity and reciprocity. Obviously the interviewee himself suggests this mixture in order to appeal to people's support, which he doubts could be attained with a basic income.

One representative I interviewed from the PvdA, the Dutch Social Democrats, proposed a partial basic income. A partial income is provided to every citizen, but its level is not high enough to provide a living. It is a kind of compromise. On the one hand the interviewee shares the idea of solidarity with those who do not have any individual rights to claim benefits, such as flexi-workers. In this respect the interviewee has similar ideas to the unionists to widen the inner circle of legitimate recipients. Also he shares the idea of individual autonomy, that people should have a right to live the way they want to. In this manner he agrees with the idea of a guaranteed basic income. But on the other hand the interviewee still is committed to the idea of reciprocity. It is the idea of reciprocity which makes him sceptical about the idea of providing a basic income.

> I am, I was in the past rather sceptical about the idea of the basic income, because of this lack of reciprocity. I think, if you talk and think about social security in general, well, in one or another way, you have to cope with the idea of reciprocity. It is very important for social security for, well, to get legitimacy for the social security system. There has to be some kind of reciprocity, I think, well, that's my opinion.

However, the interviewee combines the idea of reciprocity with a strong sense of individual autonomy. He continues:

> In practice, this is very problematic, because there are not enough jobs, for example, and secondly, well, you can ask people, I think so too, about doing some re-training, if their labour market prospects are bad. But, well, you can't say, if you are unemployed now, well, do some re-training now. There must be some time. There must be some relationship to what are your capacities, and in some respects to what you are after, what you want to achieve or not. There should be some boundaries, but well this needs to get balanced.

His interpretation of reciprocity gives room for some individual freedom. Job willingness as an eligibility criterion needs to be balanced with individual demands. Thus, his interpretation of social justice goes along with the proposal of a partial basic income, but not a full basic income. A full basic income would be in conflict with his general acknowledgement of reciprocity.

The most far-reaching reform proposal I found among those aimed at reorganizing the welfare state came in the interview with an economist who is working as senior researcher for one of the main government advisory organisations, the Social Planning Bureau of the Netherlands. He suggests an unconditional basic income should be introduced.

Following his proposal the basic income would be financed via a value added tax. The pay-out of the basic income might be organized through a system of negative income tax. The level of the basic income should be defined as a proportion of national welfare. His main idea in legitimizing his proposal is that in general everybody in society contributes to the production of national welfare in one way or another.

> In fact the idea is, that everyone contributes in one way or another to national welfare. Therefore everyone has an equal right to a particular part of that welfare. And only people who have a job have an extra right to part of national welfare, because of the kind of job they do.

This proposal is by far the most universal approach to social security provision. The interviewee includes in the inner circle everybody in society. In this way he asks for the most universal form of solidarity. Moreover, in arguing that more or less everybody in society makes a contribution to national welfare, he follows the idea of acknowledging people regardless of their status in the labour market. However, as far as those who do not contribute to national welfare are concerned, he is not asking for solidarity on moral grounds. On the contrary, he cites the principles of self-interest and economic efficiency.

> I think you always have a small part of the population who don't add anything to the total welfare and we always accept that. For example, there are always people who are drug addicts who don't seem to be of any use to society, but still we find it necessary for those people to have enough money to live on, perhaps only because they will involve themselves in criminal activities if they don't have enough money to live on. So, it might be in the interest of the rest of the population to even guarantee those people who don't contribute anything to national welfare, to give them some decent income to make sure that they don't turn to be a burden to society by all kind of activities which we don't like.

To summarize: if we look at the proposals in favour of reorganization we see that the images of justice are made up of different elements: The idea of solidarity is accompanied either by the idea of reciprocity or more often by universal participation rights, as well as by ideas of individual autonomy. The specific mixture of these elements determines which type of reform proposal the person advocates.

At the other end of the spectrum of reform proposals we find those who aim at the reduction of welfare state provision. The first position advocated by a representative of the Liberal Party VVD represents on-going government policy. The interviewee suggests major reform shifts within the given structure, and also opts for privatization.

Arguing against a basic income he first refers to the idea of reciprocity.

> We as Liberals in Holland, we say, well, if people do not want to work, they should not earn money from the state, if they refuse to work, and in the system of a negative income tax, in fact that is the case, that is the problem.

Later on he admits that the negative income tax might be a good option economically but for political reasons he is strictly opposed to it.

> If I or another person within the party, if we propose a negative income tax, people get very emotional, they do not react pragmatically, but they are very emotional. So, my opinion is that it would be, well, it would have a lot of advantages, a system of a negative income tax. But the reaction of people ehm in our country to the basic income system, to the negative income schedule is, that people who refuse to work get money, and people who don't need money, because they are wealthy or they have a husband or a wife that earns a lot of money, those people also get the basic income and that is against their thoughts about what is just. It is not part of my theory of justice, they say.

So, in this case the interviewee sees reasons of economic efficiency favouring the idea of a negative income tax, but when he takes people's reactions into account, he opposes the idea.

The representative of the CDA I interviewed is opposed to the idea of a basic income because of the individual's need to take personal responsibility. However in this reform proposal called 'responsible community', the idea of solidarity is not given up completely, but re-defined by the idea of subsidiarity. He is mainly asking for a shift of state responsibility to units other than the state, such as social partners in the insurance sector and families in the social assistance sector. The parliamentarian from the CDA, the Christian Democratic Party in Holland, argues:

> The welfare state was formed because there was a common sense of giving more rights to the individual. But in a society there needs to be a balance, a balance between the rights of the individual and the rights of society.

This balance between individual rights and the rights of society shows one possible interpretation of reciprocity. The interviewee combines it with the following interpretation of solidarity:

I think the criterion [for solidarity, R.P.] is: Does the person have the capacity to do a job or look for other activities or not. This is essential.

He continues by defining old people and disabled people as those who undoubtedly deserve the solidarity of the society. Along with this idea of social justice goes a social reform proposal for tightening the eligibility criteria concerning willingness to work on the one hand and on the other, acknowledging further the special needs of families and those with special needs like disabled people in the Social Assistance Act.

Well, at present a young couple where both have studied and both have a good job in this individualistic system they are pretty well off. And I ask myself whether this group could not be a little bit more solidaristic with those groups who have it harder. Well, this is a question of solidarity too and I think there should be a balance between individual possibilities to find a job and income but also what solidarity means. Also in this respect there should be a balance and if one just talks about individual possibilities and disparities in the tax system or social security system and one doesn't pay attention to solidarity, well, I don't think that's right. But of course this has to do with political values.

To summarize again, then: the different reform proposals do not simply refer to one dominant principle of social justice. This brief illustration of images of justice held by Dutch social policy experts demonstrates that first, empirically one finds a variety of interpretations of social justice. Second, they do not follow just one principle of social justice but represent combinations of various principles of social justice.

Comparing ideas of social justice in Germany and the Netherlands

I conclude with some remarks about a general comparison of the images of social justice found in the reform debates in Germany and the Netherlands. And finally I compare the range of images of justice as well as the diversity of reform proposals. All together, the reform proposals reflect a broad range of images of justice. At one end of the spectrum we find the general principle that the market provides the best means of assessing benefit. Then at the other end there is the principle of universal participation by all citizens in the creation of national wealth and income in the provision of some kind of an unconditional basic income. The outcome of my study is that in the Netherlands, the range of diverse images of justice held by the social policy experts I interviewed, as well as the range of reform proposals they presented, is significantly broader than in Germany. In the Netherlands one finds more far-reaching reform proposals for a reduction of the welfare state than in Germany. But at the same time one finds, at the other end of the continuum, more reform proposals directed towards the idea of a basic income than in Germany. Thus, the range of diverse images of social justice as well as the range of different reform ideas seems to be broader in the Netherlands than in Germany.

In Germany, at the end of the spectrum oriented towards the idea of market equivalence one finds the reform proposal by Saxony's Minister Kurt H. Biedenkopf who suggests a privatization of social insurance while at the same time introducing a citizens' pension scheme. His proposal derives from an idea of social justice where equivalence on the one hand, and solidarity as a duty of humanity to the community on the other, are combined in such a way that neither principle obstructs each other. In Germany, at the other end of the spectrum, one finds the reform proposal of basic security by the Socialist Party, PDS, which evolved from the SED in Eastern Germany. They are in favour of income redistribution, but remain committed to the idea of reciprocity by claiming a right to jobs. Nowadays the Greens, contrary to their party programme of the eighties, are not in favour of a basic income anymore (Pioch, 1998b). They adhere to the idea of reciprocity, in which everybody receiving benefits has to contribute to society by undertaking some kind of activity. The Green representative argued as follows:

> We want to let those on social assistance know: We still want you. We feel responsible for you. But as we take on responsibility, we expect also that you do something. This can be different things, a job, raising children and so on.

In the Netherlands, at the end of the spectrum towards market equivalence one finds the proposal provided by the Liberal Party, VVD, that comes close to Biedenkopf's ideas about social security. Still, one has to notice that the VVD is going much further by proposing privatization of the whole insurance sector and not just the pension scheme, while respecting the social minimum as a 'bottom line' of the Dutch welfare state. Second, the VVD in the Netherlands is a party in the governing coalition and not an isolated protagonist as Biedenkopf often seems to be in Germany. The image of social justice held by the CDA representative, which in my study I called communitarian social justice, I only found in the Netherlands and not in Germany. Nevertheless, one can assume that it could be found in Germany, if one continues the research. However, due to the former *verzuiling* system of strong religious involvement in politics in the Netherlands, it is not surprising to find such a moral plea even in a rather small Dutch sample.

Most important for the discussion of social exclusion is the empirical result that in the Netherlands, one finds more reform proposals discussed than in Germany, which reflects the notion of a basic income as some kind of need for universal solidarity. In the Netherlands the Social Democratic Party, the PvdA, still has the proposal for a basic income in its programme, even if Prime Minister Wim Kok currently gives priority to other ideas such as job creation. The representative of the PvdA to whom I talked presented an idea of social justice combining reciprocity and solidarity, in the sense of giving people some autonomy. Thus, he was open to the idea of a partial basic income. Among the Dutch unions one finds the so called cappuccino model, which provides an individual basic income - like the coffee part of a cappuccino - under the condition of showing willingness to work by registration at the employment bureau. A senior researcher of the Social Planning Office SCP even presented a well-elaborated reform proposal to introduce a full basic income in the Netherlands.

I suggest that the broader range of reform proposals as well as the wider diversity of images of social justice in the Netherlands can be best explained with the social minimum as an institutionally established 'bottom line' in the social security system in the Netherlands. My findings demonstrate that the discussion over measures to prevent social exclusion differs between welfare states, depending on the degree of a social security system being categorically oriented towards wage workers like the German welfare state, or having the principle of solidarity institutionalized by universal elements such public insurance in the Dutch welfare state. This phenomenon can be described as 'path-dependency' - that is, normative ideas in welfare reform debates depend on the institutional context in which they are raised. The breadth of welfare reform discussions is linked to and depends on the institutions already established in each welfare state.

Comparing the Dutch and German social security debates, in the Netherlands we find on the one hand social policy experts, who courageously propose a privatization of workers' insurance, while keeping the social minimum provision as a 'bottom line' of the Dutch welfare state. On the other hand, we find social policy experts who are open minded about integrating reciprocity and basic income, like the representatives of the cappuccino-model, or partial basic income, or those arguing for a basic income by pointing to the positive employment effects of disconnecting labour and social security costs. All in all, then, in a comparison of the German and Dutch reform debates the Netherlands show more flexibility in thinking about new ways to reform the welfare state than Germany. There is a more creative debate over welfare state reforms in the Netherlands than in Germany. Having the principle of solidarity institutionalized in the Dutch welfare system is, I conclude, one of the positive effects for the whole society in the long term. A broader range of reform proposals can be discussed, while or because at the same time the danger of social exclusion is restricted to the limit of the social minimum provided in public insurance and public assistance. The implementation of any future proposal, whether it be to extend the principle of solidarity or to enforce demands for reciprocity, will depend not only on normative ideas about social justice held by policy makers, but also on the political interests and the decision-making structures in each country. The creativity and openness for developing new ideas, however - as my study demonstrates for the Netherlands - might be the best precondition to open the floor for a debate about how to prevent social exclusion in modern welfare states.

References

Cox, R. H. (1993), *The Development of the Dutch Welfare State. From Workers' Insurance to Universal Entitlement,* University of Pittsburgh Press, Pittsburgh, London.

De Swaan, A. (1988), *In Care of the State. Health Care, Education and Welfare in Europe and USA in the Modern Era,* Polity Press, New York.

Durkheim, É. (1991), *Physik der Sitten und des Rechts. Vorlesungen zur Soziologie der Moral,* Suhrkamp, Frankfurt/M.

Durkheim, É. (1992), *Über soziale Arbeitsteilung. Studie über die Organisation höherer Gesellschaften,* Suhrkamp, Frankfurt/M.

Esping-Andersen, G (1990), *The Three Worlds of Welfare Capitalism,* Polity Press, Cambridge.

Lampert, H (1996), *Lehrbuch der Sozialpolitik*, Springer-Verlag, München.

Mitschke, J (1997), 'Fluch der knappen Kassen. Neue Jobs sind von der geplanten Steuerreform kaum zu erwarten', in *Die Zeit,* 7.2.1997, 23.

Müller, H-P (1995), 'Soziale Differenzierung und Gerechtigkeit. Ein Vergleich von Max Weber und Michael Walzer', in H-P. Müller and B. Wegener (eds),

Soziale Ungleichheit und soziale Gerechtigkeit, Leske-Budrich Verlag, Opladen, 135-155.

OECD (1996), *Employment Outlook 1996,* Organisation of Economic Cooperation and Development, Paris, July 1996.

Oevermann, U., T. Alert, E. Konau and J. Krambeck (1979), 'Die Methodologie einer objektiven Hermeneutik und ihre allgemeine forschungslogische Bedeutung in der Soziologie' in H-G. Soeffner (ed.), *Interpretative Verfahren in den Sozial- und Textwissenschaften,* Stuttgart, 352-433.

Offe, C. (1990), 'Akzeptanz und Legitimität strategischer Optionen in der Sozialpolitik', in C. Sachße and H. Tristram Engelhardt (eds), *Sicherheit und Freiheit. Zur Ethik des Wohlfahrtsstaates,* Suhrkamp, Frankfurt/M., 179-202.

Pioch, R. (1996), 'Basic Income: Social Policy after Full Employment' in A. Erskine (ed.), *Changing Europe. Some Aspects of Identity, Conflict and Social Justice,* Avebury, Aldershot, 148-160.

Pioch, R. (1998a), *Gerechtigkeit in der Sozialpolitik. Eine vergleichende Untersuchung in der Bundesrepublik Deutschland und in den Niederlanden,* Dissertation, Universität Leipzig.

Pioch, R. (1998b), 'Changes in Government - New Chances for Basic Income in Germany?' in *Citizen's Income Newsletter,* London School of Economics, Issue 2, 4.

Pioch, R. (1999), 'Die untere Grenze des Sozialstaats: Ergebnisse einer qualitativen Studie über Gerechtigkeitsvorstellungen sozialpolitischer Experten in Deutschland und den Niederlanden' in H. Schwengel (ed.), *Grenzenlose Gesellschaft,* 29. Kongress der DGS, 16. Kongress der ÖGS, 11. Kongress der SGS, Kongreßband II, Centaurus, Pfaffenweiler.

Rawls, J.(1972), *A Theory of Justice,* Oxford University Press, New York.

Rawls, J. (1994), *Die Idee des politischen Liberalismus,* Aufsätze 1978-1989. Suhrkamp, Frankfurt/M.

Schütze, F. (1976), 'Zur Hervorlockung und Analyse von Erzählungen thematisch relevanter Geschichten im Rahmen soziologischer Feldforschung' in, Arbeitsgruppe Bielefelder Soziologen (eds), *Kommunikative Sozialforschung. Alltagswissen und Altagshandeln. Gemeindemachtforschung. Polizei. Politische Erwachsenenbildung,* München, 159-260.

Vobruba, G.(ed.) (1990), *Strukturwandel der Sozialpolitik,* Suhrkamp, Frankfurt.

Walzer, M. (1983), *Spheres of Justice. A Defense of Pluralism and Equality,* Basic Books, New York.

8 Stigma and Non-take up in Social Policy
Re-emerging properties of declining welfare state programmes?

STAFFAN BLOMBERG and JAN PETERSSON

The concept of stigma

The sociological conceptualization of *stigma* was developed by Erving Goffman in his seminal book on the subject in 1963. He defines stigma in the following way:

> While the stranger is present before us, evidence can arise of his possessing an attribute that makes him different from others in the category of persons available for him to be, and of a less desirable kind - in the extreme, a person who is quite thoroughly bad, or dangerous, or weak. He is thus reduced in our minds from a whole and usual person to a tainted, discounted one. Such an attribute is a stigma, especially when it its discrediting effect is very extensive; sometimes it is also called a failing, a shortcoming, a handicap. It constitutes a special discrepancy between virtual and actual identity (Goffman, 1963, pp. 12-13).

It should be understood that the operationalization of the concept is especially fruitful in relation to group attributes. This entails that the stigma is associated with belonging to a certain group. Paul Spicker, however, further notes that not just *attributes* are at work in the creation of a stigma. It is further mediated through *attitudes* of others as well as the *feelings* of the stigmatized person. As a result the stigmatized person is treated as deviant. To conclude, if stigma is freed from being perceived solely as an individual problem, it is discrediting because of the social construction that is put on it (Spicker, 1988). Further, the complex interactions between levels in explaining stigma leads van Oorschot to remark that it is surrounded by 'conceptual obscurity' (1995, p. 47).

Stigma and social policy

In debates about the extensiveness of the welfare state a lot of attention has been paid to the *attractiveness* of social welfare, such as personal social services and social security. Some economists have argued that, where welfare provision is relatively generous, there is a lack of incentives for individuals to cope with the situation either on their own or partly so. Too many problems are considered social instead of private. The focus taken by such economists has been on the negative effects created by welfare arrangements, such as the development of a dependency culture, 'free-riding' and 'scrounging'.

In the transformation process involving the shrinking welfare state, this focus on attractiveness might still be appropriate in some respects (although the attractiveness is diminished in the process), but in a downsizing context more attention should be paid to the problems connected to and involved in the concomitant processes of marginalization and exclusion. The problems resulting from the contraction of the welfare state are different from those when it is expanding. From this perspective, the attention directed towards 'scroungers' ought to be exchanged for an interest in individuals who actually do not exercise their rights - that is, the problem of non-take up (van Oorschot, 1995). Further, in the ongoing process of increased targeting in the reshaping of social policy which has been taking place in several of the European welfare states during the 1980s, the relation between non-take up and stigma has become a major issue.

This echoes arguments first heard in the early periods prior to the full development of the welfare state. Titmuss argued forcefully and enduringly during the 1960s in numerous publications that stigma as a phenomenon was *the* central issue of social policy. Titmuss took a rather optimistic view, and argued that stigma could be eliminated if social policy were to be made universal and based on general rights.

Institutional and residual welfare

In discussions on social policy the distinction between universality and selectivity is considered to be of major importance in designing a welfare system. The notions express two different distributive principles and methods regarding the delivery of social goods. A universal distributive system, on the one hand, brings in all individuals in a society into public welfare arrangements. Entitlement to these social goods is based on social rights. Financing is based on taxes. In a selective welfare system, on the other hand, the social goods are directed towards certain groups. This means that the distributive rationale is one of targeting the poor. Eligibility is confirmed after some form of means-testing.

In a society where a great number of social goods are based on universality, one talks of an institutional model of welfare. Individuals in such a society will become aware that they can exercise a large number of social rights, to use a concept first developed by T.H. Marshall in his famous lectures at Cambridge in 1949 (Marshall and Bottomore, 1992). Generally these rights are formulated as legal rights. In a broader sense, however, the notion of institutional welfare also includes wider welfare commitments on behalf of the state. Such commitments are not legally claimable, but are instead moral rights based on a *social contract*. In Sweden, which is regarded as a prototype of the institutional welfare state (Esping-Andersen, 1990), these moral rights are applied to employment and housing conditions, i.e., a right to work and to have a decent housing-standard.

In societies where social goods are distributed mainly on principles of selectivity, the commitment to welfare on behalf of the state is low. The state is thought to have no obligations as to moral rights, and its position can be characterized as residual - 'the lender of last resort' (Olsson 1990, p. 265). Instead, welfare is mainly a matter for the individuals themselves and accommodated through a low-tax policy. A typical example is the United States.

We can sum this up in Figure 8.1:

Figure 8.1 **Degrees of Universality in Institutional and Residual Welfare**

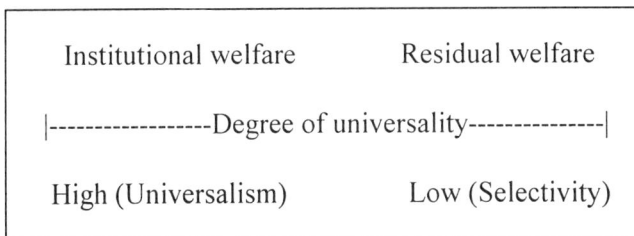

Institutional welfare	Residual welfare
|------------------Degree of universality---------------|	
High (Universalism)	Low (Selectivity)

Universalism is, as we have noted already, closely related to the notion of *citizenship*. A society with a developed institutional welfare model, seeking to apply the same standard to all individuals, implies a strong position for citizenship as a base for social rights. Citizenship becomes a key concept in deciding on the extension of collective provision instead of individual choice, or from another point of view, recognizing a large number of social needs in relation to private wants. Citizenship brings attention to values in and effects of social policy, and leads on to problems of social inclusion and exclusion, legitimacy and, as we shall see, stigma. These are central areas of concern in modern societies.

Further, on a political-philosophical level, the argument in favour of universalism is closely related to a *communitarian* perspective on state and society. According to this, society must be arranged to constitute a *community*. By community is meant 'a society that embodies (1) a sense of solidarity and (2) a sense of significance for all those who are within the group' (Goodin, 1988, p. 72). With regard to claims on the state, the advocacy for communitarism is built on the ideal that the state in actions towards its citizens should defend specific collective moral principles. It implies that the state takes a stand on what is seen as the appropriate life-course of individuals, and is non-neutral in relation to connecting values (Rothstein, 1994, p. 44). Society comes out as a 'single-status moral community' (Goodin, 1988, p. 74), which in turn becomes the basis of both institutionalism and universalism.

Titmuss bases his general thesis along lines that have been presented above. His more specific argument will be summarized in the next paragraph, and so will the forceful, contrasting view of Robert Pinker.

Titmuss *versus* Pinker

To Richard Titmuss the problem of stigma, or *spoiled identity* in Goffman's phrase, was the central issue regarding the 'conflict between universalist social services and selective means-tested systems for the poor' (Titmuss, 1968, p. 142). He dismissed the idea of selectivity: a welfare policy targeted towards those groups that for one or another reason fail to satisfy their needs on the market could not overcome the problem of discrimination or stigmatization. A selective or residual welfare system would fail 'to further the sense of community and participation; to prevent alienation; and to integrate the members of minority groups, ethnic groups and regional culture into the total society' (*ibid.*, p. 65); on the contrary it would make matters worse.

Means-testing, crucial in selective systems, reinforces the experience of personal failure. Since the foremost aim of this administrative procedure is the prevention of ineligible persons from gaining access, rather than caring for those in need, the latter are treated as socially inferior, not as citizens with social rights. Besides, Titmuss argues, 'separate discriminatory services for the poor have always tended to be poor quality services' (*ibid.*, p. 134).

The principle of universality, on the other hand, paves the way for an order where the receiver of social services is not confronted with a loss of status, dignity and self-respect. Rationing based on needs rather than means implies 'a shift from the stigma of deterrence to the concept of social right' (*ibid.*, p. 68). A key concept for Titmuss was the creation of autonomy, which is reinforced by this extension of social rights. Condemning the rationing of the economic market, Titmuss also argues that distribution according to need would create a sort of 'altruistic merging of self with others' (Goodin, 1988, p. 78), allowing social goods to be founded on a sort of *gift relationship* in a social market (Titmuss, 1968, p. 22). The welfare state creates a form of 'institutionalised altruism', which is the very embodiment of the gift relationship (Goodin, *ibid.*).

Titmuss's arguments are closely linked to communitarian values. Goodin summarises: 'Fraternal feelings and generalized altruism thus constitute at least the historical core of the communitarian case for the welfare state' (Goodin, 1988, p. 78). Titmuss himself pins down the communitarian principle that should be operating in social policy in the following words:

> The real challenge resides in the question: What particular infrastructure of universalist services is needed in order to provide a framework of values and opportunity bases within and around which can be developed acceptable selective services, provided as social rights, on criteria of the *needs* of specific categories, groups and territorial areas and not dependent on *individual tests of means*? (Titmuss, 1968, p. 122).

The questions Titmuss is posing here lead to a discussion of particularism. By particularism is meant that 'different standards are appropriate in different circumstances for different individuals and groups' (Thompson and Hoggett, 1996, p. 22). Particularism based on what is called positive selectivism is favoured by these authors, since this involves 'additional services and resources for certain disadvantaged groups, without reference to means (i.e. need: our comment)' (*ibid.*, p. 23). This is what Titmuss to some extent favours in the quotation above. Negative selectivism is identified by Thompson and Hoggett as means testing, which is clearly in line with Titmuss's distinctions.

The area of social insurance has so far been omitted from the main arguments above. In discussing stigma Titmuss concentrates on social services and social assistance, but elsewhere he has argued that social insurance is of another order altogether. A disability pension, for example, should not be considered a benefit, but a compensation: it becomes a compensation for the depletion of physical capacity resulting from working for a specific employer. The relation over time with the employer thus becomes a sort of *fair exchange*. From another angle social insurance, typically in the case of old-age pensions, can be seen as a sort of horizontal redistribution over the life-cycle. This implies that times of benefiting from the social insurance system are balanced by times of contributing to the system. Ivar Lödemel (1990) makes this very clear. Only non-contributory welfare schemes share the characteristics of citizenship rights.

Now we turn to consider the work of Robert Pinker. He agrees with Titmuss on the importance of stigma: 'The imposition of stigma is the commonest form of violence used in democratic societies' (Pinker, 1971, p. 175). But its connection to social policy is different, according to Pinker. In general he takes a more pessimistic point of view as to the possibility of creating a social market parallel to an economic market. 'The problem we face is that of establishing the extent to which these notions of reciprocity (gift exchange: our comment) are also shared by the community. Consequently, we cannot assume that the legal imposition (or preservation) of an "infrastructure of universalist services" will "provide a framework of values and opportunity bases"... that are most likely to minimize stigma' (*ibid.*, p. 135).

In essence, Pinker is sceptical about Titmuss's arguments concerning the receipt of social services. It may well be that individuals will 'experience humiliation in all forms of unilateral exchange when they are the recipients' (*ibid.*, p. 136). It seems clear that Pinker requires empirical evidence in support of a Titmuss's claims, rather than just the theoretical discourse he provides. Pinker questions whether the idea of citizenship embedded in principle of the universalism has any authenticity at all in a society dominated by market exchange. Referring to Marcel Mauss, Pinker instead points out that 'all services are systems of exchange' (*ibid.*, p.

157). He argues that this is largely a matter of subjective evaluations. The gift relationship might well be incompatible with 'an experience of guilt of getting something for nothing' (Reisman, 1977, p. 53). His standpoint becomes relativistic and non-normative: '... it is no more true to say that all universalist services always endow status than it is to claim that selectivist services always stigmatize' (*ibid.*, p. 141).

In effect, the problem of stigma descends to a problematization about feelings of dependency and a sense of inferiority, linked to the relationship between the giver and recipient. The variables of *depth, time* and *distance* have to be brought in, Pinker argues. By *depth*, Pinker means that the status as recipient is enhanced due to elements of restitution, compensation or increased giving potential at some time in the future, that is, connected to some sort of fairness. Pinker would not deny that being a tax-payer will legitimize the use of a range of social services to the average individual in society. The *distance* (social and spatial) of the recipient from the giver is also of importance according to Pinker. Social distance relates to inequality in class or status, while physical institutionalization reinforces the effect of spatial distance. With distance, there generally follows isolation, which in turn makes individuals 'more aware of their stigmatized identity' (*ibid.*, p. 173). Lastly, *time* is of importance: 'The longer the period of dependency persists, the more likely the dependent is to redefine his total social life in terms of the stigma' (*ibid.*, p. 174).

To sum up, Pinker has serious doubts about the possibilities of eliminating the existence of stigma through institutional welfare, since 'the dominant values of an acquisitive and capitalist society are such that stigmatization is a functionally necessary part of the system' (*ibid.*, p. 165). In turn, his belief is that social exchange can not coexist with and be built on a value structure (gift relationship) of its own. At the same time, however, as Pinker believes that we have to live with stigma, he is open to the possibility that on the social-administrative level, things can be done to diminish its incidence.

Implications for social policy administration

Ivar Lödemel (1990) has studied how feelings of dependency and a sense of inferiority are connected to administrative solutions in social policy. His aim was to investigate how administrative measures can be used to reduce the imposition of stigma.

Following the direction set out by Lödemel, let us explore some examples. To reduce stigma the receipt of a social service should not be conditional on the loss of other rights. This used to be the case in old days, when the right to vote was lost when one became a recipient of social assistance. Benefits in kind should be substituted for benefits in cash, which may increase the autonomy, i.e. decrease the feeling of dependency. Further, individual tests of eligibility, face-to-face and leaving assessment to discretion, should be replaced by standardized bureaucratic routines. This is in line with Pinker's argument 'that the most anonymous forms of social provision tend to be the least stigmatizing' (Pinker, 1971, p. 151). It is also connected with Titmuss's claim for universality, not because of its value-orientation, but due to the lesser importance of individual testing in such schemes.

Anonymity and degrees of standardization seem to be vital areas for concern in the construction of an administrative solution designed to reduce the incidence of stigma. On a more general level the following classification of provision systems according to levels of decision-making and principles of distribution can shed further light on the subject.

Figure 8.2   Forms and Levels of Distribution

Form:	UNIVERSAL	SELECTIVE
Level:	STATE	LOCAL

Selective distribution implies that a low level of standardization and local administration increases the risk of recognition and loss of anonymity. The combination of locality and selectivity thus increases the risks of stigma.[1] Further, the trend towards decentralization, i.e., a move from state to local level, tends to be followed by tendencies towards increased selectivity. There seem to be strong political incentives in the local environment to make social rights more conditional in different ways. This may be due to the shorter distance between financing and need. In Sweden, for example, the right to child care has changed its status to becoming conditional on employment, in the process of transferring this service from the domain of the state to that of local government.

Stigma and the process of stigmatization is 'a complex topic engaging sociologists, psychologists and political scientists as well as those in the social policy arena' (Corden 1995, p. 15). The aim in the rest of this paper is to use it as a heuristic device in an analysis of changes in social policy.

Stigma and (non-) take up

By non-take up we mean that an individual who would be entitled to a social good does not consume (i.e., take up) that good. Stigma may cause non-take up, but may also be attached to the recipient as a cost for take up. In other words, there exist two opposing connections between stigma and claim/use that will be examined below, as shown in Figure 8.3.

Figure 8.3   Stigma, Take up and Non-Take up

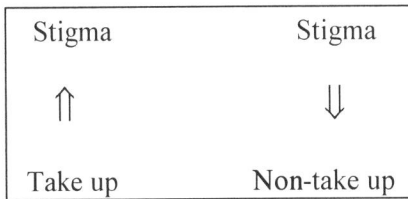

Stigma	Stigma
⇑	⇓
Take up	Non-take up

A *take up* may take place even though stigma is attached to the social good. An economist would say, using a rational choice theoretical approach, that stigma is a cost (social or psychological) connected to the use of the good (Moffitt, 1981, 1983; Blundell, Fry and Walker, 1988; Craig, 1989; Duclos, 1992). If the individual still decides to take up the good, this indicates that its utility exceeds the costs of the stigma attached. To sum up, economists treat stigma as an individualistic concept.

There are two qualifications to be made to the decision to take up. The first is that the likelihood of claiming the social good increases with the generosity/quality accorded to it, since this increases its value. In such cases there may be an increased suspicion of the possibility of fraudulent behaviour. An illustration of this situation might be when an early retirement pension is very generous and attractive. The second is that the cost connected to stigma might vary between individuals and within subgroups. This suggests that there might exist immunizing strategies towards the apprehension of stigma. An extreme case might be that, again when a social good is generous, take up might even be regarded as a sign of 'smartness' among some individuals.

Economists look upon stigma as a component in a rationing process. Some would even find it a legitimate rationing device, if it is effective. Only those really in need become beneficiaries. The recipient actually proves the need by taking up the good. Social psychologists, like the economists, focus on the claiming process in their understanding of non-take up. But instead of using the rational choice model, they use other types of decision-making models based on behaviour, among which the *threshold model* presented by Kerr (1982) has been the most influential. The threshold model recognizes the behaviour as involving passing across a number of necessary consecutive thresholds to make a claim. Kerr identifies six thresholds, but the actual decision to claim becomes the result of a trade-off between positive and negative consequences connected to individual beliefs, attitudes and feelings. Stigma is recognized as one negative factor in the formation of these beliefs, attitudes and feelings. In effect this tradition ends up rather close to that of economists, since the decision to claim in both cases depends on individualistic explanations of 'demand' behaviour. Within this epistemology extensive non-take up, as an indication perhaps of a shortcoming of a welfare programme, ceases to be problem.[2]

From other points of view, however, non-take up of social programmes indicates their failure. From within one such perspective, non-take up becomes a sign of a lack of effectiveness, that is, a poor implementation of the social policy scheme. From yet another perspective, non-take up indicates social injustice: 'If non-take up means that people are deprived of their rights and entitlements, then the resulting injustice is a cause for concern' (van Oorschot, 1991, quoted in Corden, 1995, p. 2). In contrast with the economists' and social psychologists' individualistic models of explanation, these latter perspectives accentuate structural and organizational factors, i.e. have a 'supply' side orientation. This will be investigated more thoroughly later on.

From quite another perspective, stigma can, as from the economists' standpoint, also be looked upon as the price a recipient has to pay, although there is a kind of 'moral price' for access to social policy. This line of argument emanates from an institutionalist, neo-marxian approach. Following O'Connor (1973) and later Offe (1984), social policy in a capitalist society is seen as necessary corollary of profit maximization in terms of the mutual contradictions of accumulation and legitimization. This approach is normative in its treatment of social policy as a necessary means to maintain the capitalist mode of production. The practical consequence for social policy, revealing its contradictory position, is that while it should be used, it should not be used too extensively (by increasing the risk of discouraging wage-labour, for example). From this point of view, social rights are always dubious in character. Or to be more precise, a moral price (stigma) is seen as a one of necessary factors of social policy in preserving the normative and moral orders of the commodification of labour (along with other sanctions and coercion) (Berge, 1995).

(Non-) take up and stigma

Let us now reverse the order of approaching stigma and (non-) take up by starting with the latter. If we look at degrees of take up in terms of the effectiveness of a welfare programme, it becomes pertinent to study why entitled individuals do *not* take up a specific benefit. Besides, low take up rates seem often not to be a marginal phenomenon. Evidence from means-tested programmes in Great Britain (van Oorschot, 1991), show variations in non-take up rates of between 7 per cent and 46 per cent, depending on the benefit. In the US, rates of non-take up of means-tested benefits are even higher. In Sweden, only a few take-up studies have been initiated. In 1986, take up rates in social assistance were investigated by Gustavsson (1987). The conclusion was that a majority of entitled individuals preferred to stay outside the system of social assistance. This observation is partly contradicted by the later findings of Salonen (1993). This longitudinal study of two larger Swedish cities showed that a fairly substantial number of citizens took up social assistance over the time-span of his investigation, although only on single or few occasions, and for short periods.

In looking for explanations of non-take up, the obvious place to start is with stigma as outlined above - i.e., non-favourable attitudes towards recipients. Social assistance is theoretically *the* support system vulnerable to stigma creation, since in its case needs-testing coincides with means-testing. Non-take up becomes a protest (*exit-behaviour*, to use Hirschman's (1970) notion) in order not to be associated with poverty. At the same time, low take up rates are always in a sense a paradox, since they suggest that the official recognition of need is not shared by entitled individuals, i.e., results are in conflict with aims. Meagre benefits, as in Britain clearly, decrease the propensity for take up. Further, a high degree of non-take up, i.e., a small number of recipients, might in itself increase the stigma associated with take up, which might reinforce the avoidance behaviour of others. We require a more complex understanding of behaviour.

A combination of factors will also shed some light on the Swedish paradox of the early 1990s, i.e., that even in a wealthy society a substantial number of citizens take up social assistance. First, the benefit level was fairly generous and social assistance was also available for temporary problems likely to be faced by everyone. Second, most recipients were so for only a short time, which meant that an identity linked to the status of dependency on state welfare did not have time to develop. These explanations relate closely to Pinker's discussions about what could be done to diminish the incidence of stigma in social policy. In Sweden, time, depth and distance in the relation between givers and recipients seem to favour a low incidence of stigma connected to the take up of social assistance.

But let us return to the paradox of the British case: high needs but low take up rates. It indicates that there could be other factors than purely behavioural ones at work. The price of stigma cannot sufficiently explain non-take up. An examination of possible factors leads us to two further ones. First, imperfect information can be a cause. It could simply be the case that some entitled individuals are not aware of their social rights. This case should be viewed as a failure of the design of a welfare scheme or its administration. It suggests that the general dissemination of information from the authorities who administer a particular social right is insufficient. Further, there may be imperfections in the means provided for gaining access to information and being able to claim, which could also be caused by such simple things as overload of work and low availability. An important question here is whether the lack of knowledge of a right is random or systematically associated with certain groups, which would suggest the possibility of discrimination. Is there neutrality in terms of gender, race and region? Second, administrative routines might consciously or unconsciously serve as a gate-keeping procedure. Gate-keeping involves claiming procedures which debar individuals who are borderline cases. In times of budgetary cutbacks, one explanation is that the double loyalty of administrative personnel, serving clients on the one hand and being aware of costs on the other, leans over in favour of the latter. Their actions take on the form of gate-keeping behaviour in such cases. The two cases can be summed up as being cases of *ignorance* and *non-access* respectively. We can thus portray the three explanations of non-take up in Figure 8.4.

Figure 8.4   Explanations of Non-Take up

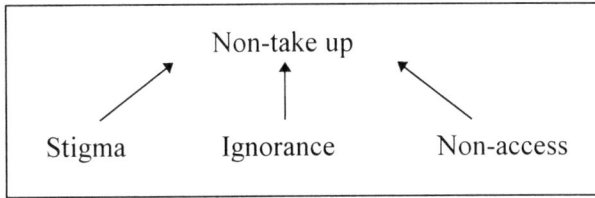

Stigma and social policy in a modern society

The term *social exclusion* has become a key concept in debates on the state of member countries in the European Union. There exist numerous definitions, but following Abrahamsson (1995), social exclusion can be seen as 'a post-modern condition for a minority of people who are marginalized from mainstream middle mass society' (*ibid.*, abstract). The author further argues that it is the modern equivalent of poverty. A definition that can elucidate the issue even more, taken from 'A Communication from the commission in 1992' (also in Abrahamsson, 1995), runs as follows:

> The concept is a dynamic one ... referring both to processes and consequent situations .... More clearly than the concept of poverty, understood far too often as referring exclusively to income, it also states the multidimensional nature of mechanisms whereby individuals and groups are excluded from taking part in the social exchange, from the component practices of rights of social integration and of identity .... More generally, by highlighting the risk of cracks appearing in the social fabric, it suggests something more than social inequality and carries with it the risk of a fragmented society (*ibid.*, p. 5).

Our investigation into the design of social policy and its relation to stigma and non-take up bears a clear relation to the concept of social exclusion as it is presented here. Let us make some observations.

Universal social policy arrangements enhance the notion of a social citizenship and in mainstream analysis this is believed to prevent developing into a *fragmented society*. From a post-modern approach, the desirability of incorporating any significant element of universalism into social policy can be questioned. For example, it is possible to interpret a feminist approach in these terms, when emphasizing that a universal construction should rather be seen to reproduce gender inequalities in society and sustain fragmentation. 'A universalist principle *deliberately* abstracts from differences between persons and groups in order to treat all of them fairly' (Thompson and Hoggett, 1996, p. 31).

Stigmatization refers to the qualitative aspects of taking up selective social policy and widens the issue beyond merely poor material conditions explaining (non-) take up behaviour. Stigmatization is furthermore a process, since it involves recurring 'inspection rituals'. The duration of one's status as a recipient is crucial to the development of a 'spoiled identity'. The attitudes of authorities as well as of other citizens are important in this process, from the point of view of labelling theory. Thus the mechanisms identified are of a *multi-dimensional* nature.

Let us sum up. The relation between social policy and social exclusion is somewhat paradoxical. On the one hand, social policy is designed to help individuals in need. In residual regimes social policy is directed towards individuals with no or low income to gain an acceptable living standard. Material inclusion, so to speak, is the aim. On the other hand, the taking up of selective benefits at the same time creates a stigma. In this way, take up enhances the risk of rejection, enforcing social exclusion. The residual model of welfare in creating a wealth gap, creates a situation of 'negative exchange' (Sahlins, 1974); that is, poor people receive benefits but are rejected as a result.

From the opposite perspective, non-take up means being deprived of the social rights to which one is entitled. But at the same time, non-take up implies a non-recognition as a social beneficiary, which, at least temporarily, relieves the threat of being openly recognised as being, or risking becoming, socially excluded. An element of 'rational' *self-exclusion* is at hand.

From this point of view it is our profound belief that a European route to combating social exclusion must be mapped out on the basis of a discussion about a generous social citizenship (a large range of basic social rights) within the European Union. This would create a basis for a *fraternal society*, to use a term by Hobsbawm (1975), combating fragmentation. But the strong arguments in favour of positive selectivism, i.e., the recognition of individual and group claims, take the social philosophical consideration back to the crucial and always present issue of the optimal blend of universalism and particularism.

At the same time, it must be recognized that the advocacy of universal social policy dates back to arguments put forward by Titmuss in traditional industrial society. This implies that one has to ask whether values and attitudes are static - that is, still stigma-creating for marginal groups - and also whether potential receivers do actually apprehend the stigma that is put on them (when still strongly enforced on them). The fact that 'techniques of neutralization' might change obviously further complicates the issue.

It is our view that negative values connected to take up of social goods have strengthened rather than weakened. Neo-liberals have repeatedly preached about the evils of welfare arrangements, focusing on 'scrounging' and the development of a 'welfare dependency culture'. This is also indicated by the development of welfare provision in the direction of increased targeting in the whole of Europe. As a consequence there is a strong case in favour of the belief that the pressure has increased rather than decreased.

On the other hand, the notion of a 'welfare subculture' indicates a specific set of behaviour and as it develops might indicate the emergence of a dual value system. It is possible that recipients of social policy can find a sort of logic of fair compensation in taking up social benefits, formed around the rationale that society has deprived them of access to the social good (i.e., a conception of impoverished citizenship). They will in turn find no shame in using social policy. But this could also be transformed into the opposite extreme with the existence of groups in society with little or no feeling of obligation to the welfare state. They may in extreme cases constitute groups deliberately resorting to fraudulent behaviour. The issue of different strategies has been studied by Dean and Melrose (1996), who distinguish between four respondent groups, each with a different strategy - subversive, desperate, unprincipled or fatalistic - towards benefit fraud. The demarcation between the groups is made by their different degrees and combinations of reflexivity and anxiety.

The growth of a dual value system might be related to age and ethnicity. First, it might be grasped as a generation issue. Younger individuals do not have a negative view towards using social policy. This might be a persistent or temporary phenomenon. It might well be temporary when values within the specific deprived group linger on in relation to values surrounding the more extensive welfare state. Older generations tend, on the contrary, to have formed values shaped by a residual model, which in turn persist even when social policy becomes more universal. The older, 'traditional' generation never came fully to grasp the idea of a social citizenship. What we are suggesting is the existence of a time-lag between the design of, and attitudes towards, welfare arrangements. Second, yet more complex to analyse, are groups of refugees and foreign citizens migrating to new nations. These groups have specific native value systems, which might have implications of a negative or positive kind in relation to the take up of social policy in their new country. Their new social citizenship is further generally secondary and incomplete, based on both a common lack of political citizenship, as well as the fact that work-related social rights, such as pensions, tend not to be fully developed.

Another aspect of post-modern difference might be encompassed in the concept of 'life-styles', developed within the sociology of culture. This concept refers to an individualization of the life-course and implies the weakening of group values and identities in general, and in relation to traditional parameters such as class position. This social fragmentation could also be relevant in relation to stigma-bearing groups. In a society where life-courses become more flexible, the locking into one central identity is weakened as well as made more temporary.

These last remarks must be seen as merely provisional. Possible changes in attitudes and behaviour must be reflected in empirical data. In addition, current changes in society are rapid and the phenomenon of social exclusion becomes ever more complex and fluid. Research is required to monitor these changes and their effects, and to inform those concerned with the development of new social policies.

Notes

[1] At first sight this argument might seem to contradict Pinker's argument that distance increases the risk of stigma, but this is a mere illusion. Distance in terms of spatial and social distance refers to the formation and confirmation of stigmatized group identities; the distance in moving from local to state provision implies a weaker identification of the individual. In fact, locality and selectivity both contribute to social distance.

[2] The refusal by the Thatcher government to accept criticism that current welfare programmes in the UK were weak was, according to Corden (1995), legitimized through reference to arguments grounded in individualistic decision models. The decision not to take up is seen as an individual choice, not as a weakness in a particular social policy.

References

Abrahamsson, P. (1995), *Social exclusion in Europe: Old wine in new bottles?*, Roskilde University.

Berge, A. (1995), *Medborgarrätt och egenansvar: De sociala försäkringarna i Sverige 1901-1935*, Arkiv, Lund.

Blundell, Fry and Walker. (1988), 'Modelling the take-up of means-tested benefits: The case of housing benefits in the United Kingdom', *The Economic Journal* 98 (Conference 1988), pp. 58-74.

Corden, A. (1995), *Changing Perspectives on Benefit Take-Up*, HMSO: SPRU, London.

Craig, P. (1989), 'Cost and Benefits: A review of Research on Take-up of Income-Related Benefits', *Journal of Social Policy* 20, 4.

Dean, H and M. Melrose (1996), 'Unravelling citizenship: The significance of social security fraud', *Critical Social Policy*, vol. 16, pp. 3-31.

Duclos, J-Y. (1992), *The Take-up of State Benefits: An Application to Supplementary Benefits in Britain Using the FES*, Discussion paper, WSP/71, L.S.E (London School of Economics).

Esping-Andersen, G. (1990), *The Three Worlds of Welfare Capitalism*, Polity Press, Cambridge.

Goodin, R.E. (1988), *Reasons For Welfare: The Political Theory of the Welfare State*, Princeton University Press, Princeton.

Goffman, E. (1963), *Stigma: Notes on the Management of Spoiled Identity*, Penguin Books Ltd., London.

Gustavsson, B. (1987), Som ett isberg? - Om underutnyttjande av socialbidrag. *Nordisk Sosialt Arbeid*, no.3.

Hirschman, A. (1970), *Exit, Voice and Loyalty*, Harvard University Press, Cambridge.

Hobsbawm, E. J. (1975) 'Fraternity', *New Society*, 34, pp. 471-3.

Kerr, S. (1982), 'Deciding about Supplementary Pensions: A Provisional Model', *Journal of Social Policy*, no. 11, pp. 505-517.

Lödemel, I. (1990), *Citizenship in the Social Division of Welfare. The Case of British and Norwegian Income Maintenance 1946 to 1966* (Working Paper). FAFO, The Norwegian Trade Union Research Center.

Marshall, T. and T. Bottomore (1992), *Citizenship and Social Class*, Pluto Press, London.

Moffitt, R. (1981), 'Stigma of Welfare Receipt: Estimation of a Choice-Theoretic Model', *Southern Economic Journal*, 47 (3).

Moffitt, R. (1983), 'An Economic Model of Welfare Stigma', *American Economic Review*, no. 5.

O'Connor, J. (1973), *Fiscal Crises of the State*, St Martin's Press, New York.

Offe, C. (1984) *Contradictions of the Welfare State*, Hutchinson, London.

Olsson, S-E. (1990), *Social Policy and Welfare State in Sweden*, Arkiv, Lund.

van Oorschot, W. (1991), 'Non-Take-Up Of Social Security Benefits In Europe', *Journal of European Social Policy,* (1), pp. 15-30.

van Oorschot, W. (1995), *Realizing Rights: A multi-level approach to non-take-up of means-tested benefits,* Avebury, Aldershot.

Pinker, R. (1971), *Social Theory & Social Policy,* Heinemann Educational Books Ltd., London.

Reisman, D.A. (1977), *Richard Titmuss: Welfare and Society,* Heinemann, London.

Rothstein, B. (1994), *Vad bör staten göra? Om välfärdsstatens moraliska och politiska logik,* SNS Förlag, Stockholm.

Sahlins, M. (1974), *Stone Age Economics,* Tavistock, London.

Salonen,T. (1993), *Margins of Welfare. A study of modern functions of social assistance,*: Hällestad Press, Torna Hällestad.

Spicker, P. (1988), *Principles of social welfare. An introduction to thinking about the welfare state,* Routledge, London.

Thompson, S and P. Hoggett (1996), Universalism, selectivism and particularism. Towards a post-modern social policy, *Critical Social Policy,* vol. 16, pp. 21-43.

Titmuss, R. (1968), *Commitment to Welfare,* Allen and Unwin, London.

9 Schooling, Exclusion and Self-Exclusion

PAUL LITTLEWOOD

Introduction

In this chapter I consider some of the purposes and effects of schooling in contemporary Europe in relation to processes of exclusion and self-exclusion of pupils and school leavers. I start by considering what various users of the term 'exclusion' appear to mean by it in the specific context of schooling. I then concentrate largely on certain, somewhat arbitrarily chosen, aspects of schooling in the United Kingdom, and especially England. In the conclusion I suggest that first, the conceptions of exclusion separately developed by Frank Parkin and Pierre Bourdieu have more explanatory value in the context of schooling than do those currently in use by European research agencies; and second, the history of mass compulsory schooling might be said to mark a movement from explicit, unconcealed exclusionary policies to ever more subtle strategies in which exclusion is presented in the concealed, mystificatory form of self-exclusion.

Social exclusion, education and functionalism

In the Introduction to this volume, we described the paradigms which tend to predominate among major European research agencies, suggesting that they are currently based on a functionalist perspective. This perspective tends to ignore or at least downplay the prevalence and salience of major structural inequalities, their origins and their persistence in our society. Thus there is the implicit assumption that those not socially integrated can be found in pockets on the margins of society, as suggested by the use of the term 'underclass' and the lack of reference to major social groupings and categories identified by social class, gender and ethnicity. In the

175

absence of substantial reference to social class, 'underclass' takes on a *lumpen*, fragmentary sense of not-in-the-mainstream. Instead the emphasis is placed on unspecified notions of 'community' and 'communities', the allegedly order-threatening characteristics and practices of those dispersed on the margins, and the need to integrate them into a more cohesive social order.

If we relate this paradigm to schooling, then the school becomes a principal means by which 'society' seeks to socialize younger generations for active and integral roles at work and as citizens. In Durkheim's words,

> Education is... the means by which society prepares, within the children, the essential conditions of its very existence... Education is the influence exercised by adult generations on those that are not yet ready for adult life. Its object is to arouse and to develop in the child a certain number of physical, intellectual and moral states which are demanded of him by both the political society as a whole and the special milieu for which he is specifically destined. It follows... that education consists of a methodical socialization of the young generation (Durkheim, 1968, p. 71).

It is this conception which has arguably provided the basis for a widely held understanding of the function of education in contemporary society, although not perhaps as Durkheim might have intended. Implicit within this understanding is the moral judgement that education is intrinsically 'a good thing', comprising useful training for work, preparation for responsible citizenship, self-fulfilment and so on; and the moral prescription to attend compulsory school or to ensure that one's children do so. Thus wilful non-attendance or parental acceptance of non-attendance is viewed as truancy, or collusion in truancy - an essentially deviant, even pathological form of behaviour, anti-social and morally wrong. One of the tasks of the sociologist, of course, is to stand back from and analyse the nature and origins of such judgements.

Levitas in her analysis of EU research strategies identifies within the discourse elements of Durkheimian functionalism as well as monetarist economics, but not at a refined level of theory: 'rather, a punk Durkheimianism of the 1990s replaces (or joins) the punk monetarism of the 1980s. The relationship between these strands of thought may ultimately be no more contradictory than the relationship between neo-liberalism and neo-conservatism in New Right discourse and policy, with the twin themes of the free market and the strong state' (Levitas, 1996, p. 13).

She finds the role of formal education accorded importance in the European Commission White Papers. She quotes references in them to the alleged need to develop "'a mastery of basic knowledge (linguistic, scientific and other knowledge) and skills of a technological and social nature, that is to say the ability to develop and act in a complex and highly technological environment'" and "'the failure of education ... (as) a particularly important and increasingly widespread factor of marginalization and economic and *social exclusion*. In the Community, 25 to 30 per cent of young people ... leave the education system without the preparation they need to become properly *integrated into working life*'" (Levitas, 1996, p. 11, her emphasis). Her comment on this is that the sense of exclusion in use here is largely restricted to the economic exclusion from paid work, which obscures the presence of other important forms of social exclusion. I would add that in relation to education, there are also the taken-for-granted assumptions that first, somehow qualifications *create* jobs and second, the absence of such preparation is somehow a failing of those without it. This conception of the relation of schooling to work is arguably another instance of punk Durkheimianism.

Alternative notions of exclusion and schooling

I now want to turn to the use of contrasting notions of exclusion as developed by other sociologists, all of which are also related, more or less directly, to schooling. In general terms such a notion is based on a treatment which places much greater emphasis on schooling as a means of rejecting or eliminating large numbers of pupils rather than on developing them to their fullest potential (see for example Holt, 1969). Let me elaborate. Schooling - and formal education more widely - can be construed as being in part not just about the transmission of knowledge in the sense of enlightenment - 'leading people out', the 'blossoming of the flower', 'broadening of horizons' etc. - but also about *selection*. And selection involves not just identifying certain candidates as acceptable for inclusion, but also identifying those not acceptable, and rejecting or excluding them - from certain types of schools and other educational institutions, from particular types of course, from or through examinations and so on. This is basic to much of the formal purpose of schooling.

In addition to this emphasis on schools as excluding institutions, some sociologists have also been aware of another, less overt aspect of the process of exclusion - whereby the educators seek to convince those excluded that it is not so much the system which is excluding the 'failed' candidate as certain characteristics or deficits within those candidates themselves. A relatively early account of this can be found in Clark's 1960 description of the 'cooling-out' function in higher education in the United States, a notion he draws from Goffman's still earlier account of the successful confidence trickster's technique of 'cooling the mark out' - not merely tricking the mark (target of the trick), but also convincing the mark to believe that either they have not been tricked or that being tricked was their own fault (Goffman, 1952). Clark applies this notion to the processes of de-selection in junior college, whereby many students accepted for college and later deemed as not being of high enough calibre are convinced that it is in their best interests to ease themselves out of continued participation at higher levels of education.

While this treatment of exclusion is interesting and enlightening, it tends to be piecemeal and lacks a broader theoretical framework. As we saw in the Introduction to this volume, at least two other sociologists have been concerned to provide such frameworks, derived more from the works of Weber and (although much less directly) Marx than from those of Durkheim.

Parkin on exclusion and credentialism

Of particular relevance to the theme of this chapter, Parkin considers the nature of closure strategies in contemporary western capitalist (and, given the nature of his thesis and the period when he was developing it, also socialist) societies:

> In modern capitalist society the two main exclusionary devices by which the bourgeoisie constructs and maintains itself as a class are, first, those surrounding the institutions of property; and, second, academic or professional qualifications and credentials (Parkin, 1979, pp. 47-8).

Parkin goes on to claim that

> Of equal importance to the exclusionary rights of property is that set of closure practices sometimes referred to as 'credentialism' - that is; the inflated use of educational certificates as a means of monitoring entry to key positions in the division of labour (*ibid.*, p. 54).

Following Weber, Dore, Berg and Jencks, he suggests that 'the universal tendency among professions to raise the minimum standards of entry as increasing numbers of potential candidates attain the formerly scarce qualifications' has little or nothing to do with the greater complexity of tasks or levels of performance required, but much more 'because they simplify and legitimate the exclusionary process'.

> Credentials are usually supplied on the basis of tests designed to measure certain class-related qualities and attributes rather than those practical skills and aptitudes that may not so easily be passed on through the family line (*ibid.*, p. 55).

Parkin's next step is to adopt Bourdieu's notion of cultural capital, relating it to Berg's claim that '"Educational credentials have become the new property..."' (*ibid.*, p. 59). Parkin, however, finally rejects this conflation of the two senses of property, not of course on the conventional Marxist grounds of confusing the productive with the distributive systems, but because the vocabulary of closure does not require it and because in different societies there are other, similar but distinct forms of closure, apart from productive and cultural capital, such as 'party membership, racial characteristics, lineage, etc.' (*ibid.*, p. 61).

In the instances drawn from the development of British schooling which follow later, we shall see how the processes of school exclusion are similarly based on class and other major forms of social identity. But where Parkin is perhaps less useful is in his rather narrow treatment of exclusion through the restrictive distribution of qualifications. The analysis for the most part remains at the level of the ways in which various professions have sought to establish and maintain their professional monopolies in the context of credentialist inflation. In addition, Parkin's tendency to conceive of exclusion as a set of strategies or devices suggests perhaps a degree of conscious purpose on the part of the excluders which they may well in fact not have. We must turn to Bourdieu for a far broader paradigm of formal education as a system of exclusionary practices - and, very importantly, of self-exclusion - and, moreover, one which recognizes the lack of awareness on the part of the excluders as to what they are actually doing.

Bourdieu on scholastic exclusion and self-exclusion

As we argued in the Introduction, Bourdieu is one of the current champions of the notion of exclusion and the associated notion of self-exclusion - although neglected in many contemporary analyses of social exclusion. In his and Passeron's Foundations of a Theory of Symbolic Violence, two key propositions are:

> In any given social formation, the PW (Pedagogic Work) through which the dominant PA (Pedagogic Agency) is carried on always has the function of keeping order, i.e. of reproducing the structure of the power relations between the groups or classes, inasmuch as, by inculcation or exclusion, it tends to impose recognition of the legitimacy of the dominant culture on the members of the dominated groups or classes, and to make them internalize, to a variable extent, disciplines and censorships which best serve the material and symbolic interests of the dominant groups or classes when they take the form of self-discipline and self-censorship.

> In any given social formation, because the PW through which the dominant PA tends to impose recognition of the legitimacy of the dominant culture on the members of the dominated groups or classes, it tends at the same time to impose on them, by inculcation and exclusion, recognition of the illegitimacy of their own cultural arbitrary (Bourdieu and Passeron, 1977, p. 40-41).

The theory that Bourdieu and Passeron are developing here is intended to be universal - hence the abstract terms in which it is couched - but it is arguably highly applicable to schooling in late twentieth century Europe, as the authors seek to demonstrate in their subsequent application of it to formal education in contemporary France in the second part of the book, Keeping Order. For Pedagogic Work we can read teaching and any other means of formal instruction; and for Pedagogic Agency, the whole of the formal educational apparatus from policy makers in government to school employees, including but not exclusively so, the teachers. Crudely put, teachers in schools 'keep order' - that is, contribute to the reproduction of prevailing power relations in contemporary society, through the teaching and by the selection of pupils, by means of persuading them to internalize the superiority or rightness of the dominant culture and the inferiority of the culture of the dominated social groups and categories. This process of persuasion the authors term 'symbolic violence' in that it involves - and indeed depends on - the exercise of power vested in the teacher by the dominant class.

Processes inherent in education lead the teacher to conceal from the taught the real nature of this process, and for both the teacher and the taught to misrecognize their roles in it. This is where self-exclusion comes in. By learning to misrecognize the culture of the dominant class as superior, or even as the only 'true' culture, members of dominated groups are either inculcated into adherence to the tenets of the dominant culture, or are excluded from it. By recognising the supposed inferiority of their own culture, those excluded tend to regard the reasons for their exclusion as lying in their own inferiority. Moreover, members of the dominant class have the added advantage of having been brought up in the culture which from which much formal education derives - that is, they come already equipped with what Bourdieu terms 'cultural capital', which they can 'invest' and later reap the profits in terms of high educational achievement. But those from subordinate classes lack such capital.

It is not my purpose in this chapter to explore Bourdieu's theory in depth, still less to offer a critique of it; but it is far more encompassing and rich than the crude summary above suggests. Nor am I going to consider other elaborations of the notions of exclusion and self-exclusion, except to note one quite remarkable feature of at least some of them.

Other uses of exclusion

An intriguing aspect relating to both Parkin's and Bourdieu's work on exclusion is the relative lack of reference to either in much of the more contemporary work involving the concept. In for example one of the major recent explorations of social exclusion, that of Jordan (1996), I cannot find a single reference to either author, despite Jordan's aim to provide 'a *theory* of poverty and social exclusion'. Yépez del Castillo's account of social exclusion in France and Belgium makes no reference to Bourdieu (let alone Parkin), despite claiming to attempt 'to place the French concept of social exclusion within its context' (Yépez del Castillo, 1994, p. 613). The 'French concept' clearly excludes Bourdieu. While Silver's very full and useful account of three paradigms of social exclusion does cite both Bourdieu and Parkin, the references to each are fleeting (Silver, 1994/5). Similarly with Crompton and Brown (1994), in whose Introduction to a volume on economic restructuring and social exclusion there is a single and brief treatment of Weber and Parkin (pp. 5-7). Significantly, perhaps, this treatment dwells on Parkin's argument that 'during the 20th century there has been a gradual shift from "collective" to ... "individualist" exclusion rules' (*ibid.*, pp. 5-6). Following Marshall as well as Parkin, the authors go on to suggest that there has been a decline in collective strategies of protection, as marked by economic and technological restructuring and the weakening of trade union power. 'Thus, increasingly, much everyday behaviour is not geared directly towards the exclusion of others, but rather to ensuring the inclusion of individuals or their family members, in terms of access to educational credentials, superior jobs, promotion opportunities, etc.' (*ibid.*, p. 6).

I would suggest that there appears to be a shift in the authors' discussion of the collective and individualist aspects of exclusion away from concern with changes in the nature of exclusion rules towards one focused on changes in inclusionary strategies. Although they tacitly acknowledge that individualist criteria of exclusion still mask collective exclusion strategies, the authors appear to downplay the role of social class as a source and strategy of social exclusion and instead stress the fragmentary nature of those excluded - 'immigrants, guest workers, and working class women' - in their subsequent discussion of poverty and contested claims about an underclass (*ibid.*, p. 7). To me this dilutes the strength of Parkin's thesis about the move from collective to individualist rules of exclusion. He is clearly arguing, not only in the original (1974) article to which they refer but also in his later and much fuller 1979 account, that while bourgeois liberal ideology has become ever more couched in terms of individualist values, bourgeois practice ensures continued exclusion of large collectivities by class, gender and ethnicity, using both individualist and collectivist criteria. 'In non-fictional societies individualist and collectivist modes of exclusion always co-exist' (Parkin, 1974, p. 9); and later, 'It is not, then, difficult to show that bourgeois ideology despite its formal opposition to ascriptive norms is supportive of a class system having a greater degree of self-recruitment than seems consistent with the liberal doctrine of the open society' (Parkin, 1979, pp. 65-6).

I perceive a parallel here with a possible implication in Bourdieu's thesis on self-exclusion, which I attempt to develop in the second half of this paper: in a sense, Parkin's argument that 'changes in class conditions over the past century or more can be seen as representing a gradual shift from collectivist to individualist forms of social exclusion' (*ibid.*, p. 7) is commensurate with a shift from, in Bourdieu's terms, exclusionary to self-exclusionary strategies. To the extent that this is accepted, each shift is one of class-based exclusionary *strategy*, still utterly dependent on the preservation of the dominance of one class and the continued subjugation of the subordinate class, albeit by changing methods. I fear that the vast majority of contemporary treatments of exclusion tend to neglect the continued existence of a dominant class, as well as the path-breaking contributions of Parkin and Bourdieu.

Brown on social exclusion and cultural capital

An important exception to this neglect of Parkin's and Bourdieu's treatments of exclusion, however, can be found in a more recent article by Brown in which he develops a much more sustained analysis of both exclusion and cultural capital in relation to recent trends in education, employment and the labour market (Brown, 1997, although the article was originally published in 1995). His account merits comment here not least because of first, his critiques of what he labels 'exclusion theory' and Bourdieu's thesis on middle-class reproduction and second, his sustained, perceptive treatment of the concept of exclusion and its continued applicability, despite the rapidly changing circumstances characterizing the end of the twentieth century.

Brown's critique of social exclusion theory is in fact levelled at Collins's thesis on credentialism (Collins, 1976). He argued that in advanced industrial societies the rapid expansion in education and training has progressively less to do with the demands of industry or required occupational skills. But Brown accuses Collins of three errors. First, his denial that technological innovation has affected at least to some extent the increasing demand for credentials has been shown in retrospect to be exaggerated. Second, again contrary to Collins's thesis, this demand can now also be seen to have been affected by changes in management and work organization and their impact on recruitment processes. And third, Collins did not foresee that the dislocation between education, credentials and the occupational structure might be affected as much by economic restructuring, recession and unemployment as by the exclusionary tactics of élite occupational groups (Brown, 1997, p. 738). While these criticisms are amply substantiated by Brown, they do *not* constitute a critique of the applicability of the concept of social exclusion (a term barely if ever used by Collins in his book on credentialism), particularly when its use is tied to exclusionary *strategies*, as intended by Parkin. In other words, acknowledgement of the impact of the rapid rate of technological innovation, the reorganization of management and work organisation and more generally the economic restructuring marking the latter part of this century, does not invalidate or even weaken the applicability of social exclusion as *an* important influence on recruitment for work.

Brown's other major criticism is levelled at Bourdieu, and in particular his allegedly exaggerated claim as to the inevitability of middle-class reproduction. Again the criticism seems justified; many other commentators have suggested that Bourdieu's work shows at times a tendency to be overdeterministic, despite his disavowals. The criticism does not, however, invalidate Bourdieu's thesis on exclusion and self-exclusion as *practices* performed by pedagogic agents. Within this conception there is surely room for some members of the subordinate class to be *in*cluded by fully assimilating dominant values, just as there is for some members of the dominant class to be *ex*cluded by refusing to misrecognize the nature of the symbolic violence being inflicted on them. Brown's subsequent use of the notion of cultural capital is, however, far less critical (perhaps surprisingly, given the unease that others have expressed with it), although Brown's treatment does seem at times to elide cultural with economic capital (*ibid.*, pp. 738-9).

In the rest of Brown's article he provides an excellent summary of the destabilization of bureaucratic structures in both the private and public sectors through flexibilization, restructuring, down-sizing and so on, and its effect on middle-class employees - in particular, greater economic insecurity with the move from 'bureaucratic' to 'flexible' careers (*ibid.*, pp. 739-41). This he argues 'will lead to an increasing emphasis on (acquiring) academic and professional credentials as an insurance policy' (*ibid.*, p. 740), 'at a time when employers are finding it increasingly difficult to absorb the growing number of highly educated students' (*ibid.*, pp. 741). Thus employers become more selective, by favouring applicants graduating from élite institutions and by developing selection techniques favouring 'charismatic' over 'bureaucratic' personality characteristics (*ibid.*, pp. 741-44). Citing Bourdieu's thesis on distinction he writes,

> Within the middle classes, the development of the 'charismatic' qualities of their children is becoming as important as arming them with the necessary credentials, contacts and networks. There is nothing new about this focus on the 'rounded' person, but whereas a range of broader interests and hobbies which offered time-out from academic study was seen as a form of cultural *consumption* which was to be enjoyed for its own sake, it has increasingly become a form of *investment* as part of the construction of a 'value-added' *curriculum vitae*. This involves an increasing 'commodification' of the socio-emotional embodiment of culture, incorporating drive, ambition, social confidence, tastes and inter-personal skills (*ibid.*, pp. 744, his emphasis).

Brown then turns explicitly to exclusion and the changing strategies developed by the middle class, given the weakening of its monopolizing influence over labour markets and its increasing dependence on access to market power.

> This competition for 'positional' advantage is not only directed against the working class but between social groups which can be loosely described in terms of the 'old' and the 'new' middle class. The 'old' has its power base in material property and the 'new', a large proportion of whom are employed in the public sector, have theirs in 'expert' knowledge systems which are wrapped in a professional ethos of service to the community... Historically, this has involved a conflict over property rights between the 'entrepreneurial' ideal of the 'old' middle class and the 'professional' ideal of the 'new'. In the context of the early 1990s, this conflict over property rights has been broadened into a more intensive distributional struggle over cultural capital in the reproduction of family status, life-style and property (*ibid.*, p745).

The ever increasing competition for credentials is now, however, being held under new 'rules of engagement': whereas in the immediate post-war period these rules were couched in an ideology of *merit*, thus legitimating middle-class pre-eminence, they are now couched in terms of the *market*, with increased importance placed, once again, I would add, on material advantage, on market power. Thus those with the resources to send their children to the more expensive élite educational institutions will accrue for them even greater advantage in the market place, given employers' continued preference for such graduates, on the grounds not so much that their education is superior but that such institutions require higher entrance qualifications in the first place. At this point Brown seems to abandon or at least downplay his earlier stress on the growing importance of transferable skills, suggesting that those lower-status institutions which accord them importance in their course programmes are in effect providing a form of 'compensatory' education for their students - who are disproportionately working class, female and from ethnic minorities (*ibid.*, p. 746). I would add that this is a strategy in Parkin's terms of 'usurpation', but one likely to be doomed to failure given the growing polarisation between classes and within the middle class.

Despite his earlier criticisms of the exclusion thesis, Brown is clearly working very much within the paradigms developed by Parkin and Bourdieu. I now intend to do the same, by looking at a somewhat randomly selected number of processes in contemporary British schooling which seem to validate the applicability of this interpretation of the concept, rather than that of the punk functionalists. (I believe also, however, that my treatment could well be applicable elsewhere in Europe. One example is Stoler's thesis on the colonial order of things and in particular, 'nationalist discourses ... predicated on exclusionary cultural principles', which contains an incisive account of nineteenth-century Dutch liberalism and social reform in relation to race, class and sexuality (Stoler, 1995, pp. 7-9, 121-136).) I want to suggest that the institution and practice of schooling has always been very importantly about social exclusion, of whole social groups and categories; and that its development over the last century has been towards ever more subtle forms of self-exclusion, couched in individualist ideology, masking the persistence of explicit social exclusion on a vastly pervasive scale.

The establishment of mass compulsory schooling

As stated in Littlewood and Jönsson (1996), by the late nineteenth century states throughout Europe had established systems of, at least in principle, free, compulsory elementary schooling for all the children of their respective citizens. There we pointed to three sets of inter-related forces behind these developments: first, changes in the nature of work, with in many areas rapid industrialization and the accompanying process of urbanization, the capitalization of industrial and agricultural production, and the growth in the demand for graded levels of literacy and numeracy in a rapidly diversifying workforce largely comprising employees dependent on wages and salaries; second, the expansion of the welfare role of the state as provider or at least facilitator of certain basic social services: primarily those of health, sanitation and hygiene, communication and transport and - the concern of this paper - education; and third, the establishment and development of representative government by nation states and the concomitant elaboration of the political and juridical rights and duties of their citizens, requiring their willing support through the ballot box and the payment of taxes. Thus the relatively new and growing demands in the nineteenth century for an appropriately trained workforce and a literate electorate were met in part through the establishment and development of national systems of schooling throughout Europe.

The orthodox or dominant treatment of education (that is, education as intrinsically good), when applied to this historical context, is based on the assertion that the establishment of mass compulsory schooling by the state was essentially a mark of progress, bringing enlightenment to those who would previously have been unschooled, training them up for 'useful' work and to meet the developing 'needs' of industry, and educating them to be citizens respectful of their social responsibilities and mindful of their rights. But critical sociologists would reject this view, pointing to the fundamentally exclusionary nature of such schooling.

In England, for example, the whole school system underwent a series of far-reaching reforms in the mid- to late-nineteenth century, the result of which was the establishment of a massively stratified structure. At the top, so to speak, were the Public Schools which, prior to the mid-nineteenth century, had become at best anachronisms dating from a medieval past and at worst, dens of iniquity and vice largely run by their pupils, and shunned by the parents of the ascendant bourgeoisie. They did, however, often reserve some places for sons of the local poor. Following the 1861 Clarendon Commission, set up because in the words of Clarendon, Public School provision was in danger of placing "'the upper classes in a state of inferiority to the middle and lower'" (Simon, 1974, p. 304), reforms ensured that they could provide an exclusive and highly elitist private education suitable for both the mid-Victorian bourgeoisie and the aristocracy.

> All in all, by insisting on the preservation of the classics as the main core of teaching, and by ensuring the final separation of the Public Schools from those for other classes, the Clarendon Commission created an efficient and entirely segregated system of education for the governing class... (*ibid.*, p. 318).

As for the sons of the traditional petty bourgeoisie, their needs were catered for by reforms emanating from the 1864 Taunton Commission, which sought to reshape and integrate a very diverse array of private secondary schools. A three-tiered system was introduced, comprising 'third grade' schools for the children of small tenant farmers, tradesmen and self-employed artisans, terminating when the pupils reached 14 years; 'second grade' schools for those leaving at 16, primarily the children of wealthy tradesmen; and 'first grade' schools for the children of the upper-middle and professional classes. In the words of one of the Commissioners,

> 'You shall be a good lower middle class school, you shall be a middle middle class school and you shall be a higher middle class school, that which is now called a grammar school' (*ibid.*, p. 323).

And as far as gender was concerned, middle class girls could enrol in secondary schools - but with little hope of proceeding to higher education.

The children - both girls and boys - of the working class, except in the very rare case of the 'scholarship boy', were restricted to the elementary school where they were taught in a highly disciplinarian fashion only the most basic skills in literacy and numeracy, respect for one's superiors and for girls domestic skills - a situation which was to prevail until after the Second World War. One of the chief architects of compulsory state schooling, Sir James Kay-Shuttleworth, was in no doubt as to the purpose of such provision; writing of an imaginary visitor to mid-nineteenth century Manchester, he said,

> 'he contemplates the fearful strength of that multitude, which lies like a slumbering giant at his feet. He has heard of the turbulent riots of the people - of machine-breaking - of the secret and sullen organisation which has suddenly lit the torch of incendiarism, or well nigh uplifted the arm of rebellion in the land' (*ibid.*, p. 166).

And the solution? Shuttleworth again:

> 'The radical remedy is ... such an education as shall teach the people in what consists their true happiness, and how their interest might best be served' (*ibid.*, p. 168); 'a general system of public education [aimed at] rearing a loyal, intelligent and Christian population' (*ibid.*, p. 357).

The result: in 1870, the establishment of free education for all the children of the working class, made compulsory over the next few years. This highly stratified system of education was to remain basically unchanged until the end of the Second World War.

My argument here is that the origins and development of state compulsory schooling were based as much on mass exclusion as they were on mass education. The system was firmly rooted in the emergent class and patriarchal structures, in 'knowing your place'; it was explicitly exclusionary, with little space for subtle forms of self-exclusion. Pupils' schooling was tied to the social class of their fathers and to their gender, and this was to endure throughout much of Britain until the mid-twentieth century.

'Secondary education for all'

But by the end of the Second World War, a very different discourse was in the ascendant: that of 'meritocracy', whereby access to different forms of schooling should be based not so much on the occupation of one's father as on one's own learning potential and academic ability. In England, Wales and Northern Ireland this took the form of the tripartite system of secondary education, which became compulsory for all. Three types of secondary school in principle were established, although in practice one type - the technical school, designed to develop the aptitudes of children for skilled manual and many routine white collar occupations - was only sparsely established. Those children who passed the 11+ - a series of tests taken at about the age of eleven - qualified for entry to the grammar school, with a relatively academic syllabus and the possibility of a university education for those who did well. Those who did not pass the 11+ were sent to the secondary modern school, in which learning programmes were far less academically oriented and in which vocational skills were emphasized. The vast majority of children failed the 11+, indicating their restricted academic abilities, and went to the secondary modern school.

The 11+ had certain significant characteristics. First, it was widely regarded as an intelligence test, although it transgressed the criteria of intelligence tests in a number of ways - principally in its dependence on a lot of culturally based knowledge. Second, the 11+ pass rate was not geared to the achievement of a certain standard in the test, but to the number of local grammar school places. Since the provision of grammar school places tended to be greater per head of population in middle-class neighbourhoods than in working-class neighbourhoods, working-class children had to achieve a higher level in the test than did middle-class children. (It should be added, however, that grammar school provision varied regionally; in Wales, for example, a greater proportion of places enabled a higher proportion of pupils to attend grammar schools than elsewhere in the United Kingdom.) And third, while girls were found to achieve higher levels in the test than boys, the numbers of grammar school places were divided equally between girls and boys - so girls, like working-class pupils, had to achieve more to pass the test. These three factors together are important in terms of not just exclusion but also self-exclusion, because pupils who failed the 11+ were widely regarded as having done so through their own lack of intelligence and intellectual aptitude. In other words, it was now widely believed that it was a personal failing, not the occupation of their fathers or their gender, which resulted in the exclusion of children from grammar school. Yet quite clearly, many girls and working-class children were being excluded *not* because of their relative lack of intelligence, but because of their sex or the location of their homes. These biases in the system were only to become widely recognised much later - in the case of class bias, in the 1960s (Floud and Halsey, 1961) and, in the case of gender bias, still later (Weiner, 1986).

Testing and the construction of intelligence

The widespread belief in the 1950s and 1960s that the 11+ was an intelligence test leads me to consider briefly the claim that intelligence itself is a natural quality, largely innate, unchangeable and inherited. This was certainly the justification for the development and widespread use of the 11+ as the principal selection mechanism for secondary schooling. This belief was increasingly being challenged in the 1960s, however, by evidence concerning the phenomenon of the 'late developer' - a term referring to those pupils who had failed the 11+ but who later in their secondary school careers were found to be capable of passing academic examinations. Many sociologists among others in the 1970s began to question received notions about the nature of intelligence and methods of measuring it (Simon, 1971, Ryan, 1972, Kamin, 1974, Henderson, 1976, Evans and Waites, 1981). First, defining intelligence was found to be much more problematic than the developers of intelligence tests acknowledged; in particular, attempts to define a single universal factor common to all intellectual activities were disputed. Second, claims that intellectual ability was largely fixed were challenged, as were claims that such ability was largely inherited. Third, the validity and reliability of tests of intelligence were questioned; in particular, claims that they were objective were shown to be largely false. Finally, the whole project of defining and measuring intelligence was argued to be the product of social class interests. Thus,

> My argument is that because of their dominance in the class structure, the middle class are able to *select* and *define* those behavioural characteristics which are to be considered 'intelligent'. Furthermore, that the characteristics selected and defined are those characteristics that they themselves are most likely to be in command of, which arise from their location in the class structure and the way of life which stems from this location. Finally, with respect to the view held that assessments of intelligence measure some kind of absolute quality, the worth of a person to society..., assessments of intelligence

measure no such thing, but are instead a mechanism by which control over social mobility is maintained: a mechanism finding its source in a situation in which such control was becoming weakened (Henderson 1976, p. 148).

Comprehensive schools

The recognition that one's intellectual potential could not be accurately measured at the age of 11 was one of the factors behind the widespread introduction of comprehensive secondary schools from the mid-1960s, with no entrance qualifications or other form of selective intake. The basic thrust of the comprehensive school reform was 'inclusionary', bringing all secondary school pupils in a given catchment area under one roof, with equal access to a far broader range of equipment and facilities than the old system allowed. But, just as in the case of grammar school provision, there were significant regional variations. In Scotland the reform was carried out more uniformly and rapidly than south of the border. In contrast, there the reform was never fully carried out, in that in Northern Ireland and in many areas in England, grammar schools with selection still based on the 11+ coexisted with comprehensive schools, 'creaming off' the arguably more able pupils. In addition, within comprehensive schools a variety of selection techniques were introduced to separate pupils by ability and by subject choice. Streaming in a variety of different forms prevailed over the so-called 'mixed-ability' classes which had been seen as essential by many of the proponents of the comprehensive school reform.

But for current purposes, the key issue in the comprehensive school reform is the extent to which it marks a move from an explicitly exclusionary to a self-exclusionary form. For now pupils and their parents were led to believe that the comprehensive school represented the achievement of 'equality of educational opportunity', with in principle all subjects and all courses open to anyone with the requisite personal abilities. Thus failure came to be seen not so much as the result of a school system discriminating on grounds of social class, gender and ethnicity, as a consequence of personal inadequacies on the part of the failing pupil. There were, of course, many discriminatory practices within comprehensive schools, as followers of the so-called New Sociology Education were to demonstrate (Young, 1971, Flude and Ahier, 1974). The nature of the curriculum remained very much geared to that of the traditional grammar school, arguably more accessible to children from middle class backgrounds (Bernstein, 1975) and teachers' assessments of pupils' abilities were found to be influenced by their preconceptions about class, gender and ethnicity (Goodacre, 1968, Keddie, 1971, Stanworth, 1981, Troyna, 1987).

But such discriminatory practices were at least in part hidden, both from the pupils and from the teachers themselves, through a process of misrecognition. Thus children from working-class backgrounds tended to be disproportionately placed in academically the lower streams, with restricted access to courses leading to higher status qualifications. Girls tended to be steered away from science-based subjects, towards the humanities, or to have much lower expectations placed upon them (Byrne, 1978, Deem, 1978, Stanworth, 1981). And pupils from certain ethnic minorities, particularly children of Afro-Caribbean origins, were disproportionately represented in subjects such as music and sport (Carrington, 1983), and in statistics for school suspension and expulsion, or 'exclusion' as it is now called. Indeed, school exclusion in general is currently rising in Britain, partly at least because of schools' perceived need to compete with each other over academic results in order to be favourably placed in the so-called 'League Tables'. Although some commentators interpret this rise in exclusion rates as very much the product of individual schools' policies to present a more attractive image to prospective parent-customers, the more conventional, common-sensical understanding is of course that those excluded are trouble-makers whose anti-social behaviour eventually necessitated their exclusion. This common-sense view ties in closely with notions of the 'underclass', a minority of deviants who have separated themselves from the majority through their own actions. This is a theme I wish to consider further in the context of one of the most talked-of books in recent years in the sociology of education in Britain and elsewhere - Willis's *Learning to Labour* (Willis, 1977).

'How working class kids get working class jobs'

Willis used participant-observation techniques to study a small group of male pupils in the early 1970s at a school in a working class town in the English Midlands. His aim was to explore the various factors affecting the transition from school to work. His basic thesis is that the boys in his study actively *chose* to reject their period at secondary school as a time for study with the intention of getting qualifications in order to widen and strengthen job opportunities. In fact, the boys chose to do the opposite: styling themselves 'the lads', they identified themselves as separate from the other pupils (whom they termed the 'earoles'); and their principal aim at school was 'having a laff' and avoiding as much scholastic work as possible. Willis argues that instead they developed their attitudes and behaviour in school on the basis of their received impressions of working-class culture on the factory floor. As a direct result, argues Willis, the 'lads' were not so much being condemned by a classist school system to getting working-class jobs, as actively *choosing* that occupational destination.

In order to develop the relevance of Willis's research in the context of this paper, one has to consider the theoretical underpinnings of his particular sociological approach. Willis, one of the original researchers in the Centre for Contemporary Cultural Studies at Birmingham University under Stuart Hall, was concerned to challenge the then prevalent form of Marxist sociology epitomized in the work of the Americans, Bowles and Gintis (1976). They had developed the notion of the Correspondence Principle, whereby schools in capitalist society were seen to replicate the social relations of production of such societies. The major criticism of this structuralist Marxism is its over-determination of people's behaviour by impenetrable and immutable state institutions - a criticism developed by Willis and the cultural Marxists of the CCCS, who accorded a central role to the choice-making, decision-making of active, rational human beings, an approach derived from the early writings of Marx in *The German Ideology* and *The Grundrisse* and developed in the Marxism of Gramsci.

By extension, the same criticism can be levelled at other Marxists who were influential in the Marxist scholarship of the time, such as Althusser; and it can be further extended to other sociologists deeply influenced by Marx, such as - crucially for our purposes - Bourdieu. Bourdieu's whole thesis on the symbolic violence of schooling, and indeed on the pivotal role played by cultural capital or the lack of it - has been similarly criticised for its over-determination, its refusal or failure to take account of the possibility of social subjects actually determining, at least in part, their own destinies. There appears, according to this criticism, little or no chance to escape the overwhelming power of the processes of exclusion and self-exclusion.

But against Willis's thesis it has been argued, among other things, that his 'lads' represent an atypical section of school pupils and that his thesis cannot be generalized to the whole of the working class. Many working class children are 'earoles' and do not go to school merely to 'have a laff', and yet still end up in working class jobs - or more likely in present economic circumstances, unemployed. His thesis cannot explain their school and subsequent careers. Indeed, in the context of the theme of this paper, it might seem that Willis's analysis is based on precepts much closer to those championing the ESRC notion of exclusion and self-exclusion, with the implication that it was not the school which led to the exclusion and self-exclusion of the 'lads', but their own chosen and active resistance to it.

Willis's thesis, however, is much richer and more complex than this assertion would allow, and he does recognize the massive probability that what schools teach and how, and what employment constraints and possibilities there are, will ensure that working class pupils will not be able to aspire to any significant level of upward occupational mobility. That is to say that the 'lads' at least, unlike the 'earoles', recognize this probability and resist attempts from within the school system to make them misrecognize it. In other words, they see through the concealing veils of Pedagogic Work and exclude themselves from a system they know in all probability will exclude them anyway - and at the same time have the extra benefit of 'having a laff'.

Conclusion

The somewhat arbitrarily selected issues described above could be said to support two basic contentions. First, they appear to validate both Parkin's arguments about collectivist and individualist exclusionary strategies, and Bourdieu's thesis on exclusion and self-exclusion, at the expense of the notions outlined in various research agencies' priorities. But there is also an irony here. It could be argued that development and application of these latter notions are in fact an illustration of the force of Bourdieu's thesis, in that the act of individualizing, marginalizing and rendering pathological those who, through their allegedly *personal* failings, are treated as research problems, presents their exclusion as if it were self-exclusion.

My second contention is that the examples I have used suggest that there may well be a historical development in the applicability of Bourdieu's dual concepts in the sense that, while at the outset the establishment of free compulsory schooling was overtly and explicitly exclusionary, the growth of schooling over the next century incorporated ever more hidden and subtle forms of self-exclusion. And as I have suggested earlier, there appear to be close similarities between such a historical development and the shift Parkin noted from collectivist to individualist strategies. Indeed, current tendencies to deny the relevance of such collective identities as social class, to stress the primacy of free market forces, to treat what were once regarded as public services now as private goods, and to portray society as made up of a vast diversity of individual consumers empowered to choose between commodities, suggest to me at least that more and more emphasis is now being given to the self-exclusion of those apparently unwilling, but in reality often unable, to take advantage of what the market has to offer. The commodification of schooling is a case in point.

References

Bernstein, B. (1975), *Class, Codes and Control, Vol III*, Routledge and Kegan Paul, London.

Bourdieu, P. and J-C. Passeron (1977), *Reproduction in Education, Society and Culture*, Sage, London.

Bowles, S. and H. Gintis (1976), *Schooling in Capitalist America*, Routledge and Kegan Paul, London.

Brown, P. (1997), 'Cultural Capital and Social Exclusion: Some Observations on Recent Trends in Education, Employment and the Labour Market', A. Halsey, *et al.* (eds), *Education: Culture, Economy, Society*, Oxford UP, Oxford, pp. 736-749.

Byrne, E. (1978), *Women and Education*, Tavistock, London.

Carrington, B (1983), 'Sport as a side-track', in L. Barton and S. Walker (eds), *Race, Class and Education*, Croom Helm, Beckenham, pp. 40-65.

Clark, B. (1960), 'The "Cooling-out" Function in Higher Education', *American Journal of Sociology*, LXV, pp. 569-76.

Collins, R. (1976), *The Credential Society: An Historical Sociology of Education and Stratification*, Academic Press, New York.

Crompton, R. and P. Brown. (1994), 'Introduction', in P. Brown and R. Crompton, (eds), *Economic Restructuring and Social Exclusion*, UCL Press, London, pp. 1-13.

Deem, R. (1978), *Women and Schooling*, Routledge and Kegan Paul, London.

Durkheim, E. (1968), *Education and Sociology*, Free Press, New York.

Evans, B. and B. Waites (1981), *IQ and Mental Testing*, Macmillan, London.

Floud, J. and A. Halsey (1961), 'Social Class, Intelligence Tests, and Selection for Secondary Schools', in A. Halsey, J. Floud and C. Anderson (eds), *Education, Economy and Society*, Free Press, New York, pp. 209-215.

Flude, M. and J. Ahier, J. (eds), (1974), *Educability, Schools and Ideology*, Croom Helm, London.

Goffman, E. (1952), 'Cooling the Mark Out: Some Aspects of Adaptation to Failure', *Psychiatry*, XV, pp. 451-63.

Goodacre, E. (1968), *Teachers and their Pupils' Home Background*, National Foundation for Education Research, Slough.

Henderson, P. (1976), 'Class structure and the concept of intelligence', in R. Dale, (ed.), *Schooling and Capitalism*, Routledge and Kegan Paul, London, pp. 142-51.

Holt, J. (1969), *How Children Fail*, Penguin, Harmondsworth.

Kamin, L. (1974), *The Science* and *Politics of I.Q.*, Penguin, Harmondsworth.

Keddie, N. (1971), 'Classroom Knowledge', in M. Young, (ed.), *Knowledge and Control*, Collier-Macmillan, London, pp. 133-60.

Levitas, R. (1996), 'The concept of social exclusion and the new Durkheimian hegemony', *Critical Social Policy*, 46, Vol. 16, pp. 5-20.

Littlewood, P. and I Jönsson (1996), 'Schooling and social justice: Some current trends' in A. Erskine *et al.* (ed.), *Changing Europe: Some aspects of identity, conflict and social justice*, Avebury, Aldershot, pp. 108-132.

Parkin, F. (1974), 'Strategies of Social Closure in Class Formation', in F. Parkin (ed.), *The Social Analysis of Class Structure*, Tavistock, London, pp. 1-18.

Parkin, F. (1979), *Marxism and Class Theory: A Bourgeois Critique*, Tavistock, London.

Ryan, J. (1972), 'IQ - The Illusion of Objectivity', in K. Richardson and D. Spears, (eds), *Race, Culture and Intelligence,* Penguin, Harmondsworth, pp. 36-55.

Silver, H. (1994), 'Social exclusion and social solidarity: Three paradigms', *International Labour Review*, Vol. 133, No. 5-6, pp. 531-578.

Simon, B. (1971), *Intelligence, Psychology and Education*, Lawrence and Wishart, London.

Simon, B. (1974), *The Two Nations and the Educational Structure, 1780-1870*, Lawrence and Wishart, London.

Stanworth, M. (1981), *Gender and Schooling*, Women's Research and Resources Centre, London.

Stoler, A. (1995), *Race and the Education of Desire*, Duke University Press, Durham and London.

Troyna, B. (1987), (ed.), *Racial Inequality in Education*, Tavistock: London.

Weiner, G. (1986), 'Feminist education and equal opportunities: unity or discord?', *British Journal of Sociology of Education*, 7, pp. 265-74.

Willis, P. (1977), *Learning to Labour: How working class kids get working class jobs*, Saxon House, London.

Yépez del Castillo, I. (1994), 'A comparative approach to social exclusion: Lessons from France and Belgium', *International Labour Review*, Vol. 133, No. 5-6, pp. 613-633.

Young, M. (1971), (ed.), *Knowledge and Control*, Collier-Macmillan, London.

10 Citizenship and Exclusion in the European Union

MIKE MCGUINNESS

This chapter examines the consequences of integration in the European Union in relation to varying conceptions of nationality and citizenship, in the context of debates about the creation of a European citizenship. It goes on to explore possible exclusionary outcomes of the process of integration for certain kinds of residents within the Union and of those seeking residence, particularly third country nationals. In doing so I question the feasibility of creating such a thing as a 'real' citizenship of the Union. Roche (1997) uses the term 'social exclusion' as one aspect of a 'constitutional exclusion' and identifies both a broad and a narrow meaning. Narrowly it might refer to problems of poverty and unemployment, with 'social inclusion' linked to policies to try to ameliorate them. In the broader sense it can refer to all forms of discrimination and barriers to social inclusion including political, civil and cultural exclusions, and encompassing racism and ethnic discrimination. European citizenship was developed by the Maastricht Treaty in 1991/92, and endorsed by the Amsterdam Treaty (Maastricht 2) in 1996, and is a developing concept.

The 'deepening' of the European Union has been gaining momentum, especially since 1986 with the passing of the Single European Act and the creation of a Single Market. The representation of this is the Inter Governmental Conference (IGC) which is when the Treaties are enacted. The Amsterdam IGC was the fourth in twelve years but only the sixth in the history of the European Union since its creation as the European Coal and Steel Community (ECSC) in 1950/1951. The latest phase has produced a tension between the twin demands of 'widening' and 'deepening' as the commitment to the enlargement of the Union after the collapse of the Berlin Wall in 1989 is realized. There is enormous pressure to integrate further, as is evidenced by the creation of a European citizenship by the Maastricht Treaty whereby all citizens of member states have rights in other member states. Part of the drive towards this new European citizenship, according to Feldblum (1998), is to generate loyalty to the European Union. This climate of integration will bring with it a range of problems and we might ask whether it is possible to develop a European identity under any circumstances - or do we take the view of Raymond Aron in 1974 that there are no such animals as European citizens (Meehan, 1993)? There is a basic thesis that suggests that a European nationalism or identity, or whatever we may wish to call it, as represented by this attempt at citizenship is hard to find or to develop. Gamberale (1995) goes further and suggests that a major obstacle to the construction of a European identity is the diversity among the national identities of the member states of the Union. As Tassin (1992) states,

> how are we to understand a *community* which gathers under a principle of unity and common identity a number of individuals and groups, which have already been defined and constituted according to territorial, ethnic, socio-economic, cultural and other criteria of belonging, themselves forged in the course of common history? (p. 169)

This diversity is something that is growing with increasing developments towards devolution and regionalism in many parts of the European Union. It is more likely that more local identities will develop as citizenship will not necessarily guarantee equal opportunities for all citizens as it is too narrowly restricted, at the moment, to that which is political.

What is required is a European society which would allow some form of citizenship and identity to develop, but more so a formal citizenship which will allow all European citizens to participate equally in the rights bound up in this concept (Delanty, 1998). Much of this relates to the work of T. H. Marshall, who recognized the different dimensions beyond the traditional concerns about civil rights (Smith and Blanc, 1996). Thus some citizens, or groups of citizens, will not be able to participate fully in the broader citizenship in an economic, social, civil, cultural or political sense. There is thus a social exclusion for some groups in the EU at a time when moves are being made towards the greater inclusion of citizens. Attached to this debate is the extent to which non-member state citizens, or third country nationals who are resident in the member states, will be able to participate in this citizenship and will not find themselves discriminated against or socially excluded. Citizenship is a key issue in defining those groups who are excluded from the above rights and they have been described as 'outsiders' (Smith and Wistrich, 1997). A further category of 'outsider', who may have fewer rights and even less participation as citizenship and integration develops, are refugees, asylum seekers and immigrants. They will also find it more difficult to get into the member states as the external border tightens (note the 'Fortress Europe' debate) as the internal borders are loosened (via Schengen and the various Treaties). This is a lively debate and Jost Halfmann (1997) considers this question from the perspective of dilemmas of citizenship developing in Germany after unification, and Ian Ward (1997) takes a broader view by looking at who is defined by law as a 'European'. This is an open-ended debate as another part of the equation is to consider how far it is possible to see nations within the Union being prepared to give up their sovereignty to a supranational body, in Brussels or elsewhere.

The European Union has started along the tortuous path of attempting to integrate the member states and to set a pattern for the enlargement of the Union into the twenty-first century. Part of this process is the establishment of clear citizenship rights for all of its citizens. In the Preamble to the 1992 Treaty on European Union, otherwise known as the Maastricht Treaty, the Heads of State, amongst other things, resolved to establish a citizenship common to the nationals of their countries; and they reaffirmed their objectives to facilitate the free movement of persons while ensuring the safety and security of their peoples. Specifically under Article 8 of the Treaty it says that every person holding the nationality of a Member State shall be a citizen of the Union and shall enjoy the rights conferred by the Treaty and will be subject to the duties involved. This involves the right to move and reside freely within the territory of member states (Article 8a) and the right to vote and stand in elections in the local (municipal) and European elections in the Member State in which they reside (Article 8b). Further there is the right to protection by diplomatic or consular staff in the territory of a third country by the staff of any Member State on the same basis as their nationals (Article 8c). There is a right to petition the European Parliament and use the services of an Ombudsman (Article 8d). A final provision states that provisions may be adopted to strengthen or add to the above as a means of further developing this citizenship (Article 8e). These lofty aims are part of a longer term programme of moving towards a more integrated Europe, building upon the developments started when the first six states came together in the 1950s. What is clear is that the provisions produced in the Treaties deal solely with the political role of citizenship and have, at this stage, ignored other areas, as indicated by Smith and Blanc (1996).

Integration

One of the problems with this debate is that there is a lot of potential confusion about the term 'integration' or the 'deepening' of the Union, especially if one is looking at it from a British perspective. It is increasingly obvious that more citizens and states are getting cold feet as we move towards a new stage in the process (Franklin, Marsh and McLaren, 1994). Initially, at least, integration was taken to mean an integration of national economies. Stephen George (1991), however, suggests that for many Europeans outside Britain this is only one aspect of a wider process that will eventually involve the integration of national political systems. The Schumann declaration of the 9th May 1950 stated that the intention of establishing the co-operation in coal and steel production was to 'build the first concrete foundation of a European federation which is indispensable to the preservation of peace' (Pinder 1998). In trying to arrive at a definition of integration Brigid Laffan (1992) saw it as a process for the creation of political communities and as a process of transforming previously separate units into components of a coherent system. In moving towards a more formally integrated structure it has created a counter-reaction, despite the relatively low level of integration at the moment.

But one still has to ask how far it is possible to create a European identity that can be transformed into a European nationalism (note Aron above). Tonra and Dunne (1997) consider that while most people appreciate the value of building a European identity, distrust remains. This distrust is based on two emotive deterrents: the threat to national sovereignty and the threat to national identity. In the former case, sovereignty is a legal concept which has a hold on national consciousness; but national *identity* is more pervasive, in that many Europeans can only comprehend the Union in terms of the nation state. In some ways a European 'national' identity is the most difficult thing to achieve and, despite the moves towards economic integration, both official and unofficial, the political dimension is proving to be problematic. In some cases it is the thought of a premeditated construction of European identity that evokes either 'hope or hostility' in European debates (Tonra and Dunne, 1997). Even during the 1994 European elections it was suggested that most election campaigns were fought in predominantly a national rather than a European context. They were more about national rather than European issues, in particular the general performance of the respective member state governments. Indeed the only campaigns on European issues seem to have come from the anti-Maastricht parties in Germany, Britain, Denmark and France with, for example, the British Conservatives attacking the 'federalist' positions of the Labour and Liberal Democrat opposition parties, and attacks in Germany on Chancellor Kohl's European record (Pinder, 1994). The European Parliamentary elections can be seen as 'second-order' elections, and as long as the national party agenda remains pre-eminent in the minds of parties and voters, European Parliamentary elections must be seen as events dependent on a national political agenda (Reiff and Schmitt, 1980).

Haas (1993) goes as far as to suggest that the only way to achieve an authentic identity is where a state-building tradition precedes the growth of nationalism, that is where the state 'built the nation' (p. 518). If there is to be any way forward for the European Union then it may be necessary to attempt to forge an identity amongst the diverse nations making up the Union at the moment. But he goes further by suggesting that multi-cultural settings are inhospitable to the establishment of nation states, if this is the intention of the European Union. The idea of a European identity replacing loyalty to separate nation states is a bit fanciful, and has been strongly resisted by such diverse figures as Margaret Thatcher and Charles de Gaulle. Even the development of multiple loyalties '...in which the mental maps of European citizens would add an additional dimension to those national and regional loyalties they already possessed...' has also not been realised (Wallace, 1990, p. 17). The notion of European identity is also linked to the concept of citizenship as developed in the Maastricht Treaty, whereby the view that we are all European citizens seems to be focused on concerns about one's political status, that is, the right to vote outside one's own member state and to approach the European Ombudsman (Church and Phinnemore, 1994). It seems more likely that the 'citizens' of the Union are, at the moment, unaware generally of their 'citizenship', and the battle to create an identity will take a long time. Developments in the opposite direction seem to be taking place, with the creation of a more 'local' awareness or identity, especially as there are perceived threats from outside the Union and as inequalities develop between regions.

Citizenship

Citizenship can come in many forms and for the purposes of this debate we may, for example, consider the attempts to get people more involved in society as good citizens, developing activities with youth organizations where one may acquire a citizenship badge, as well as a broader societal debate, which has gone on for many years, about what it actually is. Definitions of citizenship are generally relatively easy to find, although no attempt is made in the Treaties which deal with citizenship to produce such a definition. A standard approach is that provided by Roberts and Edwards (1991) who describe the position of a citizen as:

> ... a member of a state entitled to such civil and political rights as exist in that state, and owing obligation in respect of those rights, as contrasted with others, including residents, who do not possess such rights or obligations. The extent to which citizenship is conferred depends on the state and its regime......Citizenship can be distinguished from nationality: not all citizens will also possess the rights of 'nationals' within a state (p. 16).

That is, traditional citizenship has meant full membership in a polity, normally the nation state, and institutionalized by rights, benefits and obligations that distinguish members from non-members (Feldblum, 1998). More specifically Barbalet (1988) suggests that citizenship is as old as settled human communities and defines those who are, and who are not, members of a common society. Putting it more simply, he says that citizenship can readily be described as 'participation in or membership of a community' but different types of community give rise to different forms of citizenship. It constitutes a legal relationship between the state and a person or group of persons which is usually exclusive, permanent and immediate. This can be described as political inclusion in that citizenship is inclusion into the state (Halfmann, 1997). Baykan (1997) suggests that citizenship can also be defined as a set of practices which define a person as a 'competent member of society' and which shapes the flow of resources to persons or social groups. Barbalet (1988) takes this further and argues that at a time when all persons are conceived of as being equal before the law as citizens, as defined above, the provision of citizenship across the lines dividing unequal classes or groups is likely to mean that the practical ability to exercise rights or legal capacities which constitute the status of citizen will not be available to all who possess them. That is, although in theory we can all share in citizenship rights, in practice gross inequalities persist.

With the creation of a European citizenship one would hope that the inclusion of all citizens would apply but, again using Raymond Aron (and Barbalet's comment above concerning the possibility of inequality), how far is such a citizenship either logically impossible or politically unlikely?

In 1974 Aron wrote a searching article titled 'Is multinational citizenship possible?' (reprinted in Meehan, 1993), indicating the difficulties associated with attempting to develop such a citizenship. The main points of his argument were as follows. First, national and Community (Union) authorities provide sets of rights of a different order from one another. Second, European citizenship involves a transfer of legal and political powers from the national to the European Community (Union) level. Third, citizens can insist that a nation-state respect their rights because the state can demand that citizens fulfil their duties to defend the state, whereas there is not an inter- or multi-national polity which has such authority. Fourth, in 1974 there was no popular demand for a European federation which would be simultaneously responsible for legal-political rights and economic regulation, and which could command duties from its citizens. One has to consider how relevant this fourth statement is in the 1990s, as the European Union takes further and more rapid steps towards integration.

In general terms the approach to integration has not been greeted enthusiastically in a number of ways. The Maastricht Treaty stepped away from federalism and substituted subsidiarity; referendums across Europe, but especially in France and Denmark, have been less than enthusiastic; the German Constitutional Court only allowed Maastricht to be ratified because it did not take away the sovereignty of the German state; and some states have 'rejected' membership, at least for the moment, e.g. Norway, Switzerland and Malta. How many of Aron's concerns can be related to these events? There is little doubt about the enthusiasms of the political elites, but ultimately it is the consent of the peoples of Europe that needs to be considered.

As indicated earlier, the Maastricht Treaty affirmed that every national of a member state 'shall be a citizen of the Union' and 'shall enjoy the rights conferred by this treaty and be subject to the duties imposed thereby'. Although the Treaty contains this important section on European citizenship, the provisions are essentially concerned with directly political matters. Apart from reinforcing existing mobility rights, the treaty itself contains little that is relevant to, for example, industrial or economic aspects of citizenship (Grahl and Teague, 1994). Roche and van Berkel (1997) argue that pressures are being applied to promote both economic and non-economic (that is political and social) forms of interdependence and integration, but it is the economic logic of the integration process which is the main concern. There is, however, a perceived need to legitimize and popularize the Union in the eyes of the 'peoples of Europe' by 'constitutionalizing' and democratizing the relations between the people and the institutions.

The EU had already established a multitude of rights in the economic and related social fields but the treaty neglected to make clear to the citizens what such rights might be (Pinder, 1995). Interestingly, in the nineteenth century Karl Marx insisted that mere political emancipation in citizenship is inadequate and advocated a general human emancipation in which persons are freed from the determining power of private property and its associated institutions (Barbalet, 1988). This is not likely to be the situation we will find in the European Union as the main integrative pressure is the perceived need, according to the political, economic and bureaucratic elites in Europe, to respond '...constructively to the new techno-economic logic of globalized and high technology capitalism' (Roche and Van Berkel, 1997, p. xxi). It is in this environment where the potential for exclusion, social or otherwise, is likely. There need to be compensatory developments between the move towards economic and monetary union, and a political process to build a democratic and social union; otherwise exclusion will be made worse (Roche, 1997).

Citizenship offers a more varied account than merely political rights and it is because of the implications of a 'deepened' Union that more questions have been asked. A lot of interest has been rekindled in the work of T. H. Marshall who considered the broader aspects of citizenship. His definition of citizenship has been considered as the most popular, at least in British social science, and can be simply described as membership in a community (Anthias and Yuval-Davis, 1993), or in Marshall's terms it is actually 'full' membership of a community and a mechanism for social inclusion (Halfmann, 1997). But how far does citizenship convey with it an equality of rights and opportunity for all people within the Union in more than just political terms? In *Citizenship and Social Class and Other Essays* (1950), Marshall presents a relatively conventional view of citizenship, in that citizenship is a status attached to full membership of a community, and those who possess this status are equal with respect to rights and duties associated with it. He further identifies three distinct parts or elements of citizenship arising in English society at different historical times, civil, political and social. Civil citizenship is composed of rights necessary for individual freedom, and the institution most directly associated with it is the Rule of Law and the system of courts and is rooted in the eighteenth century. Political citizenship consists of the right to participate in the exercise of political power and it is usually associated with Parliamentary institutions and is rooted in the nineteenth century. Social citizenship is made up of the right to the prevailing standard of life and the social heritage of the society associated with social services and education, and is rooted in the twentieth century.

On the surface these seem straightforward but Bryan Turner (1992) says that at the heart of Marshall's account of citizenship lies the contradiction between the formal political equality of the franchise and the persistence of extensive social and economic inequality. Turner also adds to this the cultural dimension and emphasizes that citizenship is a complex set of social practices (see Baykan, 1997 and Delgado-Moreira, 1997 for a general discussion of this). In attempting to integrate the 15 member states, with more to follow as the European Union enlarges in the twenty-first century, it is difficult to imagine how it will be possible to ensure that all elements are adequately fulfilled in the type of Europe we have now. Marshall, according to Turner (1992), fails to produce a theory of the state alongside his theory of citizenship, making the maintenance of citizenship more difficult. As it is the state which implicitly provides the principal element in the 'maintenance and development of social rights' then this is the political instrument through which political movements seek to redress their circumstances. Baykan (1997) states that these definitions of citizenship place the concept squarely in the debate about inequality, power differences and social class, since citizenship is 'inevitably and necessarily bound up with the problem of the unequal distribution of resources in society' (pp. 62-63).

Further assessments of this have been considered by John Pinder (1995) where he treats European citizenship as an uncompleted project. The political element seems relatively easy to achieve as rights associated with voting and participation are more tangible. He looks at Marshall's elements in turn and tries to assess how effectively the European Union has been able to deal with them. As far as civil citizenship is concerned, secured through the Rule of Law, he feels that it has been created in as far as it guarantees a wide range of economic and social civil rights. These are the rights necessary for individual freedom - liberty of the person, freedom of speech, thought and faith, the right to own property and to conclude valid contracts, and the right to justice (Marshall as discussed in Twine, 1994). This stems from the principles of freedom to buy, sell, invest, establish economic activities or seek and obtain work throughout the Community regardless of frontiers and without discrimination on grounds of nationality. This is enforced by the Rule of Law, and the European Court of Justice in Luxembourg, on the basis that all citizens are equal before the law for all EU purposes.

The issue here is that if the law is to be applied even-handedly to all EU citizens, it has to have primacy over any of the laws of member states that may run counter to it. How far is it then possible to expect member states to countenance laws that contravene the rights and freedoms guaranteed under their constitutional traditions? Equally there is the problem as to how far citizens of the member states will want their rights and freedoms to be entrusted to a new and higher authority. Inevitably there are major gaps in this process causing tensions between the levels of government in the EU. Jurisdiction of the Court of Justice is confined to the Community/Union treaties and there is a question as to how far it should go, perhaps by introducing the European Convention on Human Rights over its jurisdiction. Although the EU requires all member states to be democratic as a condition of membership, there is no guarantee that rights and freedoms will be applied.

Pinder (1995) also observes that political citizenship in Marshall's sense is still underdeveloped as the Rule of Law without representative government is an anomaly. Thus, a European citizenship lacks legitimacy without an effective parliamentary structure. Although recommendations were made by Spain in 1989 to give the European Parliament equal powers with the Council of Ministers after Maastricht to overcome the democratic deficit, this was not achieved. Maastricht only went as far as extending voting rights to vote in local and European elections to citizens of member states resident in another member state. What is missing is crucially the right to vote in national elections in the country of residence. This would give the European citizen a clear role in that society and would reflect true citizenship rights as long as the European level institutions, especially the European Parliament, remain not as powerful as the national parliaments. However, this is a controversial debate as to how far it is possible to allow the European level powers to grow and to move away from the 'second-order' nature of European elections (see Reiff and Schmitt, 1980) This is also not surprising when we consider that the European Parliament, despite being given increased roles, is still not a true Parliament. Fulvio Attiná (1990) stated,

> When we think of a Parliament in a democracy, we think of an elective institution that legislates and controls other political institutions - an assembly of representatives... we speak of parliamentary accountability... In the case of the European Parliament, such political and institutional requisites are missing (p. 557).

Attiná's assessment of the European parliament helps explain the negative attitudes towards European institutions and which thus works against the development of a European civil society. Elections to the European Parliament have reflected this negativity as we note that the average turnout fell from 62 per cent in 1979 (the first elected European Parliament) to 56.4 per cent in 1994. It is possible to argue that this figure may be significantly overstated as in two states, Belgium and Luxembourg, voting is compulsory. In most cases, including Belgium and Luxembourg, there has been a fall in the turnout (although the United Kingdom has shown a steady, if small, rise in turnout over the four elections). As long as the European Parliamentary elections do not offer the prospect of a change in government, switches in policy or the making and unmaking of reputations, then negative attitudes towards the institutions are likely to continue. Further, the possession of a political citizenship, or at least some rights, has little validity as the chamber generally lacks an effective representative role.

The concept of social citizenship relates to the need for positive integration. The single market, created after the 1986 Single European Act, required the removal of barriers to economic transactions across borders, but it also requires a parallel development of welfare integration. How far this can be developed is limited somewhat as the Maastricht Treaty emphasized that decisions should be taken as closely as possible to the citizens. This notion of subsidiarity can conflict with the idea that there are common problems that may be better dealt with on a broader level, for example unemployment; but actions by member states may have a knock-on effect in other states. Jacques Delors's attempt to develop a Union-wide approach to this with the White Paper, 'Growth, Competitiveness, Employment: The challenges and the way forward into the 21st Century' in 1994 was not universally supported.

What needs to be recognized are the potential problems that can develop as states and citizens look inwardly instead of Community-wide. Marshall considered that social rights of citizenship should be regarded as providing an equality of status that cuts across social classes and, more importantly, civil and political rights must be supported by social rights. If they are not then the 'three legged stool of citizenship', as he called it, will be unbalanced (Twine, 1994). Closa (1995) suggests that although social rights mark the final stage in the development of citizenship, Marshall failed to take into account the possibility of a setback - for example, a crisis in the welfare state which may then imply a crisis for social citizenship.

The position of third country nationals

Citizenship is an issue which has emerged in recent times as the borders between states begin to fall, but it must be clearly distinguished from nationality. According to Closa (1995) the concept of nationality derives from 'nation' which in turn derives from *nascere*, to be born. Thus it is an undetermined attribute of a person generally ascribed at birth. Citizenship, on the other hand, has a history which not only involves inclusion but is also marked by the exclusion of certain categories of individuals. The issue of citizenship has assumed ideological as well as political significance and is at the root of a great deal of conflict. The possession of citizenship will take on greater importance as the Union develops, given the tension between the European Union's commitment to human rights *per se*, and its concern to protect its own citizens relative to non-EU nationals. For citizens of the European Union there are certain rights and/or obligations that obtain to that notion of citizenship. Both the Maastricht Treaty of 1991-1992, and the Single European Act of 1986 (developing the 1957 Treaty of Rome provision) promoted and developed the idea of a 'free' movement of goods, capital, services and, importantly, persons; but King (1993) sees this as a movement for some whilst at the same time restricting 'outsiders'. An immediate result of this is the impact it has on the position of residents within member states who are not citizens of one of the member states - that is, are third country nationals. They will find their status being adversely affected with the Europeanization of rights and the consequences for the treatment of 'outsiders'.

Adrian Favell (1998) provides an interesting discussion on the Europeanization of immigration politics whereby migrants and minorities can no longer be seen as immigrants who will eventually be integrated into their host nations. Third country nationals are unable to exert political pressure to ensure their rights to free movement, etc., are included in the new provisions of citizenship. Citizenship status is a key issue in defining those groups who are excluded from social welfare, from political representation and from civil rights. It is a study of the position of third country nationals which allows an evaluation of the meaning of social exclusion and clarifies the nature of citizenship. That is, a look at what Deakin (1969) called 'the outsider... the minority' (see Smith and Blanc, 1996, p. 70, and Smith and Wistrich, 1997, p. 229). Central to the concept of the Union is the free movement of citizens, initially that of workers, and it is an important issue of democracy and human rights for the minorities who are not citizens of member states. Free movement within the EU for all member state citizens may be won *at the expense of* third country nationals, who could face threats to their rights of entry, mobility within the Union and access to jobs, benefits and general security of life. It is the abolition or relaxation of internal frontiers that has created increasingly strict external control, as, it could be suggested, is entailed by the Schengen Agreement of 1985.

The Schengen process has had the function of distinguishing those who 'belong' from those who are outsiders, and thus its function is to exclude others. How far is it the case that a person who does not possess the nationality of one of the member states will be excluded from the rights which are presently bestowed upon Union citizens (see d'Oliveira, 1995)? Betz (1993), writing before the full implications of the Maastricht Treaty were realized, suggested that the European Community (Union) had contributed to a two-track status of residence and citizenship. It has become relatively easy for European Union citizens to move across borders but non-European Union citizens find it increasingly difficult to enter and find employment. He cites Craig Whitney in the *New York Times* of December 29th 1991 who said of the European Union that '.......its walls are intended to keep out people...' but, ironically, not commodities (pp. 195-196). It is of concern that third country nationals are not only being excluded from a wide range of rights but that the situation is developing in a climate of xenophobia and growing racism. The situation is further complicated by the fact that some non-citizens have rights which are denied to other non- citizens, for example nationals of European Economic Area (EEA) countries like Norway (d'Oliveira, 1995). An interpretation of this might suggest some form of discrimination that tends to exclude more easily citizens of non-white states.

The Schengen Agreement has as its goal the creation of a Europe free of internal borders, as set out in the Single European Act, and to create a *citizens' Europe*. This goal was originally taken up by Chancellor Kohl of Germany and President Mitterrand of France, with the aim of accelerating the process and acting as a trend-setter (Schutte, 1991). In 1985 the under-secretaries for Foreign Affairs of Belgium, Luxembourg, the Netherlands, France and Germany came together to sign an agreement on the gradual abolition of checks at their common borders. They were later joined by Spain and Portugal. This is somewhat problematic as it is an illustration of what we might describe as a 'two speed' Europe; that is, it is outside the Union framework but it is within the Union orbit in the sense that all of its members are members of the Union. But it has only been achieved by 7 of the 15 member states (CMLR, 1995).

The rationale behind the agreement is the notion of 'compensatory measures', that is, when the borders are opened to the free flow of people and goods, internal security can only be maintained if the border controls are compensated for by the introduction of alternative measures. Conversely, compensatory measures in the form of intensified internal controls should not be implemented until the external borders have been removed (Ahnfelt and From, 1993). The fear is that this will increase actions against visible minorities as more frequent internal non-frontier controls are introduced as a means of dealing with the perceived growth of international organized crime, the problem of drugs and terrorists and illegal immigration (CMLR, 1995). Indeed, the Contracting Parties have undertaken to criminalize illegal immigration (Schutte, 1991). A relevant feature of the agreement is in relation to the free movement or circulation of aliens within the territory of the contracting parties. The Implementing Convention (its proper title) defines aliens as persons other than nationals of a member state, thus nationals of member states not party to the convention are *not* constituted as aliens (Schutte, 1991).

Within the Convention there is the development of a European Union concept of territoriality, a process of integration which has become more holistic, with internal and external policies intended to transform the spatial reference of the populations of the nation states towards the European system boundaries (see Magone, 1994), which has major implications. In attempting to remove the psychological barriers between member states in terms of boundaries it appears to be creating different outcomes from those intended. On the one hand there is the reaction against this loss of identity, even when accepting some of the economic advantages which go along with it; and on the other hand there is the reaction against the process of immigration from outside the European Union. It is, as indicated above, such immigrant groups who will find their citizenship rights most severely affected.

The definition of nationality is at the heart of some of the problems encountered by the minorities, the 'outsiders'. The determination of citizenship depends upon the determination of nationality that is in the hands of the member States. This nationality, according to the Treaty on European Union (Maastricht), is settled solely by reference to the national law of the member state concerned. However, the creation, albeit in a rudimentary form, of a community of states marks a significant departure from the traditional link between nationality and citizenship in the nation state. According to d'Oliveira (1995) it represents a loosening of the 'metaphysical ties between persons and a state and forms a symptom of cosmopolitization of citizenship' (p. 83). The problem with this is that it will potentially produce inequalities in rights, since there are great variations in the way in which states of the European Union allow third country nationals to acquire citizenship (see Closa, 1995). Germany represents an extreme case in having a restrictive system which makes it difficult for such people to become naturalized even when they were born in the country. This has been highlighted by the position of the Turkish population in Germany which has become established but has had great difficulty in obtaining citizenship. A series of violent reactions against Turks and other groups, especially asylum seekers and refugees, has highlighted the issue that there is not necessarily a political majority in favour of easing their path to naturalization. Jurgen Habermas said in 1993 that they 'live in the paradoxical role of Germans with foreign passports' (Smith and Blanc, 1996, p. 76).

In other states naturalization is a much easier process; or nationality and citizenship is gained by place of birth or territory, as in the case of colonies. Despite the problems which may develop because of the disparities there is no Union mechanism or attempt to harmonize the acquisition of citizenship (Closa, 1995). Equally Betz (1993) suggested that with the strengthening of the external borders (associated with the debate about Fortress Europe), the European Union needs to arrive at a comprehensive immigration policy. He goes as far as to suggest that a Europe without internal borders can only become a reality if there is an agreement on this issue.

Conclusion

One of the concerns of this chapter has been a worry that a 'drift' had taken place towards the 1996 Intergovernmental Conference and it may have produced less commitment to the dream of Schumann and others for an integrated Europe with peace and harmony as the basic themes. The Amsterdam Treaty, despite reiterating the concept of European citizenship and pushing the aims of a Single Currency, has not developed the concept of a European citizen any further than at the administrative level. Despite the surface enthusiasm for the Euro, it illustrates, once again, the conflict between the elite and the popular perceptions of European integration. The politicians have embraced the ideas wholeheartedly, in most cases, but citizens in the member states remain to be convinced. The national perspective still has a hold on many European citizens' assessment of

European integration or disintegration. Nevertheless there is an accepted view that what has been produced is a significant period of peace with no physical conflict between nations in Europe, (ignoring, that is, the internal conflict in the former Yugoslavia). This is not to say that there are no tensions existing between member states of the European Union or that there are no tensions within states.

The myth of 'shared nationality' (Goodin, 1995) comes more strongly to the fore as we move towards a more integrated future, a 'deepening' of the Union. This works in conflicting. First, within states there are growing demands for the independence or recognition of minorities or nations, that is (as with the Scottish National Party in the United Kingdom), for independence in the European Union. There is the recognition that power, policy and decision-making are moving away from the nation state towards a more concentrated and centralized Union. Second, there is pressure to bring together the states of Europe into a closer relationship with a European identity, while still recognizing and acknowledging the cultural diversity of Europe. Both of these competing tensions have the ability to fuel the nationalistic, xenophobic and racist tendencies inherent within all societies. What impact this might have on citizenship is not entirely clear as the whole thing is in the process of developing and we have little experience of how this might work out in the future.

At the start of this chapter it was suggested that Aron's assertion that there is no such animal as a European citizen seemed a little dated since a form of citizenship has since been created. But, as Ward (1997) states, the issues of nationality and citizenship are intimately bound up with the question of exclusion and inclusion and, as much of this is linked to the idea of 'privilege', it ensures that some citizens will be excluded. It is a matter of how effectively policies can be put into place to ensure that all can participate fully in the process, assuming that this is not a forlorn hope. Jo Shaw (1997) makes the point that there is a consistent gap between rhetoric and concrete proposals on citizenship in the European Union. Drawing heavily on the work of Gráinne de Búrca, she warns that although citizenship has had a central place in the proposals for enhancing the legitimacy of the Union, it is not necessarily effective. In fact, the suggestion is, again from de Búrca, that citizenship is not necessarily an integrative force and may indeed be exclusionary and divisive. This is partly because it is so effectively linked to the notion of member state nationality as the basis of European citizenship, thus excluding third country nationals even where they are lawfully established and contributing to the 'economic health and wealth of the Union'. Thus they have no European rights despite contributing to its development via, for example, taxation and the Common Agricultural Policy.

At all levels the notion of citizenship can be questioned and Percy B Lehning (1997) asks whether European citizenship is just a 'mirage'. For him the difficulty starts with the basic debate as to whether the European Union is to be conceived of as an association of states with some political independence, or as a representative of a single people. Further, it has been suggested that the emphasis has been mainly economic via the Single Market and in this context a shared citizenship identity is not necessarily required. If it is the former structure rather than the latter, through the idea of subsidiarity (although what this means is also open to debate), then it is likely that all citizens will not necessarily be equally treated across the Union. The more matters are left in the hands of the member states, then the more likely it is that some groups will be excluded and inequalities will develop across Europe. This is assuming that the thrust of European integration is to ensure that all citizens share equally in the process. As was discussed earlier there are those who will be excluded as a clear boundary is drawn between members of the Union and the rest of the world. Increasingly member states of the European Union are tightening their borders and making it more difficult for various groups, for example immigrants (legal or illegal), refugees and asylum seekers, to get in. Even when having gained access their status is still inferior since, as they do not possess citizenship of the member state even if they may possess rights and can participate in the society, they are therefore excluded from European citizenship and all of the rights that this offers.

The exclusion, social or otherwise, of the above groups should be a major factor in discussions about European citizenship. As indicated above, it is not clear that those people possessing full citizenship of a member state will be able to enjoy a full citizenship across the Union, apart from the partially political, using Marshall's categories. It is especially difficult for those residents of member states, whether new or established, who hold the citizenship of a third country to have any of the rights enjoyed by their neighbours. To achieve these rights, new definitions of citizenship, separating it from nationality, may have to be developed, providing equality of treatment for all citizens legally residing in member states (Venables, as cited in Smith and Blanc, 1996). This model has been proposed by the European Migrants' Forum and involves each individual retaining the nationality of their original nation state. If permanently resident in a member state, under criteria to be defined, they would be allowed to qualify as new and established citizens of the European Union and would thus be entitled to European citizenship irrespective of nationality (Smith and Wistrich, 1997). A broad recognition of these rights would have to be backed up by legislation, especially in the area of racial discrimination, to ensure that all persons in the above category, who are for historical reasons most likely to be non-white, can actually enjoy them.

At the Union level, however, this recognition has been very slow to develop and we are only just seeing the emergence of the first recommendations for national obligations. But since the publication of the Evrigenis Report in 1985 (Report on the Findings of the Committee of Enquiry into Racism and Fascism in Europe) there has been a growing awareness of the problem. This has culminated in the Kahn Report (Report of the Consultative Committee on Racism and Xenophobia) in November 1994 following the Corfu Summit of July 1994. The speed of their deliberations was heightened by their view that this was an extreme problem that had to be dealt with to ensure the stability of the Union. One of their recommendations was that immigrants, or third country nationals, who had been legally resident in the European Union for at least five years should enjoy the same rights and duties and freedom of movement as Union citizens, thus sharing in a European citizenship (see Carvel, 1995).

But the Kahn Report has so far met with little response. It was stated at the time that the heads of government would find it difficult to ignore this as part of the Maastricht review, that is, the Amsterdam Summit, but that is what they did. A European Citizenship for all of the peoples of Europe is still a long way off - if, indeed, it can ever be achieved. Europe, and its identity, can only spring from a denationalization of states and the development of a non-national political community that will incorporate all peoples, including third country citizens resident in member states (see Tassin 1992). There is little doubt that 'Fortress Europe' is beginning to develop and that, unless strong action is taken now, the position of third country nationals will be that of the excluded: excluded in that they will have great difficulty gaining entry to the Union; excluded in that they will not have the same rights as those afforded to the holders of European citizenship; and excluded in that, as Roche (1997) suggests, they will encounter forms of discrimination including racism.

References

Ahnfelt, E and J. From (1993), 'European Policing', in S. Andersen and J. Eliassen, (eds), *Making Policy in Europe. The Europeification of National Policy Making*, Sage, London.

Anthias, F., N. Yuval-Davis, *et al.* (eds), (1993), 'Whose Nation? Whose State? Racial/ethnic divisions and "the nation"', in F. Anthias and N. Yuval-Davis (eds), *Racialized Boundaries. Race, nation, gender, colour and class and the anti racist struggle*, Routledge, London.

Attiná F. (1990), 'The Voting Behaviour of the European Parliament members and the problem of Europarties', *European Journal of Political Research*, Vol. 18. No. 5, September, pp. 557-579.

Barbalet, J. M. (1988), *Citizenship*, Open University, Milton Keynes.

Baykan, A., (1997), 'Issues of Difference and Citizenship for 'New Identities': A Theoretical View', *Innovation. The European Journal of Social Sciences*, Vol. 10, No, 1, pp. 61-67.

Betz, H-G. (1993), 'Fortress Europe or Promised Land?' in A. Cafruny and G. Rosenthal (eds), *The State of the European Community. Vol. 2: The Maastricht Debates and Beyond*, Lynne Reiner Publishers/Longman Boulder, Colorado/Harlow, Essex.

Carvel, J. (1995), 'EU must join the fight against racism', *The Guardian*, 2nd May.

Church, C. and D. Phinnemore (1994), *European Union and European Community. A Handbook and Commentary on the Post Maastricht Treaties*, Harvester Wheatsheaf, London.

Closa, C. (1995), 'Citizenship of the Union and Nationality of Member States', *Common Market Law Review*, Vol. 32, No. 2, May, pp. 487-518.

CMLR (1995) Editorial. 'Schengen: The pros and cons', *Common Market Law Review*, Vol. 32, pp. 673-678.

Delanty, G. (1998), 'Social Theory and European Transformation: Is there a European Society?', *Sociological Research Online*, Vol. 3, No. 1, http://www.socresonline.org.uk/socresonline/3/1/1.html

Delgado-Moreira, J. (1997), 'Cultural Citizenship and the Creation of European Identity', *Electronic Journal of Sociology*, Vol. 2, No. 3, http://www.sociology.org/vol002.003/delgado-moreira.article.1997.html.

d'Oliveira, H. (1995), 'Union Citizenship: Pie in the Sky?', in A. Rosas and E. Antola, (eds), *A Citizens' Europe. In Search of a New Order*, Sage, London.

Favell, A. (1998), 'The Europeanisation of immigration politics' *European Integration online Papers* Vol 2. No 10 http://eiop.or.at/eiop/texte/1998-010a.htm

Feldblum, M. (1998), 'Reconfiguring Citizenship in Western Europe' in C. Joppke (ed.), *Challenge to the Nation-State. Immigration in Western Europe and the United States*, Oxford University Press, Oxford.

Franklin, M, M. Marsh and L. McLaren (1994), 'Uncorking the Bottle: Popular Opposition to European Unification in the Wake of Maastricht'. *Journal of Common Market Studies*, Vol. 32, No. 4, December. pp. 455-472.

Gamberale, C. (1995), 'National Identities and Citizenship in the European Union, *European Public Law,* Vol. 1, No. 4, December, pp. 633-661.

George, S. (1991), *Britain and European Integration since 1945,* Blackwell, Oxford.

Goodin, R. (1995), 'Conjectures on the Nation State', *Government and Opposition*, Vol. 30, No. 1, Winter, pp. 26-34.

Grahl, J. and P. Teague (1994), 'Economic Citizenship in the New Europe' *Political Quarterly*, Vol. 65, No. 4, October -December, pp. 379-396.

Haas, E. (1993), 'Nationalism: An Instrumental Social Construction', *Millennium: Journal of International Studies*, Vol. 22, No. 3, pp. 505-545.

Halfmann, J. (1997), 'Immigration and Citizenship in Germany: Contemporary Dilemmas', *Political Studies*, Vol. 45, No. 2, pp. 200-274.

King, M. (1993), 'The impact of Western European border policies on the control of "refugees" in Eastern and Central Europe', *New Community*, Vol. 19, No. 2, January, pp. 183-199.

Laffan, B. (1992), *Integration and Co-operation in Europe,* Routledge/UACES, London.

Lehning, P. B. (1997), 'European Citizenship: A mirage?', in P. B. Lehning, and A. Weale (eds), *Citizenship, Democracy and Justice in the New Europe*, Routledge, London.

Magone, J. (1994), 'The Territorial Politics of the European Union and Southern Europe (1986-1994): The rise of Regionalist and Nationalist Politics', Unpublished paper - conference 'Beyond Boundaries? Citizens, Cultures and Languages in the New Europe', University of Salford, 11-12 November.

Marshall, T. H. (1950), *Citizenship and Social Class and Other Essays*, Cambridge University Press, Cambridge.

Meehan, E. (1993), *Citizenship in the European Community*, Sage, London.

Pinder, J. (1994), 'The European Elections of 1994 and the future of the European Union', *Government and Opposition*, Vol. 29, No. 4, Autumn, pp. 494-514.

Pinder, J. (1995), 'European Citizenship: a project in need of completion', *Political Quarterly Supplement: Reinventing Collective Action: From the Global to the Local*, pp. 112-122.

Pinder, J. (1998), *The Building of the European Union*, Oxford University Press, Oxford.

Reif, K and H. Schmitt (1980), 'Nine Second-Order National Elections: A Conceptual Framework for the Analysis of European Election Results', *European Journal of Political Research*, Vol. 8, No. 1, pp. 3-44.

Roberts, R. and A. Edwards (1991), *A New Dictionary of Political Analysis*, Edward Arnold, London.

Roche, M. (1997), 'Citizenship and Exclusion: Reconstructing the European Union, in M. Roche and R. van Berkel (eds), *European Citizenship and Social Exclusion*, Ashgate, Aldershot.

Roche, M. and R. van Berkel (1997), 'European Citizenship and Social Exclusion. An Introduction' in M. Roche and R. van Berkel (eds), *European Citizenship and Social Exclusion*, Ashgate, Aldershot.

Schutte, J. (1991), 'Schengen: Its Meaning for the Free Movement of Persons in Europe', *Common Market Law Review*, Vol. 28, pp. 549-570.

Shaw, J. (1997),'European Citizenship: The IGC and Beyond', *European Integration online Papers*, Vol. 1, No. 003, http://eiop.or.at/eiop/texte/1997-003a.htm

Smith, D and M. Blanc (1996), 'Citizenship, Nationality and Ethnic Minorities in Three European Nations', in *International Journal of Urban and Regional Research,* Vol. 20, No. 1, March, pp. 66-82.

Smith, D. and E. Wistrich (1997), 'Citizenship and Social Exclusion in the European Union', in M. Roche and R. van Berkel (eds), *European Citizenship and Social Exclusion*, Ashgate, Aldershot.

Tassin, E. (1992), 'Europe: A Political Community?', in C. Mouffe (ed.), *Dimensions of Radical Democracy: Pluralism, Citizenship, Community'*, Verso, London/New York.

Tonra, B (1997), *A European Cultural Identity. Myth, Reality or Aspiration?*, Institute of European Affairs, Dublin.

Turner, B. (1992), 'Outline of a Theory of Citizenship', in Mouffe, C. (ed.), *Dimensions of Radical Democracy: Pluralism, Citizenship, Community'*, Verso, London/New York.

Twine, F. (1994), *Citizenship and Social Rights. The Interdependence of Self and Society*, Sage, London.

Wallace, W. (1990), 'Introduction: the dynamics of European integration' in W. Wallace (ed.), *The Dynamics of European Integration*, Pinter/RIIA, London.

Ward, I. (1997), 'Law and the Other Europeans', *Journal of Common Market Studies*, Vol. 35, No. 1, March, pp. 79-96.

11 The Socio-Cultural Exclusion and Self-Exclusion of Foreigners in Finland
The case of Joensuu

M'HAMMED SABOUR

Introduction and background

One of the most striking phenomena of modern times is the great movement and migration of people. In other words, modern times are characterised by a formidable interpenetration of symbols, cultures and values. This phenomenon is seen by many as an inevitable outcome of globalization. It creates an encounter of diversities where the clash and interfertilization of cultures create the possibility of greater awareness of otherness and greater understanding (Koser and Lutz, 1998).

Seen from the viewpoint of the expatriated, namely the immigrant and foreign workers in Europe, who are mainly in the subordinate and weakest occupational positions and status categories, this encounter is considered to be one-sided and takes place mainly according to the conditions, rules and expectations of the host societies. Many of these immigrants find themselves stigmatized and excluded because they think little or no recognition is given to their religions, ways of life or values within the mainstream culture. This state of affairs has led to feelings of marginalization which inhibit their social and cultural inclusion. Commonly, immigrants and their descendants react against the host societies by revitalizing and emphasizing their identities, and even by excluding themselves from the mainstream culture.

For historical, geographical and economic reasons Finland, compared with many other western European countries, has remained ethnically and culturally relatively homogeneous. Except for the small ethnic minorities of gipsies, Lapps, and the Tatars, the number of registered foreigners a decade ago did not exceed 1 per cent of the total population. Converted into numbers, this was around 50,000 persons. At the present date, however, the total is around 80,000 (1.5 per cent) persons out of the five millions of the total population (Figure 11.1). Most of them came originally from neighbouring countries.

Figure 11.1   Foreigners in Finland

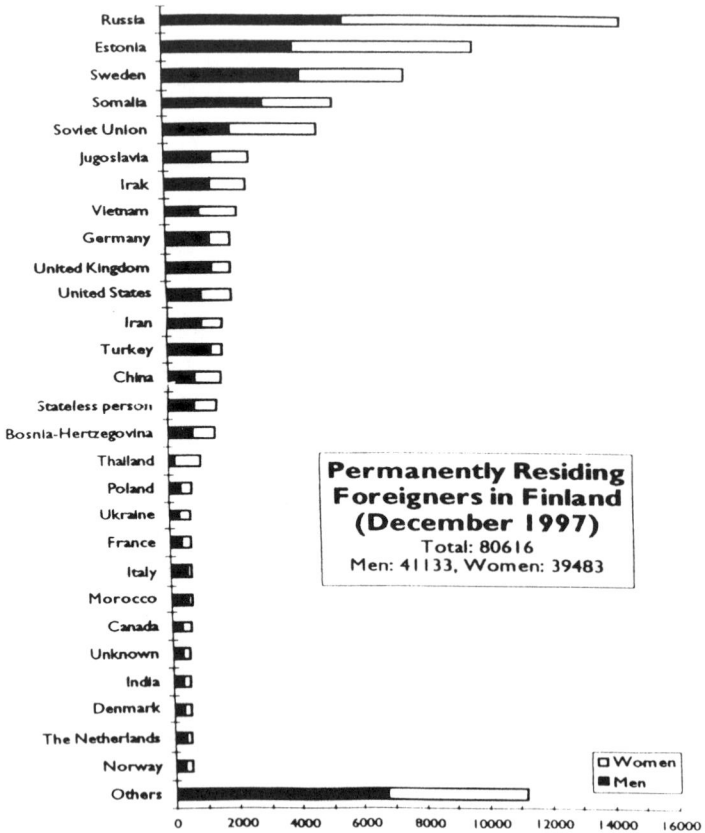

Source: Vaestorekisterikeskus. 31.12.1997 (MoniTori, No.1, 1998, p.9)

The 1970s saw the coming of Chilean and Vietnamese immigrants. The increasing internationalization of the economic sector and the increase in student mobility in the 1980s has attracted many students to the Finnish universities, which have a tuition-free policy. During the past few years there has arisen an intense academic and political debate concerning the cultural and social readiness and ability of Finland to receive and absorb foreign newcomers. The turning point in this debate took place at the beginning of the 1990s when, escaping a civil war, around 2000 Somalis came via Russia to seek refugee status in Finland (Jaakkola, 1994, pp. 50-79). This coincided with economic recession and therefore provoked a major debate in the political sphere and also at a public level. The mode of entry of the Somalis imposed into the country, the differences of their culture, religion and the cost of their stay were among the topics of this debate. The debate adopted various tonalities and contents, from a humanistic one favourable to foreigners (refugees) to a xenophobic discourse, passing on the way through nationalism and ethnocentricity (Sabour and Antikainen, 1995). This relatively 'sharp rise' in the number of asylum seekers from Africa (Somalia) and the lack of experience of those in charge of managing policy towards foreigners and refugees have provided the tabloid and populist press with sensational and scandalous subjects to create an atmosphere of xenophobia, islamophobia and racism (see the analysis of a similar case by Swyngedouw, 1995). This crystallized in the formation and galvanization of far right-wing groups such as the skinheads. This group initiated organized violence and terror against foreigners, especially black people. When some of the Somali refugees were placed in Joensuu (see map), the city became one of the hot spots for this violence. Since the beginning of the 1990s the number of crimes and violence with xenophobic and racist motivation has increased tremendously (Liebkind, 1994a, 1994b). This fact has persuaded many black people to move away from Joensuu to other cities in southern Finland. In other words, this exodus from Joensuu seems to be due to many factors: a feeling of insecurity on the part of black (African) foreigners, a scarcity of job possibilities, the *laisser-faire* attitude of the authorities regarding the organized violence of the skinhead group and, in general, the hostile atmosphere among the public. The foreigners, especially blacks, who have stayed in Joensuu are those short of alternatives or who are evidently attached by different obligations or commitments: work, marriage or studies (Sabour, 1996).

Social exclusion

As a social phenomenon, exclusion emerged in European societies because of economic development. Originally it was politically and sociologically

Map 11.1   The Location of Joensuu

coined and shaped in France during the 1970s and 1980s. As a result of various problems of unemployment, immigration, cultural alienation, social disenchantment, weakening of the welfare society, etc., exclusion has become one of the most fashionable concepts in scientific and political discourses (Rogers, 1995; Lamarque, 1996, pp. 29-31).

Expanding on a Durkheimian perspective, Nasse (1992, p. 29) defines exclusion generally as a set of mechanisms of rupture on the symbolic level (stigma or negative attributes) and on the level of social relations (break-up of social bonds that aggregate people). He specifies, however, that the mechanism of symbolic rupture seems often to anticipate the mechanism of social rupture. Moreover, Nasse contends that the process of exclusion seems to start with the loss of symbolic bonds: the rejecting group begins by imposing negative labels and categorizations which make possible the definition and classification of individuals who are not in conformity with the mainstream norms and a system of representations.

In this regard, Foucault (1975) contends that during interaction between two systems of representations, one group may win over the other when it later succeeds in imposing its own norms as a framework for assessing normality. It does so because in relationships between the mainstream native population and the foreign-born minority it is the former that sets the norms and normality. Exclusion may be the product of a process of stigmatization which is itself constructed in the field of the legitimation of collective representation. After all, when a process of stigmatization occurs it is presented in the form of symbolic exclusion: it is visible through negative and pejorative images. It may ineluctably lead to an act of concretely keeping aside, that is, a situation of social exclusion (and not only symbolic), defined as a situation of rupture of social relations (see Nasse, 1992, pp. 30-36; Xiberras, 1992; Weiberg *et al.*, 1993). From this perspective, how can cultural exclusion be defined?

Cultural exclusion and self-exclusion

To begin with, culture is an intensive productive, reproductive and interactive process in society. In other words, society lives by rules and according to cultural structures such as symbols, rites, scripts, traditions, customs, and reciprocally the practice of those structures moulds the way of life and activity of society. This interactive interdependency between culture and society gives rise to conduct and norms that inclusively integrate and characterize all those members of society who live by them. This inclusiveness entails a conscious and unconscious feeling of belongingness and a sharing of the same set of cultural values among the members of a social group. If these social and cultural values are those of the mainstream society (dominant group) they may become normative and exclusive. Those representing variant cultural values may find themselves excluded from enjoying the advantages of this mainstream. Therefore, they may be requested to embrace mainstream values and even to give up their own (Lamont, 1989, pp. 131-150). Pressure in this regard takes various forms, from the non-availability of food items consumed by the minority to the formal denial of practising one's culture and traditions. Thus, those who are different from the mainstream can find themselves, in point of fact, culturally disqualified (Hagendoom, 1993).

The question of cultural exclusion, particularly in the context of relations between individuals and groups, can be seen as the inability of an individual who does not belong to the mainstream population to enjoy his/her cultural rights (traditions, rites, religion, language, etc.). This cultural exclusion could be the result of intentionally planned policy or the outcome of unfortunate circumstances. In the former case, the individual from the minority finds himself/herself deprived of the possibility of living according to the way of life of his/her native culture. This situation may prevail because of the aloofness, the 'exoticism' and even the adversity of his/her culture in relation to that of the majority. This means that s/he must accept and live by the requirements and the rules of the majority's cultural values (Camilleri *et al.*, 1990, pp. 58-59). The prestige, status and respectability which the members of a minority enjoy in society have a decisive impact on their position. Furthermore, a society with a history of multi-ethnic tradition and a heterogeneous culture is more inclined to tolerate diversity. In contrast, a society characterized by cultural homogeneity and ethnocentricity may be very reluctant to tolerate values and traditions different from its own. The acceptance of and attitude towards a different minority may be also conditioned by the socioeconomic need of its labour force. The more there is a demand for its services by the host society, the more flexible the host society will be in accepting it. This can be exemplified by the periods of high and low economic growth in Europe. During periods of high growth in the 1960s and 1970s, a foreign labour force was welcomed with open arms to Europe. But when the demand for its services declined during the recession, these foreigners started to be the target of all kinds of rejection, discrimination and exclusion. It goes without saying that the relationships between the majority and the non-European minority are more complex than that. The difference in ways of life, difficulties of cultural identification faced by second and third generations of immigrants within European society, together with their economic precariousness and social marginalization are only a few of the aspects that could be mentioned in this context. These are potential elements which may increase the impact of exclusion and deepen the gap between the minority and the host population. Furthermore, the degree of integration and inclusion into the mainstream population remains dependent on the level of closeness or distance of a minority culture to that of that of the mainstream (Lorenso, 1989, pp. 193-207).

In addition to intentional and planned forms of cultural exclusion, there are other forms of exclusion. There is exclusion through distancing, indifference or stigmatization. In the first case, the majority, which has the power and the advantage of the initiative, spatially marks the cultural distance it thinks it occupies from the minority (e.g. immigrants) by dwelling, consuming and spending its leisure time far from it. Indifference represents a hidden form of exclusion when no attention, respect, sympathy, understanding or interest is manifested towards the minority's culture or traditions in everyday life, school, TV programmes, sport, etc. A third form of exclusion is basically suggested by consciously or unconsciously insisting, in the public sphere, the media, entertainment, social interactions, or business, on the 'negative' and disadvantaged sides of the minority's culture, history and way of life (Jodelet, 1996, pp. 68-73; Sabour, 1998). These invisible aspects of exclusion are often disguised under the misleading label of 'respect for the cultural differences' which exist between 'their' and 'our' values (Bryson, 1996). The attitude which places particular stress on exotic, 'shocking', primitive, stereotyped traits of a minority's culture are tantamount to rejection and exclusion (Liautzu, 1992), since, as I have emphasised elsewhere (Sabour, 1993), when an immigrant is presented in schools, family and public discourse as possessing only negative characteristics, s/he finds herself/himself cognitively, socially, and economically excluded from those spaces where the values of respect, tolerance, trust, human dignity and recognition are predominant and represent a symbolic currency (see also Vertovec, 1996).

It can then be inferred that cultural self-exclusion can be conceived of as a voluntary withdrawal from the field of the mainstream culture, through conscious avoidance of learning, practising, consuming or identifying with it. This withdrawal could be motivated by personal choice, social pressure, cultural variance or a disruptive experience (Murphy, 1988; Moreau, 1993). Self-exclusion could also be explained by the drive to preserve identity, to avoid assimilation into mainstream values, to encourage cohesiveness among minority members, or to stimulate the emergence of a subculture or counterculture. The status of a self-exclusive culture is linked to the status of those who have chosen it or are cornered into it. Cultural self-exclusion practised by an economically and socially dominated minority may entail a conflicting relationship with the host population (Cousineau, 1994; Fletcher, 1996). This self-exclusion can involve factors of marginalization detrimental to the minority. This withdrawal may also signify the existence of a feeling of defiant rejection of the mainstream or a desperate act of introversion. In this regard, because professional, social and economic success and mobility are basically achieved through the symbolic structures of the mainstream, any withdrawal or self-isolation of the minorities' members from it may be tantamount to an engagement in a self-undermining and self-destructive action.

The identification with certain social and cultural values and symbols implies tacit identification with all those who identify themselves with such values and symbols (Sabour, 1997). In this regard, the 'Others', whose cultural backgrounds (e.g. foreigners, immigrants) are different, may be seen as alien and therefore excluded from this identification (Affergan, 1987; Taguieff, 1987). Such an attitude of exclusion can be reinforced by the fact that the natives form part of the 'mainstream' and majority culture, while the newcomers, as a minority, form part of a different culture. Cultural exclusion could have explicit features when emphasis is placed on the native culture alone without paying due attention or consideration to the Others' cultural difference. Sometimes, the majority tries intentionally and concretely to hinder the exercise or development of the minority's culture (Bochmann, 1994). To justify their actions, the decision makers from the majority may claim the preservation of their identity and the social cohesiveness of the community. In other cases, the majority can distance itself from the minority by means of the symbolic-cultural-artistic-educational (e.g. disregard for the others' beliefs, non-use of their culture, non-consumption of their music, or arts, and by avoiding placing their children in the same school). This may push the deprived poor minority to remain outside the mainstream and to stay on the margin, and possibly to 'ghettoize' itself. Spatially, this self-ghettoization may be visible, but on cultural and mental levels it can remain latent. Evidently the minority is expected to live, in one way or another, according to the conditions and the requirements of the majority indigenous population.

Aims of this study

One of the main objectives of this study is to assess how foreigners residing in Joensuu, especially African people, evaluate their experience of social and cultural estrangement, exclusion/inclusion, tolerance or prejudice. In other words, what is their self-assessment of this experience and what kind of 'strategies' or solutions have they adopted to cope with the hostility or the misunderstanding of the host society? How do these Africans describe reflexively their own position in and attitudes towards this society? How do they themselves analyse their position among and relationship with the host population? To answer these questions my starting point is based on the assumptions that (1) the greater the symbolic and cultural distance and difference between groups, the larger is the risk of the emergence and prevalence of prejudice and misunderstanding; (2) the prestige and status of a minority in the eyes of the majority are dependent on the very success of the former and its contribution to the welfare of society as a whole; (3) the attitude of acceptance or rejection which the majority has towards a culturally different minority is relatively tied up with the degree of endorsement or questioning of the former's social and cultural values and interests; (4) cultural self-exclusion by the minority may be a sign of failure in managing diversity, in preserving its difference, and in winning recognition for this difference from the mainstream majority; and (5) the degree and profundity of inclusion or exclusion are closely correlated to the economic, social, political and religious status of this minority.

Subjects and description of method

Sixteen subjects from Africa were interviewed for this study. Three are from North Africa and the rest from sub-Saharan Africa. Six are female and the rest male. Their stay in Finland varies from two to 14 years. Their ages are between 22 and 39 years. The mean age is 26.5. Six of the interviewees have university degrees, four have finished secondary school, and the rest have elementary school education. Four of them are active students, five are working in different jobs, but mostly services. The rest are unemployed. Five originate from the middle class, the rest are from a working-class or peasant background. Except for four who came to Finland principally as students, the rest came to Finland because of marriage with Finnish nationals or with the status of immigrants. Four entered the country as 'tourists' and then married and became residents. The long itineraries of their 'odyssey' from Africa to Finland are varied. The North Africans came via France or directly from their native countries as 'husbands' and 'wives'; five from West Africa (Nigeria, Ghana, Ivory Coast, Senegal) and two from East Africa (Tanzania and Kenya) came as students via Western countries, mainly France, the United Kingdom and the Netherlands. The rest arrived from Somalia as refugees at the beginning of the 1990s via Russia.

The empirical part of this study was carried out during autumn 1997 and spring 1998. Only African foreign residents were selected because they were and are more frequently the targets of violence, intimidation and prejudice than any other ethnic group. In the selection, geographical factors are considered. The participants come from various African regions and have different life trajectories and they have different experiences in their encounters with and their status in Finnish society. Out of the 32 persons invited to take part in this study, 21 accepted. During the study or after, five of them asked to be dropped from it. Many reasons were put forward: the uselessness of the study, the risk of being recognized after its publication, fears of its consequences, doubts about the intentions for its use, etc. The 'interviews', which were carried out by the writer, took place, according to the choice and wishes of the individuals, in their homes or in those of relatives or friends or, in a few cases, in the University library. Three of the interviews were carried out through the medium of Arabic-French and the rest were in English. The translation into English was done by the writer. To achieve the authenticity of the respondents' opinions and to get their genuine thoughts, the interview, after its transcription, was given to the respondent, as was agreed beforehand, so that he or she could read it and complete or improve it. The present writer was more concerned with getting their own considered assessments rather than their spontaneous and immediate reactions.

In this regard, the interviews were based on neither closed nor open questions. I instead conducted what could be termed thematically loose and 'conversational' discussions (*entretiens*). These constitute what Bourdieu calls a 'socioanalytical' approach. Socioanalysis, according to Bourdieu (1993), aims at establishing a social relation based on a 'reflexive reflexivity', where the researcher is sensitive to the symbolic violence involved in his/her position with the studied person. Thus, despite the difference in academic capital and the social dissymetry between the 'interviewer' and the 'interviewee' he/she is able, as much as possible, to control the effects that may cause distortions and biases in this process of social relation. Bourdieu adds: 'we should try to establish a methodical and active relation of listening which is far from the pure *laisser-faire* of the non-directed interview and also from the directiveness of the questionnaire'. This approach requires a preliminary deep knowledge of the objective conditions of the individuals under study. As a result of proximity and similarity in cultural origin and foreignness it was possible for the interviewer to link a 'nonviolent communication' with the subjects and to build up a relation of trust that is necessary in this kind of approach (see also Sayad, 1991).

The selected interviewees

Because of limited space, five stories and self-analysis were chosen to illustrate and develop the theme of this study. The five foreigners are:

Arhaz: 32 years old, she comes from a working-class background. Having graduated in Human Geography (BA) in Morocco, she entered Finland eight years ago with a student visa. For economic reasons, she did all kinds of work, ranging from baby-sitting to cleaning. Unable to study or to find a job in her field she started teaching oriental dance and dancing professionally at parties and restaurants. Because the oriental dance is now *en vogue* in Finland she is making a reasonable living.

Ed: 23 years old, he is from a middle-class family. After studying in Kenya, his native country, and in Britain, he met his Finnish wife and moved to Finland four years ago. After getting divorced, he interrupted his studies in Computer Science at the University of Joensuu and took a job in a computer company. Without any clear plan for the future, he is 'ready to go back to Kenya whenever possible'.

Ham: 27 years old, he came as a refugee from Somalia via Russia at the beginning of the 1990s. He came to Finland only by chance. 'I wished to go to Britain or Canada but my trip ended in Joensuu', he said with bitterness. From what he calls a 'normal working family', Ham has a secondary level of education. Living on social security assistance, he has been practically unemployed since his arrival. His hope is, one day, to join his relatives in Britain. His stay in Finland is only transitional.

Kader: 30 years old from Tunisia, he studied physics for two years in his native country before coming to Finland seven years ago as a 'tourist'. He married one year after his arrival and got divorced three years later. He has a daughter of five years of age. He is working as a cook in a pizzeria. Originally from a lower class, Kader, owing to economic, administrative and language problems, was unable to continue his studies in Finland. He is expecting to get Finnish citizenship in two years time. Because he is divorced and without a permanent job, obtaining citizenship is a difficult goal to achieve in the future.

Mamadou: 39 years old, he is from Senegal. He has lived in France for eleven years. A friendship with a Finnish woman led him to come to Finland, where he has been living for the last eight years. After two unsuccessful marriages, he is 'free from any commitment but living on the margin of society', as he puts it. He has two children from each marriage. Having only a 'primary education but self-taught', he has been in different unskilled short-term jobs. 'Uncertainty has become a part of my life and I have learned to manage it relatively well', he declares proudly. He is, however, reluctant to speak about his background or life trajectory. Mamadou justifies it philosophically in this way: 'since the past has passed, the future is unknown; let's talk about the present, that's what counts now...'.

Social and cultural exclusion

I am undesirable, I am rejected, I am oddly different

[...] Sometimes, when I take the bus and the seats are occupied but the seat next to me is free. I am always surprised that no one comes to sit near me [...] I have the feeling, when I am sitting alone in a seat reserved for two or three persons, that I am disturbing the others' comfort [...] The passengers' avoidance behaviour makes me feel that I am undesirable, I am rejected, I am oddly different, I have some disease, I am leprous [...] (Kader)
The biggest problem a foreigner like me faces here is, besides the harassment of the skinheads, which I do not consider a very significant problem, is the feeling of exclusion and of injustice [...] (Ed)

After all the experiences I have had during my stay here I intend to leave when possible [...] Here, I will remain an outsider and excluded all my life. I like to be in a place where I feel I can belong to society and have a feeling of being accepted by the others, whatever my origin or the colour of my skin [...] (Ed)

It is a negative stigma of being educated in the South

[...] because I am not black and not white, some Finns have difficulty in categorizing me. It takes time before they get to know my origins [...] I hate to be always classified with one group or another. So, sometimes I am seen as a Somali, and sometimes I am called a "Negro", etc. The worst aspect of all these is the discrimination in finding work [...] (Arhaz)

My university degree and knowledge are negatively correlated with my native country. For them (the Finns), Morocco is in Africa and Africa has nothing positive to offer. It is a negative stigma of being educated in the South. People are suspicious about your knowledge and skill qualities. So, you have to prove yourself all the time and often [...] (Arhaz)

Social and cultural self-exclusion

Spatially I live a self-regulated existence

Compared to other foreigners my experience is not so bad because, to avoid trouble and exposure to racial aggression, I don't go to those places where the risk is high - for example, discos, bars, districts in the city, where the skinhead people are in control. Spatially I live a self-regulated existence [...] (Kader)

In this situation, I don't see myself having any future in this country. I live like an animal, I wake up in the morning, go to my miserable work and come back home and sleep, to restart the same thing, next day. So, no material or spiritual prospects for the future: no education, no saving, as we say in Tunisia 'we eat the food and wait for death' (*nakul qaut wan tsanau lmaut*) [...] (Kader)

In my native country my relation with religion was always secular. A few years' stay here has taught me that if I do not protect my cultural identity I will become uprooted and perhaps absorbed without conviction into the Western way of life. [...] I am aware that I look strange in the eyes of the Finns, who maybe consider mistakenly every Muslim who practises his religion openly to be a fundamentalist. However, I have to look at what is good for me and my kids and not at what the Finnish people says or think of me, or expect me to be. [...] (Ham)

The best way to survive here is to live like a snake

The best way to survive here is to live like a snake. I participate in some courses (organized training by the Ministry of Labour for the unemployed) in the morning and then I go back home, always keeping in my mind that I must avoid all the places where there are chances of having trouble. Well, it is living like a snake, isn't it? [...] (Ham)

Because of the difficulties linked with my adjustment to this society and the feeling of racism and rejection I felt mixed up at the beginning in my relations with people and therefore started pushing them away and isolating myself [...] It is a traumatic situation to be a rejected black person in a predominantly white society [...]. (Ham)

... it is a self-exclusion imposed on me by society

Nowadays, I feel a lot of stress in the public sphere. Consequently, I try to be indoors most of the time. I work at home, I do my banking from home through my computer, I spend much of my free time at home. I am not a hermit but the circumstances related to the outdoor hostility oblige me to live far from the others and in intimacy with myself because it is the place where I find some kind of peace [...] But is this a normal life? No, it is a self-exclusion imposed on me by society [...] (Ed)

I have no friends, I mean Finnish friends. I have, let us say, interest friends or work colleagues, but no intimate friends in the Moroccan sense of the word with whom I can share my joy and sorrow, everything [...] Foreigners cannot easily make Finnish friends. Finns are very distant and avoid being involved with foreigners (*ulkomaalaiset*, said in Finnish in the interview). I suffer very much from that. I have no contact even with my neighbours [...] (Arhaz)

What bothers me most now is that I am unemployed. I am ready to do any kind of job. You can imagine what is like to be here, cut from your roots, uncertain about your future, unemployed and harassed by this nasty skinhead group [...] (Ham)

I am a free prisoner in my own ghetto

Because I cannot live normally with the Finns there is no other choice than to withdraw early in the evening in my apartment, my own ghetto, arranged by myself, according to my own conditions [...] In this ghetto, there is only me, a free prisoner in my world of tranquillity and solitude [...] The racist Finn cannot intrude where I have the freedom to do in my psychological ghetto what I want. This ghetto may appear strange to the outside world but it represents to me a secure refuge of peace [...] (Mamadou)

Cultural difference and self-exclusion

... I am wrong and my culture is worthless

I was married [...] I did have some ideas about the problems linked with mixed marriages, but not to the extent I have experienced. It was too problematic. [My wife] continuously talked about the Finnish values and cultural points of view and did not care a bit about what I represent or my native culture. It seems to me that, like many Finns, she was always convinced that she is right and represents the best but I am wrong and my culture is worthless. In such a situation I feel that there is no use in trying to understand her or give value to her Finnishness because she did not care about me and what I represent [...] (Kader)

[...] My best means of protection and self-defence is to isolate myself, to be aloof from all the others. In this way I find my internal tranquillity. Mixing with others from a different cultural origin (e.g., in marriage) is condemned to failure and the suffering of both sides. I have in mind the sort of mixing where each partner tries to pull only to his or her side without any interest or consideration for the other side's expectations and wishes. It is better in such a case to distance myself from the Finns, for my own sake and for the salvation of my mental health and cultural integrity [...] (Kader)

Cultural difference, indifference and ignorance

I feel ... I am culturally an orphan

I have very little to do with the Finnish culture. I don't go to concerts and I am not interested in any Finnish sport. I have not even visited the Museum though I was living for seven years in Joensuu. How can I explain this behaviour? I think that the Finnish culture does not give me any of the intellectual or aesthetic pleasure or satisfaction I am in need of. (Kader)

One source of disappointment I have experienced here in this country is related to my marriage. In all economic matters there are no big problems. On the cultural level we have some difficulties. Because I am isolated here. I cannot celebrate feasts and religious events related to Moroccan traditions. As well as the contextual circumstances there is also the lack of comprehension from my Finnish husband. I have the feeling that he does not understand how much it is important to me to keep in touch with my traditions. I feel from time to time that I am culturally an orphan. [...] (Arhaz)

In social and technical achievements Finns have difficulties in hiding self-praising and self-glorifying attitudes in front of people like me coming from a developing country.

I have nothing against the Finnish way of life. But when it does not recognize me and does not give room to my culture and to my difference it becomes disagreeable to me and I started to be disrespectful towards it.[...] (Kader)

What is terrible for a black African in this society is that he has everything against him: history, media, the reality in Africa, the social prejudices, racism, etc. Whatever you try to prove to Whites (Finns) that you deserve respect and trust, no way; you must content yourself with the second class [...] (Mamadou)

There is also a problem because of the fact that some Finns, my husband included, who take for granted that their culture, compared to the Moroccan one, is better (e.g., social interactions, art, organization, etc.). Maybe, we can say that but I think that each culture has its raison-d'être, its strong and weak sides. (Arhaz)

I have noticed that the Finns are attached to their culture and education to a such extent that they lack flexibility in accepting new ideas or new ways of looking at things that may be different from those they are used to. They are extremely reluctant to change without making sure that the new direction, idea or solution is 200 per cent certain. In social and technical achievements Finns have difficulties in hiding self-praising and self-glorifying attitudes in front of people like me coming from developing countries. It is their right to be proud of their achievements and what they are; but they should give us room to be proud of ours too [...] (Arhaz)

Cultural inclusion and identity

... converting to the religion of the majority will be an identity suicide

I can compromise about almost anything but giving up my religion, or accepting a way of life that may alter or alienate it, is absolutely out of the question. I may appear rigid but for a person like me, from a minority, converting to the religion of the majority will be an identity suicide. My being will be completely annihilated, because the Islamic religion for me is the last stronghold where I protect myself. (Ham)

To begin with, I tried to socialize with them (Finns) and assimilate everything coming from them but I was always rejected. Their rejection caused me a deep crisis but it helped me significantly to find myself and give sense to my life. With other brothers, who suffered from the same rejection and unfortunate experience, we restored and transformed the basement of an old building into a mosque. For us it has become a place where we pray, we discuss our everyday problems, we exchange ideas about our traditions [...] (Ham)

The Finns may speak self-mockingly of their poor social skills or of the rural entrenchment of their culture, from time to time, but in reality they are deeply aware and proud of the 'superiority' of their way of life and cultural values, especially the quality of their work ethic and straightforwardness (*rehellisyys*). [...] (Arhaz)

When the Finns don't come to me, I have to go them. It is the only way to make myself accepted and understood by them and to gain their trust [...]
To preserve my traditions I try to respect Islamic rules. I fast at Ramadan, I celebrate the religious feasts despite the difficulties linked to the difference in the way of life between Finland and Morocco. I do my prayers five times per day. I try my best to keep up something of my identity [...] (Arhaz)

[...] a person like me who carries his racial identity, a black identity, will be laughed at if he tries to integrate too closely into the Finnish way of life [...] (Ham)

Cultural prejudice

Finns tolerate difference and others' traditions only reluctantly

As a Muslim living in this society, people always have a prejudiced attitude towards me. Whatever I try to be and however I behave they have fixed ideas about me and my origins. All what they 'know' are the negative aspects of my culture [...] (Kader)

Before coming to Finland I was very naive about a lot of things in the outside world [...] Growing up in that atmosphere I assumed that different races could coexist without friction. Once here, I realized how naive I was, it's not like that. It is very sad that people are so very prejudiced [...] (Ed)

The foreigner may work as an employee in some service (e.g. restaurant) but if he tries to start his own business, especially in technically demanding fields like the computer business, he is not trusted [...] (Ed)

Most Finns, in general, ignore most or all of our culture and religion. If they know something it is negative or exotic things that are far from the reality. (Kader)

Generally speaking, the Finns tolerate differences and the others' traditions only reluctantly. This is maybe due to the historical introversion of their culture and geographical isolation. This explanation may no longer appear   valid in this time of globalization but the Finns are an exception in world culture. (Ed)

Some may be ashamed to walk or to speak to black Africans in front of their colleagues

I think that many Finns feel very insecure in front of foreigners [...]. Some may feel ashamed to walk or to speak to black Africans in front of their colleagues. A friend of mine from Somalia told me that he once met a woman in a disco; at the end of the evening she invited him to her place but on the condition that he should not walk beside her in the street in front of everybody. She asked him to follow her a few meters behind. Can you imagine this, she likes to f... him but not to walk side by side with him [...]. (Ed)

Foreigners and natives can be blamed for cultural ignorance

I think the Finns have excellent general knowledge but it is not assimilated in a way that helps them to understand the world and things from an objective angle, there is a gap between theory and practice. Moreover, Finns remain, for reasons that I do not know, culturally and socially very ethnocentric. They look at the world from their own cultural window. This is the source of their misjudgment and misunderstanding of others and also the source of the problems they have with foreigners [...]. (Ed)

After a stay of two years in Finland I have unfortunately developed a spontaneous feeling of distrust towards white people. I cannot help it but everyday experiences have put this reaction in me. Now, to have any relationship with a Finn they have to prove to me that they're not racist [...]. (Ed)

I must confess that I did not know much about Finland before. All I knew was, mostly, positive. On the other hand, most of the Finns do not know much either about the African cultures, but the worst of it is that unfortunately they know only negative, shocking and disturbing aspects. All of these are reflected in the relationships between the two, here. (Mamadou)

... the African never brings something but always disturbs, steals, takes or breaks

Finnish society is culturally, ethnically and socially constructed in a such way that a foreigner like me, an Arab, brown skin and Muslim, will remain an outsider and stranger indefinitely in spite of my Finnish citizenship or my long stay in this country. Most Finns see in the foreigner only a troublemaker, a job-seeker, a social security-profiteer, a *pique-assiette*, a cultural parasite, an AIDS-spreader, etc. They rarely look at him/her as a person who may bring something positive to the community, may contribute with some creativity, may enrich the cultural spectrum with his/her difference [...]. (Arhaz)

Cultural estrangement

Solitude is enduring in silence

[...] The feelings of insecurity and uncertainty oblige the foreigner to live in a continuous hindering routine one day at a time. In other words, he cannot plan anything for a *longue durée*. The routine kills all ambition especially when the foreigner is stuck in the daily needs that most of the time are very basic such as economic survival. Here, all other aspirations and ideals are put aside. The foreigner is stuck in this reality and routine and therefore he can only think in the *courte durée* [...]. (Kader)

The worse side of living isolated in this society (Finnish society) is when there are no compensatory and reliable individuals, groups or associations who share the same culture and values, to whom you can turn. (Kader)

[...] I miss very much the collective spirit of society. This society is very individualistically oriented where people are suffering alone in their corner [...]. Solitude is enduring in silence. (Arhaz)

From time to time I suffer of the feeling of exclusion and loneliness. It is the hardiest thing. Compared to the problems of prejudice, racism and the threat of skinheadss, which are there outside, which I can resolve or take my distance from them, the loneliness and exclusion are terrible because they live with and in me [...] (Ed)

Discrimination and skinhead intimidation and racism

... the skinheads use foreigners as scapegoats for their own social failure

The phenomenon of the skinheads in Joensuu, despite its locality, is worldwide. Some groups of the young generation in Europe are, for economic and social reasons, living a sort of disillusionment and despair. The future is no longer as secure and bright as it used to be for older generations [...]. The skinheads use foreigners as scapegoats for their social failure and despair. Maybe they have also a feeling of uncertainty in the face of foreigners. So, hating and blaming foreigners for all stupid things is a sign of the lack of maturity of some Finns and their culturally-interiorised fear of the different and the stranger [...] (Ed)

The skinhead kids, who often are small criminals, emotionally disturbed, social marginals, use this as an excuse for justifying their aggressive and racist behaviour against foreigners [...] (Ed)

When I have to go out, I do so always during daylight. At night, I avoid going out, and if I do have to go I must do it in a group with other friends. Being in a group we can better defend each other and deter the skinheads terrorists from attacking us. However, I rarely go out at night to public places like discos, bars, the main city square, etc. I cannot enjoy being in these places because I must all the time be on the alert that someone may attack me [...]. (Ham)

My blackness is an element that creates a line of mental and physical separation

In a white society, I feel, as a black man, that I look very strange in the eyes of other people. The problem with the black-skin in a majority-white society is that you cannot hide yourself anywhere; your identity and origin are displayed on your face. This means that in Finns' eyes, as I understand it, I don't belong to the group, I am an outsider, I am a foreigner *(muukalainen*, said in Finnish in the interview). My blackness is an element that creates a line of mental and physical separation, a zone of distance, a barrier for closeness, and it awakens an attitude of prejudice between me and the Finns. [...] (Ed)

My stay in Finland has made me aware of the fact that white people still have a superiority complex although we are living in a so-called egalitarian and human rights and tolerance-cherishing international society. Just a few years back I was convinced that all races can live together harmoniously despite the differences in their traditions, religions, and status. Now, I am more 'realistic', and pessimistic as well. (Ed)

[...] Anyway, if you would really like to know my explanation for the Finnish male aloofness, my answer is that it is because I am a BLACK (said loudly) African. My black colour is seen negatively by the social context, therefore, it is difficult for the Finnish man to be in an association of friendship or any other close relation with me. He will be judged on that basis. If you mix with 'outsiders' and 'rejected' people you will be labelled accordingly [...]. (Ham)

Certainly, there are many good people among the Finns who are not prejudiced against foreigners. Lately, we can notice a clear change in attitudes. This can be seen in the increasing and alarming number of verbal and physical attacks, whose victims are particularly black Africans [...]. Earlier, we spoke about concealed racism, but now we must recognise the existence of visible racism [...] (Mamadou)

Analysis and conclusions

'Finland is a nice country but only for its own people'

These five stories, which could also be seen as points of view, statements and (self-) analyses, vividly denote the state of helplessness, uncertainty and frustration in which African foreigners live in Joensuu. Coming from different origins and through different life trajectories, the respondents have many similarities and a common denominator in their experience of Finnish culture and society. Tracked by the negative attitudes linked to their origin and culture, harassed by doubts concerning their ability and integrity, and marginalized by their failure to be assimilated into the mainstream, these foreigners are trapped in an unenviable situation.

Their state of psychological and social misery becomes like dark glasses through which they see only the grim and unfortunate sides of Finnish culture and society. In fact, their statements reveal feelings of disappointment, bitterness and grudge against the Other (the whites) who have not provided opportunities and accessibility for a decent (or comfortable) life. These feelings are a reflection of the weakness of their social position, status and prestige. Those who feel themselves to be unjustly excluded or oppressed by a group or a system are tempted to blame and even demonise it, and place exclusive emphasis upon the negative and unfortunate aspects of that group or system.

In the *entretien,* statements such as the following were expressed: 'I should like how social and political issues are democratically debated here and the way decision-making is transparent'; 'the Finns are hard-working people, they behave according to the rules and blindly respect the law...'; 'the high status and emancipation of women in this country tells about the degree of its development'; 'the straightforward and committed behaviour of the Finns has enabled them to build a prosperous and modern country, in contrast to what people have done in our countries in the south...'; 'Finland is a nice country but only for its own people'. Recognizing these facts, however, does not improve their position in the eyes of the host population because they feel themselves to be on the margin of society. A good society which possesses opportunities that cannot be obtained, gained or shared, is considered to be a bad one by those excluded. Evidently the cultural deprivation, which is concretized in foreigners' (Africans') lower educational capital, their lack of higher professional training, and their poor linguistic skills, constitutes a major disability and hindrance for such foreigners to be included in the labour market and in society. When these obstacles are added to by the problems involved in occasionally encountering prejudice and racism, we can speak of 'accumulated handicaps' which do not ease the life of Africans in Finland.

There are irrefutable facts that Africans (mostly black people) have been discriminated against and molested on racist grounds. Their experience of racism and discrimination makes black people racially conscious, and they react accordingly (Banton, 1988). Sometimes, their effort to understand and analyse problems linked with 'blackness' pushes them across the line unconsciously and so that they become guilty of their own racist attitude to 'whiteness' (see Phoenix, 1998, pp. 109-122). Sometimes, defence of the rights of blackness and of black people has encroached on the field of whiteness. This is noticeable in statements where there is 'guiltification' of the white and victimization of the black. But their exaggerations and anger have to be understood in the light of the negative and degrading social and cultural habitus which has been interiorized and assimilated throughout the history and memory of their unfortunate relationship with slavery, colonialism, immigration and economic marginalization, all of which are, in one way or another, linked with 'white' people. Africans become very sensitive to the way their social and cultural environment looks at and interacts with them (Räty and Saari, 1997). This sensitivity is concretely maintained and amplified by the very reality of their lower economic status, which makes them an easy target for stigmatization and rejection.

'Social and cultural exclusion may provoke a tendency towards a mental and physical self-ghettoization of the foreigner'

One of the striking elements the respondents continuously bring forward is how difficult it is for them to establish close relationships and friendship with the natives. If some Finns may be prejudiced, there are attitudes of caution towards foreigners anchored in certain features of Finnish culture. This can easily be observed even in situations where Finns, coming from different origins or with different levels of status, meet each other and find it very demanding and stressful to establish communicative contact and to socialize with each other (Marjeta, 1997). Foreigners coming from the 'south', who are used to initiating social contacts easily, may be surprised by this 'coldness' and reserve. The distanciation of Finns often, however, has a lot to do with their own weak social and cultural competence rather than with an unfriendly attitude to foreigners. In other words, it is often more a question of character than of attitude. It is quite comprehensible for Africans, whatever the motivation underlying the native's behaviour, that the consequence is the same: they remain outsiders socially and they are always at the 'mercy of the state of mind and humour of the natives'.

The uneasiness and uncertainty of Finns, as outlined in the respondents' statements, in coping with strangeness, foreignness, and difference are reflected in the relationship between natives and Africans and dramatically highlighted by the imbalance and variation in the cultural and economic *rapport de force* (Costa-Lascoux, 1995). Mutual ignorance of and indifference to each other's culture broadens the gap between understanding and *rapprochement*, and leaves fertile space for stereotyping, stigmatization and polemical mutual rejection. Natives who are not economically in need of foreigners (especially those from developing countries) and are socially reluctant to accept them, find themselves under pressure from humanitarian organizations to change their attitudes and their laws to accommodate refugees. Joining the European Union has also obliged Finland to adopt a more 'comprehensive' and continental policy to deal with asylum seekers.

There is evidently intentional and mutual ignorance of and indifference to the culture and values of the Other. The natives think that foreigners 'must live by the Finnish customs and the Finnish way of life if they want to stay in the country'. In others words, they think foreigners should accommodate themselves to the Finnish culture. Many foreigners, as became clear in the interviews, are unwilling to submit to the requirement of the mainstream culture and invoke their right to preserve their difference. Some reasons are to be found in the very intentions of foreigners. Many see Finland only as a transitory and temporary stage in their migration plans (in the interviews many mentioned that they were just waiting to obtain Finnish citizenship and then they plan to move elsewhere, e.g. Canada, England or the USA). Finland is not a land full of 'opportunities where an American dream could be fulfilled' nor is there 'some certainty about the future'. Many are very aware of their limited opportunities. As expressed by a former salesperson from Nigeria, now jobless and residing in Finland for five years: 'In a country of high tech, where the academically highly educated are unemployed as engineers, nurses, teachers, what people like me can expect is temporary and low-paid jobs or unemployment [...]; the future is gloomy'. This reluctance in the relationship between the natives and resident Africans and their mutual rejection creates a problem of cultural recognition and sets up a tension in multicultural coexistence.

As argued by Abdallah-Pretceille and Thomas (1995, pp. 47-51), in the case of communicative incompetence, a lack of interest in or need for a foreign minority is established, a process which they call 'cultural avoidance'. In this process emphasis is placed on unifying the social traits of the mainstream and its cultural similarities and on their role in strengthening national identity. This cultural avoidance is felt and interpreted by the minority as a form of cultural exclusion. Genuinely worried about the position of their country under the growing influence of globalization, an important segment of the Finnish population is anxious about multiculturalism and its long-term impact on Finnish identity and the well-being of society. Putting aside the racist thesis which cares more about the survival of the purity of the race, this anxiety is driven by concrete issues like employment, national identity and language, the environment, etc., though Finland is almost entirely dependent for the export of its high technology on foreign markets. It can be said, therefore, that Finland is more interested in technical than cultural exchange; its focus is on import-export.

Many Africans who feel rejected and discriminated against are inclined towards the 'interiorization of cultural rules of exclusion,' as contended by Nicklas (1995, p. 41), and subsequently withdraw into themselves through a reflex of cultural self-exclusion from the mainstream. However, many convert this cultural self-exclusion into a strategy of preserving, (re)valorizing and empowering their 'ethnic particularity and identity' (Malewska-Peyre, 1989, p. 117). This strategy was defined by Fanon (1961) as a reflex of 'revitalization of native cultural traditions', which is a means for the oppressed and the excluded to confront the dominant cultural and ideological paradigm and to challenge its power. Some Muslim minorities push self-exclusion to the extreme, that is, to a cultural self-ghettoization where the influence of the host society on the minority way of life and cultural practice is kept at the lowest level. While we can speculate, as one Algerian student suggests, that 'social and cultural exclusion may provoke a tendency towards a mental and physical self-ghettoization of the foreigner', it is self-evident that some individuals in the Muslim minorities erect numerous symbolic, religious and moral boundaries, for instance, to prevent young women from going to school or mixing with other ethnic groups, or to justify female circumcision. This strategy of self-ghettoization aims at creating '... space free of the western culture, where Islamic values can be implemented'. As can be expected, this behaviour often gives rise to a clash of cultures and values. Whatever the status of the foreigner she or he is in a weak and relatively dependent position among the majority.

The immigrants are 'trapped' in the unpredictible misfortune of their destiny

Cultural exclusion is generally seen as a set of values and common collective representations which have found a common cultural patrimony, from which are excluded not only those immigrants belonging to another culture and arriving only recently but also those whose cultural origins are different despite their long stay amidst European culture (Fournier and Vermes, 1994).

In such situations those marginalized from the cultural mainstream may be tempted consciously or unconsciously to develop a subculture or even a counterculture. This, in a way, is a process whereby they convert the stigmatization of society, which considers them to be deviant and pushes them to its margins, into a new identity of survival and self-protection. Moreover, there are cases where marginalized immigrants refuse to be seen as deviant or socially parasitic and try, as Fanon put it, to revitalize their cultural roots and traditions. This is a reaction of 'self-preservation' and defiance towards the marginalizing force of the mainstream. Marginalized, these immigrants have excluded themselves from the cultural mainstream by creating the new features of a culture of their own or by emphasising their native culture and religion (Gallissot, 1993; Gore, 1995)). This self-exclusion, which may be understandable from an identity and emotional point of view, can be prejudicial to those practising and defending it because it may amplify their distance and separation from the mainstream, a process which can be economically and socially harmful and even degrading. Cultural self-exclusion may also be done at the expense of women, as mentioned above, who are the first to be forced to submit to traditions and to restrictions on mixing with the mainstream culture. In extreme cases and as a measure of respecting one's identity and traditions, young women in a Muslim minority may be prevented by their parents from continuing their school or practising sport, etc.

Many interviewees have shown genuine feelings of disappointment and frustration at being excluded from the activities of the mainstream population. Their blackness in a white context has made them aware of the fact that there are all kinds of prejudice, discrimination, rejection and misunderstanding (Hall, 1991). Their everyday experiences with the ordinary people, and with the authorities and their peer groups have made them suspicious about the sincerity of the Other and their expressions of racial tolerance, especially with regard to black people. Many have come with great dreams of building a life in Europe and with the hope of finding a job, but they have been faced instead with the hostility of the climate, the cultural ignorance of the people, the hostile attitude of the far right-wing, and economic uncertainty. Waiting day to day in the hope of better times, they live in a continual or permanent state of transitoriness. They realize later, after several years, that the situation has not improved on all fronts, that the possibility of employment is non-existent, that integration into the Finnish society is painful, and that the economic situation is hopeless. It is a difficult confrontation with the harsh reality: the feeling of having failed to cope with life in Finland, the collapse of earlier dreams, the inability to save money to afford a trip to the home country, and the ambiguity and perplexity caused by feelings of uncertainty over whether to stay or to return. Moreover, after so many years of economically fruitless stay in Finland there is also a feeling of empty-handedness. In other words, there is nothing that the immigrant can be proud of which could be brought and shown to his or her family in Africa as an achievement. Dissatisfied by staying permanently in Finland and uncertain about the return to the native country, immigrants are 'trapped' in the unpredictable misfortune of their destiny. It goes without saying that an individual living in these circumstances can experience feelings of frustration. In addition, because of their temporal, cultural and spatial distance from their native countries and their symbolic separation from the African context, African immigrants find themselves, consciously or unconsciously, in a situation of alienation, exclusion and marginalization.

References

Abdellah-Pretceille, M. (1995), *Relations et apprentissage interculturels*, Armand Colin, Paris.

Affergan, F. (1987), *Exotisme et altérité*, Presses universitaires de France, Paris.

Banton, M. (1988), *Racial Consciousness*, Longman, London.

Bochmann, K. (1994), 'Les stéréotypes ethniques. Nature et contours d'un objet de recherche', in J. Berting and C. Villain Gandossi (eds), *The Role of stereotypes in International Relations*, the Rotterdam Institute for Social Policy Research, Center for Socio-Cultural Transformation, Rotterdam.

Bourdieu, P. (1991). 'Introduction à la socioanalyse', *Actes de la recherche en sciences sociales*, No. 90, Décembre, pp. 3-5.

Bourdieu, P. (ed.), (1993), *La misère du monde*, Le Seuil, Paris.

Bryson, B. (1996), '"Anything but Heavy Metal": Symbolic Exclusion and Musical Dislikes', *American Sociological Review*, Vol. 61, No. 5, October, pp. 884-899.

Camelliri, C. and M. Cohen-Emirique M. (eds), (1989), *Chocs de cultures: Concepts et enjeux pratiques de l'interculturel*, L'Harmattan, Paris.

Costa-Lascoux, J. (1995), 'Différences culturelles, discriminations et citoyenneté', in C. Neveu (ed.), *Nations, frontières et immigration en Europe*, L'Harmattan, Paris.

Cousineau, M-M. (1994), 'Quelques considérations sur le sentiment et la condition d'isolement des victimes de la peur du crime', *Cahiers de recherche sociologique*, No. 22, pp. 77-91.

Fanon, F. (1961), *Les damnés de la terre*, Maspero, Paris.

Foucault, M. (1975), *Surveiller et punier*, Editions Fayard, Paris.

Fournier, M. and G. Vermes (eds), (1994), *Ethnicisation des rapports sociaux. Nationalismes, ethnicismes et culturalismes*, Vol. 3, L'Harmattan, Paris.

Gallissot, R. (ed.), (1993), *Pluralisme culturel en Europe? Cultures européennes et cultures des diasporas*, L'Harmattan, Paris.

Gore, C. (1995), 'Markets, Citizenship and Social Exclusion', in G. Rodgers *et al.* (eds), *Social Exclusion: Rhetoric, Reality, Responses*, International Institute for Labour Studies, Geneva.

Hagendoorn, L. (1993), 'Ethnic Categorization and Outgroup Exclusion: Cultural Values and Social Stereotypes in the Construction of Ethnic Hierarchies', *Ethnic and Racial Studies*, Vol. 16, No, 1, January, pp. 26-51.

Hall, S. (1991), 'Old and New Identities, Old and New Ethnicities' in A. King (ed.), *Culture, Globalization and the World-System*, Macmillan, London, pp. 19-39.

Jaakkola, M. (1994), 'Ulkomaalaisasenteet Suomessa ja Ruotsissa', in K. Liebkind (ed.), *Maahanmuuttajat, Kulttuurien kohtaaminen Suomessa*, Gaudeamus, Helsinki.

Koser, K. and H. Lutz (1998), 'The New Migration in Europe: Contexts, Constructions and Realities', in K. Koser and H. Lutz (eds), *The New Migration in Europe, Social Constructions and Social Realities*, Macmillan Press, London.

Lamarque, G. (1996), *L'exclusion*, Presses Universitaires de France (Que sais-je), Paris.

Lamont, M. (1989), 'The Power-Culture Link in a Comparative Perspective',

Comparative Social Research, No. 11, pp. 131-150.

Liautzu, C. (1992), *Race and civilisation, L'autre dans la culture occidentale*, Syros-Alternatives, Paris.

Liebkind, K. (1994a), 'Maahanmuuttajat, Kulttuurien kohtaaminen' in K. Liebkind (ed.), *Maahanmuuttajat, kulttuurien kohtaaminen Suomessa*, Gaudeamus, Helsinki.

Liebkind, K. (1994b), 'Monikulttuurisuuden ehdot' in K. Liebkind (ed.), *op cit.*

Lorenzo, J-M. (1989), 'Immigrés dans l'entreprise', in C. Camelliri C. and M. Cohen-Emirique (eds), *Chocs de cultures: Concepts et enjeux pratiques de l'interculturel*, L'Harmattan, Paris.

Malewska-Peyre, H. (1990), 'Le processus de dévalorisation de l'identité et les stratégies identitaires', in C. Camelliri *et al.* (eds), *Stratégies identitaires*, Presses universitaires de France, Paris.

Marjeta, M. (1997), 'Somalinaiset kahdessa kulttuurissa: Muutos, elämänkulku ja identiteetti', unpublished MA thesis, Dept. of Sociology, University of Joensuu, Joensuu.

Moreau, I. (1993), 'Exclusions: perdre la cohésion sociale, un risque majeure', in *Espace social européen*, No.191, Février, pp.21-26.

Murphy, R. (1988), *Social Closure, The Theory of Monopolization and Exclusion*, Clarendon Press, Oxford.

Nasse, P. (ed.), (1992), *Exclus et exclusions: Connaitre les populations, comprendre les processus.* Rapport du groupe technique quantitatif sur la prospective de l'exclusion, la documentation française, Paris.

Nicklas, H. (1995), 'Identité culturelle et conflits entre les cultures', in M. Abdellah-Pretceille (ed.), *Relations et apprentissage interculturels*, Armand Colin, Paris.

Phoenix, A. (1998), 'Representing New Identities: "Whiteness" as Contested Identity in Young People's Accounts', in K. Koser and H. Lutz (eds), *The New Migration in Europe, Social Constructions and Social Realities*, Macmillan Press, London.

Rodgers, G. (1995), 'What is Special about a "Social Exclusion" Approach?' in G. Rodgers *et al.* (eds), *Social Exclusion: Rhetoric, Reality, Responses*, International Institute for Labour Studies, Geneva.

Räty, M. and Saari, S. (1997), (eds), *Nimeni ei ole pakolainen: Elämä ulkomaalaisena Suomessa*, Kosmos, Vihreä Sivistysliitto ry, Helsinki.

Sabour, M. (1993), 'Etre arabe en Finlande: le tatouage d'un stéréotype', in T. Melasuo (ed.), *Dialogue Arabo-Scandinave*, TAPRI, Tampere.

Sabour, M. and Antikainen, A. (1995), *Joensuun skiniongelmassa ei kyse pelkästä rasismista*, Karjalainen (23.11.1995).

Sabour, M. (1996), *Skinheads, Violence and Discourses about Racism in Finland: A Case Study.* Paper presented at the Fifth Conference of the International Society for the Study of European Ideas (Memory, History and Critique: European Identity at the Millennium), 19-26 August 1996, The University of

Humanist Studies, Utrecht, The Netherlands.

Sabour, M. (1997), 'The North African Intellectual Diaspora in The Nordic Countries: The Socio-political Factors of Expatriation', in M. Sabour and K. Vikor (eds), *Ethnic Encounter and Culture Change*, NSMES, Bergen, London.

Sabour, M. (1998), *Suomalainen unelma, suomalaisen yhteiskunnan kohtaamisen päiväkirja*, The Joensuu University Press, Joensuu.

Sayad, A. (1991), *L'immigration ou les paradoxes de l'alterité*, Editions universitaires-De Boeck Université, Bruxelles.

Schlesinger, P. (1994), 'Collective Identities, Friends, Enemies', in J. Berting and C. Villain Gandossi (eds), *The Role of Stereotypes in International Relations*, the Rotterdam Institute for Social Policy Research, Center for Socio-Cultural Transformation, Rotterdam.

Swyngedouw, M. (1995), 'The "Threatening Immigrant" in Flanders 1930-1980: Redrawing the Social Space', *New Community*, Vol. 21, No. 3, July, pp. 325-340.

Tabouret-Keller, A. (1994), 'De la culture idéale aux cultures de contact' in C. Labat and G. Vermès (eds), *Cultures ouvertes, sociétés interculturelles, du contact à l'interaction, Vol. II*, L'Harmattan, Paris.

Taguieff, P.-A. (1987), *La force du préjugé*, Gallimard, Paris.

Touraine A. (1991), 'Face à l'exclusion', in *Esprit*, Février, pp.7-13.

Vertovec, S. (1996), 'Multiculturalism, Culturalism and Public Incorporation', *Ethnic and Racial Studies*, Vol. 19, No. 1, January, pp. 49-69.

Weinberg, A. *et al.* (1993), 'Comprendre l'exclusion', *Sciences humaines*, No. 28, Mai, pp.12-15.

Xiberras, M. (1992), *Les théories de l'exclusion sociale*, Méridiens Klincksieck, Paris.

Index